27.6.06

Social Science

Second Edition

CONCEPTS IN THE SOCIAL SCIENCES
Series editor: Frank Parkin

Published titles

Democracy (Second Edition)	*Anthony Arblaster*
Discrimination	*Michael Banton*
Citizenship	*J. M. Barbalet*
Welfare (Second Edition)	*Norman Barry*
Freedom	*Zygmunt Bauman*
Bureaucracy (Second Edition)	*David Beetham*
Nationalism	*Craig Calhoun*
Trotskyism	*Alex Callinicos*
Policy (Second Edition)	*H. K. Colebatch*
Socialism	*Bernard Crick*
Exchange	*John Davis*
Social Science	*Gerard Delanty*
Social Darwinism	*Peter Dickens*
Power	*Keith Dowding*
Rights	*Michael Freeden*
Feminism	*Jane Freedman*
Science	*Steve Fuller*
Liberalism (Second Edition)	*John Gray*
The State	*John A. Hall and G. John Ikenberry*
Kinship	*C. C. Harris*
Sovereignty	*John Hoffman*
Discourse	*David Howarth*
Utopianism	*Krishan Kumar*
Social Structure	*Jose Lopez and John Scott*
Postmodernity (Second Edition)	*David Lyon*
Ideology (Second Edition)	*David McLellan*
Pluralism	*Gregor McLennan*
Fascism	*Mark Neocleous*
Conservatism	*Robert Nisbet*
Structuration	*John Parker*
Race and Ethnicity	*John Rex*
Postcommunism	*Richard Sakwa*
Orientalism	*Ziauddin Sardar*
Capitalism	*Peter Saunders*
Class	*Richard Scase*
Caste	*Ursula Sharma*
Ecologism	*Mark J. Smith*
Culture	*Mark J. Smith*
Polulism	*Paul Taggart*
Status	*Bryan S. Turner*
Multiculturalism	*C. W. Watson*

Concepts in the Social Sciences

Social Science

Philosophical and Methodological Foundations

Second Edition

Gerard Delanty

Open University Press

Open University Press
McGraw-Hill Education
McGraw-Hill House
Shoppenhangers Road
Maidenhead
Berkshire
England
SL6 2QL

email: enquiries@openup.co.uk
world wide web: www.openup.co.uk

and Two Penn Plaza, New York, NY 10121-2289, USA

First published 2005

A catalogue record of this book is available from the British Library

ISBN: 0335 21721 4 (pb) 0335 21722 2 (hb)
ISBN-13: 978 0335 217212 (pb) 978 0335 217229 (hb)

Library of Congress Cataloging-in-Publication Data
CIP data applied for

Typeset by YHT Ltd
Printed in the UK by Bell & Bain Ltd, Glasgow

To Gudrun von Alten

Contents

Preface to the Second Edition

In preparing this second edition I set myself the task of retaining the basic structure and rationale of the first book while at the same time adjusting it in light of omissions that have come to light in my reading and thinking over the past eight years. Some of the changes are the outcome of the anthology I edited with Piet Strydom, *Philosophies of Social: The Classical and Contemporary Readings* (2003).

While the basic structure and text remains intact, I have made changes – ranging from minor corrections to revised and in some cases new sections – to most chapters, and have substantially rewritten the chapter on constructivism. There is now a new chapter on reflexivity and a more qualified argument concerning constructivism. This is reflected in a change to the subtitle of the book.

Gerard Delanty
November, 2004

Preface and Acknowledgements

This is a book about the self-understanding of social science from the perspective of the end of the twentieth century. It offers both undergraduate and postgraduate students in the social sciences an overview of the principal philosophical debates on the methodology of the social sciences, beginning with the positivist dispute, and at the same time tries to say something about social science as an institution in modern society. It is impossible to do justice to the full range of issues that this involves in a book of this size, which has in fact been written as an introduction to a larger and more ambitious work. I hope, however, that this book will not only be an accurate and concise overview of the most important debates, but will also provide a contemporary perspective, and that it will therefore make an original contribution to debates on the social construction of knowledge and its public utility.

I have suggested that the contemporary perspective relates to the question of the public role of social science. The relationship of social science as a professional culture to the public culture of debate on society is one of the central issues facing social science today. Since the creation of permanent structures of knowledge that accompanied the rise of the modern state, the principal challenge for social science was its professional institutionalization in the university system. This goal has now been achieved and, indeed, many of the problems facing social science today relate to the fragmentation of knowledge that has arisen as a result of its being made professional and academic. The challenge facing the social sciences in the twenty-first century is therefore quite different: it is a question of the public legitimation of science. If social science is unable to meet this challenge, it will enter a crisis as far-reaching as that now faced by other structures created by the modern state. In order to begin to understand the relationship of social scientific knowledge to its publics, the philosophy and sociology of social science need to move beyond the positivist debate to deal with new problems that have arisen in recent years. I have chosen to focus on the realist–constructivist debate, since it is in this debate that the really crucial issues concerning the public role of social science arise. The main chapters have therefore been written with the aim of clarifying the terms of current debate around the question of social science and its publics.

The central thesis of the book is that social science, like all of science, must be conceived of as both a system of knowledge and as a social institution. As a socially constructed discourse, the crisis and transformation of knowledge in contemporary society has major implications for the identity and conduct of social science. The most important of these relate to the rise of new conceptions of democracy that have accompanied the decline in the sovereignty of the state and its structures of knowledge; the changed relationship of society to nature, which has placed the idea of time at the centre of debate; the reopening of culture around new issues relating to power and identity; the collapse of the unquestioned authority of scientific rationality; and new developments in natural science, which point to the limits of the Baconian-Newtonian conception of 'nature as timeless'. Viewed in the longer perspective of history, the contemporary challenge to social science can be said to be the overcoming of some of the disciplinary divisions that emerged in the seventeenth century and that became institutionalized in the nineteenth century. In order to achieve this task of forging new links with the public sphere, social science will have to recover its role as the critical voice of modernity.

I wish to express a special acknowledgement to Piet Strydom of University College Cork for much valuable advice in writing this book

Gerard Delanty
Kirchwehren, Lower Saxony, August 1996

Introduction: Challenges for Social Science

Why does society need social science? What is the current self-understanding of social science? What is the public role of social science? These questions have always been central to debates on the task of social science ever since the neo-Kantians launched their critique of positivism in the second half of the nineteenth century. However, the situation of social science today is different from the days when the neo-Kantian philosophers of the German Historical School demanded a radical bifurcation of the human and the natural sciences and, consequently, the answer to the question of what does the public role of social science consist can no longer be found in methodology, but concerns the role of social science as a mediating discourse between public culture and professional culture. This book is a plea to debate the self-understanding of social science on new foundations and to recognize that the matter cannot be resolved by methodology or philosophical reflections on epistemology alone: it is above all a question of the public role of social science. The critique of positivism has been too much preoccupied with the relationship between the sciences. The consequence of this has been the neglect of the relationship between science and other forms of knowledge.

The crisis of the social sciences, then, is no longer one of methodology nor is it one that can be conducted as a critique of positivism: it is one of the very social relevance of social science. The challenge of social science today is not the decline in high-quality social research, whether positivistic or otherwise, but derives from the failure of social science to mediate its professional culture with the public commitments of intellectual culture. One does not have to agree with Irving Louis Horowitz's (1993) reactionary claim that the 'decomposition of sociology' began when the great sociological tradition of Durkheim, Weber, Simmel and Mannheim became overtaken by ideological thinking and its mantras of race, ethnicity and gender to recognize that social science has entered a profound crisis in its relation to the object of its study, namely society. The tradition of the classics – social science as the interpretation and critique of modernity – has been forgotten as far as the practice of research is concerned, while much of contemporary sociological theory has degenerated into hermeticism, sterile and self-referential discourses. As Edward Said (1994: 8) has argued in his Reith Lectures: 'There is a danger that the figure or image of the intellectual might disappear in a mass of details, and that the intellectual might become only another professional, or figure in a social trend'.

Never before have there been so many tenured university academics in the social sciences, yet their actual public influence has never been so weak (Dettling, 1996: 28; Wagner, 1996: 34). It is surely a sign of the malaise of sociology that historians are noticeably more prominent in the public sphere than are sociologists. This is a tendency that is most evident since the revolutionary upheavals of 1989, when historians became the spokespersons on social change. Can the reason be that social science no longer has a theory of society capable of interpreting and guiding the changes that are going on today? In the past, in particular in Germany but also in France, leading social scientists such as Adorno, Horkheimer, Marcuse, Habermas and Foucault were active in shaping public debates on the key issues of social change and innovation, but there is now a noticeable decline in sociological interventions. This situation led the conservative German sociologist Helmut Schelsky (1975) to warn against the false promises of the new class of intellectuals led by the sociological elite whose radical influence he exaggerated in order to call for an 'anti-sociology'. For Schelsky, the sociologists must remain professionals. In the English-speaking world social scientists never had a strong presence in the public sphere, which perhaps explains why media pundits, popular economists and historians have such a relatively strong public profile in Anglo-Saxon culture, which has not been noted for its intellectualism. However, what has more generally ensured the silence of social science is not only a commitment to a conservative professional positivism but a pervasive cultural and political relativism. This betrayal of the critical function of sociology was something for which C. Wright Mills (1970 [1959])* in a famous book, *The Sociological Imagination*, criticized Talcott Parsons and Robert Merton. Sociology, he argued, at a time when positivism was the orthodoxy in American sociology, had an important role to play in society in criticizing power, a role he believed was reconcilable with its role as a profession and with the classic works of the discipline. This argument was reiterated by Scott and Shore (1979) in their *Why Sociology Does Not Apply*, which argued that the kind of knowledge produced by social science has become irrelevant to society. In their view, social scientific knowledge should be able to contribute to the improvement of society, otherwise it is a luxury society can ill afford. This is a theme found in much of recent debates on the identity of social science (Beck and Bonss, 1989; Wagner et al., 1991; Dierkes and Biervert, 1992; Fuller, 1993; Giddens, 1996; Stehr, 1996).

Where are the sociologists today? What is their self-understanding as a profession? The truth is that many of them have found comfort in the retreat of social science from intellectual culture into professional culture. Peter Wagner (1994: 147) is undoubtedly correct when he writes: 'my hunch is that a large number feel rather relieved under the present condition, given that the obligation to argue and justify one's procedures is much reduced'. Russell Jacoby's (1987) argument of the collapse of intellectual culture is relevant to the failure of social science to sustain its project. Although he was primarily bemoaning the obsolescence of the non-academic intellectual who could counteract the sterile discourses of academia, his thesis can be applied to the malaise of the social sciences themselves which have retreated from critical engagement and intellectual debate into an anarchy of cultural relativism and fragmented knowledge cultures that is the hallmark of the present. The social sciences seem to have been untouched by the debate raging in the humanities over the last ten years concerning the continued relevance of the literary canon. The descent of Western culture into relativism is reflected in the social sciences as much as in the study of literature: the classical works in the history of social

* The references in the text include, in cases where I have considered it relevant, the original year of publication. The date of the recent publication is given first, followed by the original date of publication in square brackets. Works referred to in square brackets only are not referenced in the Bibliography.

ideas are simply not read or made relevant to the practice of research. Relegated to undergraduate courses, the works of the classics have lost their power to influence the direction of research (Baehr and O'Brien, 1994; Alexander, 1996; Poggi, 1996).

The debate in the humanities, important as it is for the social sciences, differs in one respect: it has been primarily concerned with the relationship between professional or expert knowledge and intellectual culture. While the question of whether the social scientist is an expert or an intellectual is an important issue which cannot be dismissed, a more pertinent question for the social sciences concerns the status of scientific knowledge with respect to society. The crisis of the public role of social science concerns the relationship between expert systems and society. In other words, it relates to the question of the relationship between the production of knowledge by experts and the social institution of science in society. To what extent is science autonomous of society? Can science be made accountable to society? How are we to understand the relationship between science as a cognitive system (i.e. a system of knowledge) and as an institutional system in modern society? These questions lie at the heart of new debates on the social sciences.

While it is undeniable that the social sciences have entered a deep crisis with respect to their public role, the present situation can also be seen in more positive light as one of transition. This book is an exploration of this changing situation. One of my central contentions is that social science has always been the critical consciousness of modernity and with the revision, if not the decline, of modernity in the twenty-first century, its present situation is characterized by a less confident consciousness of its role in the world. This situation of uncertainty need not necessarily imply a crisis, but can point to new possibilities for social science to recover its critical consciousness as a framework for interpreting the social world. Yet, however we view the present situation of social science, we cannot avoid the conclusion that the public legitimation of science is going to increase, not decline, in the twenty-first century.

Just to mention four examples of the decline in modernity and the opening of new possibilities for social science: the decline in sovereignty of the nation-state; the global impact of the revolutions in Eastern Europe and the USSR in 1989/90 along with the end of the Cold War; the emergence of new conceptions of nature; and the increased importance of knowledge in society.

Firstly, social science as an institutionalized system of knowledge has been linked to the rise of the modern state, which provided it with its conditions of existence. Moreover, the unitary and territorial nation-state has been the crucible in which social science evolved. With the decline of the state as the dominant institution in contemporary society and the shifting of democracy from the state onto society, social science is finding itself about to enter new and uncertain territory.

Secondly, the revolutions of 1989/90 have also been consequential in raising new questions about the social production of knowledge. Revolutions have always been central to the construction of systems of knowledge: the scientific revolution of the sixteenth and seventeenth centuries provided the context for the first discourses on society, the American and French Revolutions of 1776 and 1789 opened up new conceptions of social science, and the spectre of Marxist revolution culminating in the Bolshevist Revolution of 1917 reopened the idea of a revolutionary social science. The cognitive systems produced by the Cold War no longer resonate in society: neither Western liberalism nor social democracy nor Marxism has succeeded in providing a social basis to knowledge.

Thirdly, nature has re-emerged as a new theme in natural and social science in recent years in response to the ecological crisis. Nature is increasingly being seen as a social construction. Social science can no longer suppose the objectivity of nature as a unchanging essence. In other words, the ontological distinction between humans and nature is breaking down. Both nature and society can no longer be conceived in dualistic terms.

Fourthly, the importance of knowledge is increasingly being recognized in society today. We are living in a society which is as much characterized by the production of knowledge as anything else. Never before have there been so many systems of meaning requiring institutionalized cultures of experts and their professionalized discourses (see Fuller, 2000; Turner, 2003). Of the many questions that this raises for social science, one is paramount: can social scientific knowledge provide society with a discourse of renewal and critique or will it suffer the fate of increased specialization and academization?

The implications of these developments – changed conceptions of nature, knowledge, democracy and sovereignty – are far-reaching for the social sciences in their search for a new identity and will have major implications for the relationship of the scientist to the research object, which can no longer be conceived of in the categories of modernity. The following anticipates some points to be taken up later in the book.

The philosophy and the sociology of science cannot be separated if we are to arrive at a full picture of the present situation of science in a changing world. This is because the problems that social science is faced with are no longer purely ones related to epistemology and methodology. These are the terms of the older debates, which have been superseded today. The new debates penetrate to the nexus of science as a cognitive system and as an institution. Thus the question of the value-neutrality of science cannot be answered by science as a cognitive system, but by its institutional context. Therefore, we need to look at the changing social role of science. This cannot be separated from looking at the kinds of debates going on in society about the politics of knowledge.

These debates relate centrally to the question of democracy and of societal responsibility for nature (Strydom, 2002). Thus we find in the foreground of new debates on the philosophy and sociology of science considerable common ground between the natural and the social sciences. Under the rubric of the 'risk society' (Beck, 1992), the 'finalization' of science by social demands (Schäfer, 1983a), the 'discourse of radical constructivism' (Schmidt, 1987, 1992; Nüse et al., 1991) the sciences have found a common voice in a concern with self-reflection on the social presuppositions and commitments of knowledge.

The emergence of new post-positivistic commonalties in the social and natural sciences was one of the principal findings of the *Report of the Gulbenkian Commission on the Restructuring of the Social Sciences*, which presents a new scenario for science in the twenty-first century. We may witness a new alignment of the sciences comparable to that in the early nineteenth century, when the modern university system emerged. In *Open the Social Science* (1996), the Gulbenkian Commission questioned the continued validity of the distinction of the 'two cultures' on the grounds that the natural sciences are now moving towards a conception of nature as an active and creative force and the laws that scientists advance are only possibilities, never certainties. The second great challenge the Commission listed for the social sciences is the weakening of the distinction between the social and the human sciences. This distinction is collapsing as a result of the rise of new 'cultural voices' which conceptualize power and identity in new ways. This cultural turn in the social sciences amounts to a new 'hermeneutic turn' (Gulbenkian, 1996: 65). Culture is one of the new master themes in contemporary social science, but rather than accept postmodernist scepticism, the authors of the Gulbenkian Commission Report stress the importance of the search for coherence as a continuing obligation of a reconstructed historical social science. We may now say that we are moving towards a non-contradictory view of the multiple domains of knowledge in which the tripartite division between the natural, the social and the human sciences is no longer as self-evident as it once was.

The spirit of the Gulbenkian Commission was one of new opportunities, a theme reflected in Anthony Giddens's (1996) *In Defence of Sociology*. Giddens argues that the social sciences, and in particular sociology, are in fact in a position of strength today despite the charge that much of social science has become over-professionalized and divorced from society; social research forms so much a part of our consciousness today that we take it for granted: 'Not only empirical research but sociological theorizing and sociological concepts can become so much part of our everyday repertoire as to appear as "just common sense".' A central question, then, is that of the relationship of social scientific knowledge to other kinds of knowledge. Giddens (1996: 77) has pointed out that scientific knowledge has always had a constructive role. The invention of the discourse of political science, for instance, helped to construct the modern state; the discourse of economics assisted in the construction of industrial society; and the concepts of social science have also entered the common language and are not restricted to professional discourse: 'Social science does not stand in a neutral relation to the social world, as an instrument of technological change; critique cannot be limited to the criticism of false lay beliefs. The implications of the double hermeneutic is that social scientists can't but be alert to the transformative effects that their concepts and theories might have upon what they set out to analyse'. The change that is occurring in the contemporary conception of a critical social science is that professional knowledge involves a reciprocal relationship to other kinds of social knowledge.

Moreover, the identity of the social sciences needs to be radically rethought in light of the shifting alignments in the disciplines. The internal differences within the various disciplines are frequently greater than the differences between disciplines. With increasing specialization of research, social scientists are reaching across the borders of the old disciplinary boundaries, and even the distinction between natural and social sciences is becoming blurred.

Chapter 1 outlines the background to the positivist debate, looking at the rise of modern science and the institutionalization of social science as a discourse around rationalism and empiricism. The chapter concludes with a look at the collapse of positivism in the twentieth century with the emergence of post-empiricist conceptions of science, such as Popper and Kuhn.

Chapter 2 deals with the hermeneutical challenge to positivism, beginning with the neo-Kantian critique and Weber's attempt to link explanation and understanding into an interpretative sociology. The chapter looks at twentieth-century developments in the philosophy of social science, in particular the significance of the linguistic turn in philosophy for constructivist social science.

Chapter 3 goes on to examine the third classical approach in social science, Marxism. The main focus here will be to trace the transformation of the concept of critique in Marxism from the critique of political economy to the Frankfurt School's critique of ideology. Marxism involves both constructivist and realist dimensions.

Chapter 4 concentrates on the reconstructive approaches of Habermas and Apel, who have sought to combine the three classical approaches into a critical hermeneutic and emancipatory social science. The advantages of their approach lie in their emphasis on the importance of communication for science in its task of human emancipation. The chapter includes a discussion of the influence of pragmatism.

Chapter 5 looks at the postmodern turn in social science from French post-structuralism, including Foucault's historical studies of power, to the so-called cultural turn in the social and human sciences in the 1980s and finally the confluence of postmodernism and the new culturalist-emancipationist sociology of globalization and post-colonialism. The aim of the chapter is to show how the explanation/understanding debate has shifted onto to new issues, which, while not being resolved by postmodernism, established the context for subsequent approaches.

Chapter 6 looks at the theme of the return of the actor with particular regard to standpoint epistemology, which can be seen as an expression of a more general reflexive turn in the self-understanding of social science. The central question in the controversy to be considered is whether a reflexive social science based on human experience can be objective.

Chapter 7 attempts to access the contemporary situation of social science in light of the constructivist debate which is contrasted to critical realism. The chapter aims to show that that a reconciliation of radical constructivism and critical realism is possible, but in a way that will entail a movement beyond these positions.

Chapter 8 discusses social science in terms of a communicative concept of knowledge. In a whole range of recent developments, it is argued, science is becoming increasingly conceived as a communicative system that interacts reflexively with society. The chapter concludes with an argument for a notion of critical social science as discursive practice.

1

Positivism, Science and the Politics of Knowledge

Introduction: Defining Positivism

Philosophical debates on the methodology and self-understanding of social science have been for the greater part shaped by the positivist dispute. Therefore a good place to begin is with positivism itself. This will inevitably involve looking at disputes on the meaning of science more generally, since positivism, broadly understood, is a philosophy which argues for the application of the methods of the natural sciences to the social sciences and thereby presupposes the unity of the sciences. Underlying positivism more fundamentally is the naturalistic notion that science is the study of an objectively existing reality which lies outside the discourse of science.

Positivism has been under attack throughout the twentieth century from a variety of different standpoints. It is customary to contrast positivism to hermemeutical or interpretative social science or to the more Marxist inspired critical social science, but positivism, which makes certain assumptions about the nature of natural science, has also been undermined by developments within natural science itself, which cannot be considered positivistic. Thus positivism, both in natural and social science, has been very much in question, particularly since the 1950s. However, the origins of the demise of positivism are to be located within neo-positivism, that is in the general turn to deductive epistemology that began with logical positivism.

To begin, let us be clear on exactly what positivism is. In the most general terms positivism entails the view that scientific knowledge can be positively verifiable, in contrast to dogmatism, speculation or superstition. Positivistic knowledge is thus knowledge that is based on sure and certain foundations. It has been a feature of all kinds of positivism that such foundations are built on the discovery of general laws. Beyond that general principle, which was a key feature of modern experimental science, it can be defined by the following five tenets, which for the purpose of illustration may be somewhat stylized:

(1) *Scientism or the unity of the scientific method* For positivism, there is no essential difference between the method of natural science and social science. In arguing for the unity of the scientific method, the natural sciences are generally taken to be the model for all the sciences. The assumption underlying this is that there is a basic unity underlying the human and natural worlds. This leads to the second point.
(2) *Naturalism or phenomenalism* Not only is there a unity of method, but there is also unity in the subject matter of science. Science is the study of reality which is external to science itself. This reality can be reduced to observable units or naturalistic phenomena. Positivistic naturalism generally entails (a) reductionism or atomism (that everything can be reduced to atomic units), (b) a correspondence theory of truth (that there is a correspondence between the truths of science and the nature of reality) and (c) phenomenalism or objectivism (an objectifying attitude to nature by which nature is seen as existing outside science and can be neutrally observed).
(3) *Empiricism* The foundation of science is observation. Positivistic science is based entirely on what is positively given to experience, in other words only that which can be subject to observation and verification. For positivists the progress from observation to verification is operationalized by means of the experimental method: the scientist carries out experiments in order to uncover objectively existing general laws from which hypotheses can be made and which can be used to predict what can happen. In general, the kinds of laws positivism seeks to uncover are causal laws and have the power of explanation.
(4) *Value freedom* Science does not make judgments on its subject matter; it is a neutral activity free of social and ethical values. Positivists therefore insist on a dualism of facts and values. Values, it is claimed, cannot be derived from facts. For positivistic social science, there are only social facts, which can be

examined. Positivism involves a commitment to the pursuit of scientific truth, which is arrived at independently of ethical self-reflection or personal subjective elements since truth is a verifiable and explanatory statement about an objectively existing reality. Thus scientific knowledge is different from all other kinds of human knowledge since it can be verified and it can therefore be said to be universally true.

(5) *Instrumental knowledge* In general the institution of science as a profession in modern society has favoured the pursuit of technically useful knowledge, though this can take a variety of political forms. Positivism has taken three political forms: (a) the classical positivistic ideology of scientific politics, as represented by Saint-Simon and Comte and by scientific socialists, (b) science as instrumentally useful knowledge but without overt political significance, as represented by reform movements particularly in Britain and the United States, and (c) instrumental-bureaucratic social science associated with the professionalization of social science in the twentieth century. In the case of the latter, which proclaims itself to be unpolitical, critics such as C. Wright Mills (1970) argue the political nature of positivistic empirical research is disguised by its claims to scientific objectivity.

It is important to appreciate, as this chapter will illustrate, that not all of these criteria were embodied in any one positivist philosophy or scientific practice. Positivism, strictly speaking in its classic form was largely a nineteenth-century French ideology of the unity of the scientific method which was held to have a radical political mission. Thus 'positive science' and the 'positive polity' formed a unity. This conception of positivism is best associated with Henri Saint-Simon and Auguste Comte. A second form it took was the more neopositivist science of the 'Vienna Circle', or logical positivism, when the idea of the positive polity was abandoned in favour of the purity of science as an unpolitical endeavor. Aside from these two classical forms, thirdly, positivism is often used to describe, in somewhat disparaging terms, modern empirical social science in general.

In what follows I shall outline the changing forms that positivism took from the New Learning of the late Renaissance to seventeenth-century rationalism and empiricism to Enlightenment thinking to the emergence of modern social science in the nineteenth century and finally to its twentieth-century proponents and critics. Though often criticized for being a conservative doctrine asserting the superiority of science over other forms of knowledge and driven by a relentless instrumental rationality striving to gain intellectual mastery over nature and society, positivism, along with empirical science, has historically, in fact, been related to liberalism and its changing forms have reflected the transformation of liberalism from early modern anti-authoritarian and anti-obscurantism to Enlightenment radicalism to liberal reformism and the rise of the modern republican state and its need for instrumental knowledge. While positivism can also be seen as related to the rise of the modern state and science as an institution, in general positivists and empiricists have been liberals, ranging from Locke (who was a Whig critic of Stuart absolutism) to the enlightened reconstructionism of Condorcet (who was a liberally inclined Ancien Regime official), to the scientific utopianism of Comte, the reformism of Mill and Spencer to the anti-obscurantist radicalism of the Vienna Circle and the Marxism of Neurath. Any account of positivism will have to take account of the rise, transformation and decline of liberalism and the belief that the republic of science and the liberal polity have a unity of purpose. In the twentieth century the most important development in positivism was the decline in the culture of the intellectual and the rise of the professional and institutionalized expert systems, with the result that knowledge became fragmented according to different knowledge producers.

The Rise of Modern Science as a Cognitive System and Institution

Positivism is primarily a nineteenth-century post-Enlightenment ideology, but its roots lie deep in Western culture. The pursuit of scientific truth as an absolute form of knowledge can be traced back to Plato's philosophy, which argued that the highest kind of knowledge which can be aspired to is the pure contemplation of the natural forms of the cosmos and that this kind of knowledge, or *logos*, was fundamentally different from other kinds of knowledge, such as opinion, or *doxa*. Moreover, those who possessed pure knowledge had a right to rule those who were trapped within the limits of the world of mere opinion. The Platonic conception of knowledge has had an enduring appeal throughout the history of philosophy, bequeathing a legacy of rationalistic inquiry in the quest for objective truth which had to be protected from democracy, which was deemed to be confined to doxa. The Platonic idea survived through antiquity and the Middle Ages in Aristotelian philosophy and Christian metaphysics, which posited as the aims of human inquiry the study of the natural laws of the universe and the search for first principles.

While Aristotle was responsible for the emphasis on first principles, he had earlier established the basis of an empirical inductive science in his *Politics*, which stressed less the quest for absolute ideals than a classification of empirically observable phenomena into categories, such as his famous classification of the three kinds of states: monarchies, aristocracies and democracies. In his *Posterior Analytics* Aristotle provided the foundations of modern inductive and deductive methodology: knowledge progresses inductively from observation of facts to general explanatory principles from which reasons can be deducted to explain the specific facts. Aristotle, however, gained influence in medieval thought only since the thirteenth century when the dominant conception of knowledge, which lasted until the advent of the Scientific Revolution, was a Christianized version of Aristotelianism known as scholasticism, developed by St Thomas of Aquinas. Aristotelianism shifted from a concern with the inductive-deductive approach to an emphasis on first principles. With the rejection of scholasticism, Aristotelianism fell into disrepute.

Positivism was a product of modernity. Although not unrelated to the older philosophical traditions, it did not emerge until the development of the experimental method in the Renaissance, which witnessed the Scientific Revolution and the rise of rationalism. While Platonic epistemology (or theory of knowledge) was metaphysical and idealistic (oriented towards the pursuit of transcendental realities, or 'ideals', to be uncovered by philosophical knowledge), modern positivism was on the whole empirical: based on the observation of reality with the help of experimental science. Platonic knowledge, in contrast, rejected knowledge derived from sense experience as being inferior to knowledge of the 'eternal forms'. Nevertheless, despite being post-metaphysical and anti-idealist, positivism can be seen as a continuation of the Platonic quest for truth and objective knowledge.

An early exponent of positivism was the thirteenth-century predecessor of the Renaissance, Roger Bacon, who stressed the importance of observable data as the basis of knowledge, and

William of Ockham, who also argued that knowledge must proceed in a 'razor'-like manner from an examination of empirical cases in order to exclude the superfluous. Thus evolved the notion of 'Ockham's Razor', which states that the simplest explanation is to be preferred. From the Renaissance thinkers and scientists, such as Leonardo da Vinci, to those of the sixteenth and seventeenth centuries, such as Giordano Bruno, Galileo Gallilei, Desiderus Erasmus, Michel de Montaigne, Robert Boyle, Johannes Kepler, Nicolas Copernicus, Francis Bacon and Issac Newton, the experimental method developed along with the progress of modern science.

The experimental method was epitomized in the writings of Francis Bacon, who advanced an inductive methodology of observation without philosophical presuppositions: theory is arrived at from presuppositionless observation and not from prior knowledge. The Renaissance artists, but most of all Leonardo da Vinci, gave expression to the new consciousness by evolving new techniques in the representation of reality which allowed the object to appear in its natural form. The scientists, such as Galileo, replaced the principle of clerical authority with the experimental method, which was to be the demarcation of science from non-science. In this way, modern science began with a gradual attack on clerical authority which asserted that knowledge derives from the ancient authority of the Church. This attack, however, it must also be pointed out, was more implicit than outright for the Renaissance thinkers were not always anti-Christian; many, such as Thomas More and Erasmus, sought to reconcile their ideas to the prevailing Catholicism, and the seventeenth-century pietistic proponents of rationalism, such as Francis Bacon, were also ardent Protestant reformers who argued for a separation of divine laws from natural laws in order to make science possible and to preserve a space for belief. In this way the Reformation greatly facilitated the rise of modern science since it gave theological justification to the freedom of science, which could also be used to provide rational justifications for the existence of God. This was the 'paradox of modernity' which Max Weber believed marked the entry of the modern age. This paradox can be explained by the fact that both the pietistic Reformation and rationalistic science were expressions of the modern turn to radical subjectivity which brought about the de-centring of consciousness and established the self-confidence of the individual as the bearer of knowledge. Despite this paradox, science and belief were bifurcated: science was to be based on method, belief was free of the burden of empirical proof.

By the mid-seventeenth century rationalism had finally replaced Aristotelian scholasticism and the Platonic legacy of metaphysics as well at the unitary Christian world-view of the Middle Ages. Modern rationalism was born in the de-centring of consciousness from the divinely ordained laws of the universe to those which modern science is capable of uncovering. Classic statements of the new spirit of rationalism were Nicolas Copernicus's *De Revoluntionibus Orbium Coelestium* [1543], Francis Bacon's *Novum Organum* [1620], René Descartes' *Discourse on Method* [1637] and Issac Newton's *Mathematical Principles of Natural Philosophy* [1687]. This was a period that had witnessed major conflicts over belief, leading to the necessity in the view of many to separate science from belief. As Stephen Toulmin (1992) has argued, the seventeenth-century quest for certainty must be seen in the context of the Thirty Years' War, which plunged Europe into war fought over religious doctrine and political legitimacy. Rationalism and empiricism alike were attempts to find a certain basis for knowledge, beyond clerical-autocratic dogma. Objective and presuppositionless observation was a means of emancipation from the past and from myth and metaphysics. So, too, was rationalism, with its typical belief in the superiority of intellectual designs based on rational systems of knowledge such as logic and mathematics.

The New Learning, or New Science, of the Scientific Revolution and the pietistic humanism of the Reformation period was accompanied by programmes for radical social reform, of which Thomas More's *Utopia* [1516] was a famous example and also one which can be read as one of the first works on modern social policy. The provision of health care, universal education and the abolition of poverty were among the aims of new conception of a utopian polity and were also central to the Baconian reform movement. Francis Bacon himself wrote about the advancement of learning and defended the intellectual resistance of science against the canons of antiquity (such as Aristotle, Ptolemy, Thomas of Aquinas) and, like Thomas More, wrote one of the early utopias: *New Atlantis* [1627]. Other examples of early social utopias are James Harrington's *Oceana* [1675] and Campenalla's *City of the Sun* [1623]. The New Learning was not then only about philosophical arguments; it was also about the emancipation of knowledge from the old monopolies exercised by the corporate professions in the universities and Church. The movement can be described as an early Enlightenment, for it strove to further the cause of universal enlightenment through knowledge emancipated from the past. This period, too, saw the emergence of radical scientific currents (such Paracelsian physicians, alchemists, mystical-hermetic thinkers, magic) from outside the mainstream New Learning and which were later suppressed with the institutionalization of science by the absolute state (van den Daele, 1977: 32/3).

It is important to see that modern science emerges at a time when the institutions of the Middle Ages, such as the Church, the universities and the established professions of jurisprudence and medicine, were collapsing but when the social and political order of modern society had not yet consolidated. It was in this period of transition and upheaval that modern science emerges as part of a project of social reconstruction. Creative or constructivist utopianism was part of the early conceptions of science. Of course, the distinctions between the modern disciplines had not been clarified; more significantly, the distinctions between the sciences were not strongly pronounced. Modern natural experimental science begins as anti-authoritarian, progressive, anti-elitist and based on a programme of educational and social reform. The New Learning, accelerated by the Puritan reform movement (Hill, 1988), implied nothing less than social reconstruction involving the universal availability of knowledge and its employment for the public good (van den Daele, 1977: 36). The radicals of the English Revolution wanted to end the dominance of Greek and Latin and to drive the scholastic theologians out of the universities. Winstanley and the Levellers wanted to the end the distinction between lay and professional knowledge by enlisting science in the democratization of society. The connection between science and its public commitment to society was firmly established in the formative period of modern science and cannot be explained by the notion of positivism, which was a later development. We can say, then, that modern science in its formative period involved the creation of a new cognitive system (or system of knowledge) which sought to link scientific knowledge to social and political goals while preserving its autonomy within the institution of science.

However, this was all to change by the late seventeenth century when the Age of Absolutism reaches its zenith. In England the Restoration in 1660 marked the end of radical science and the association of science with social reconstruction. The Restoration government purged the reformed universities of the adherents of the new experimental natural philosophy and reestablished the authority of the Church and state censorship. In this period the institutionalization of science under the auspices of the absolute state and its mercantilist economy commences. This was marked by the foundation of the Royal Society in London in 1662 by Charles II and the *Académie des Sciences* in Paris in 1666 by Louis XIV (van den Daele, 1977: 29). In France science in the Ancien Regime had an institutional role since the foundation of the *Académie française* in 1635, but one subordinated to the court (Heilbron, 1995). By the end of the century this state control was much strengthened. The political incorporation of science by royal edicts into the state compromised its radical function, which henceforth became one of social administration led by expert systems. At about this time, alternative challenges to modern experimental science, such as hermeticism, had all but disappeared and a state sponsored positivistic Baconism became the dominant framework for science. The consequence of these developments was that the possibility of a radical social science, the first intimations of which were in the utopias of More and Bacon, was aborted and natural science underwent its own path of development as an autonomous expert system linked to the administrative state. In place of social science, literature, in particular in England since the Restoration, took over the role of social science. The relationship between knowledge and its public utility fell apart. It was in this spirit of the differentiation of the sciences that modern rationalism developed: the subversive elements and the project of social reconstruction were abandoned and became the concern of intellectuals who were isolated from the culture of science and a depoliticized cultural humanism flourished in the university. The incorporation of science into the state apparatus and the suppression of alternative forms of knowledge occurred at a time when the modern university system had not yet emerged as an institution capable of sustaining a permanent structure of social scientific knowledge.

Rationalism, Empiricism and the Enlightenment

Beginning with the sceptical humanism of writers such as Erasmus and Montaigne, rationalism reached its apogée in the Cartesian method of Descartes, who established the foundation of a rationalistic conception of science as the search for absolute truths based on first principles. The Cartesian method consists of a belief in the certainties of the 'clear and distinct perceptions' of the solitary individual contemplating an external reality. Everything else is to be treated with scepticism. For Descartes the path to certain knowledge consists in putting everything into doubt so that only those things which can be clearly and distinctively perceived remain. Knowledge thus consists of the pure objects of reason and presupposes psychologism or solipsism: reason is a property of the psychology of the mind of the individual and can in principle be practised by anyone who casts systematic doubt on the objects perceived by the mind.

The Cartesian method exemplified the spirit of modern rationalism, but did not quite encapsulate the core tenets of positivism, which was closer to the doctrine of empiricism. Yet, it was a precursor of positivism in that it established that the demarcation between rational knowledge (knowledge of what is true) and false knowledge is determined by the sceptical power of the mind. Cartesian dualism also laid the basis of one of the tenets of modernity: the dualism of body and mind, spirit and nature, mind and matter. This distinction, which parallels the bifurcation of the sciences, stipulated an absolute demarcation between knowledge of the world of nature and the subjective world of society and its psychological constructions.

While Descartes had established the foundation of true knowledge to be the inquiring and sceptical power of the mind which gains mastery over the external world, positivism has been mostly (until the early twentieth century) inductive rather than deductive. Descartes advocated a deductive approach from first principles, while empiricists argue for an inductive approach: observation of data and the conducting of experiments can lead us to general laws. In other words, Descartes was able to conduct the quest for knowledge seated by the fireside simply by proceeding from the universal to the particular, while the empiricists (such as Newton and Bacon) advocated the gathering of observable data in order to see what universal laws they revealed. The main difference between rationalists and empiricists is that the former regard knowledge as depending on *a priori* logical structures, while the latter emphasize sensory perception or experience as the criterion of valid knowledge. But they were each routes to modernity and marked the separation of science from belief in different ways.

Two of the classical exponents of empiricism were Thomas

Hobbes and John Locke. It is important to see a difference between Cartesian rationalism and English empiricism. The latter is more illustrative of positivism in the conventional sense of the word. According to Hobbes in his famous *Leviathan* [1651], which can be said to have laid the foundations of modern political science, scientific knowledge is based on the search for causal laws. The data the scientist examines are meaningful only as a laws. One of the laws for which Hobbes is famous is the principle of methodological individualism, which was the basis of his political theory, and became the foundation of modern liberalism, influencing in particular the disciplines of politics, economics and psychology. This law claimed that social action can be explained by the behaviour of isolated individuals the sum of whose action is society. Society is thus reduced to the behaviour, in Hobbes quite literally, of the psychological motives of rationally acting individuals seeking to realize their interests. John Locke was also an exponent of empiricism. His *Essay Concerning Human Understanding* [1690] argued for a common-sense theory of knowledge in which science severs all connections with religion. The sole criterion for valid knowledge is determined by sensory experience. This view must be seen in the context of its time for it in effect amounts to a defence of the democratic nature of knowledge against clerical and state censorship: all human beings can have access to scientific knowledge, which cannot be reduced to the pronouncements of clerical or political elites. Locke's empiricism was a liberal and anti-dogmatic conception of science: valid knowledge is that which can be put to the test of experience. In this sense, both rationalism and empiricism were expressions of the turn to radical subjectivity which characterized the modern worldview.

In embracing rationalism and empiricism, the philosophers of the sixteenth and seventeenth centuries brought about a major revolution in the conception of science. However, rationalism and empiricism in this period did not automatically imply a genuinely modern understanding of science. In the case of George Berkeley, empiricism was a critique of science and a defence of theological ideas, and Descartes believed he was incumbent to provide proof of the existence of God. The modern scientific outlook did not occur until the eighteenth century, in the period known as the Enlightenment which radicalized many of the earlier ideas.

From the mid-eighteenth century several schools of thought developed around the *leitmotif* of reason. The philosophers of the

Scottish Enlightenment, in particular David Hume and Adam Smith, were important figures in the history of modern social science. In his three-volume *Treatise of Human Nature* [1739 and 1740] and the later, *An Inquiry Concerning Human Understanding* [1748], Hume advocated an extreme scepticism which brought empiricism beyond the limits of natural laws to which it had previously been bound. He defended Locke's empiricism to the extent that all knowledge derives from sensory experience but drew different conclusions. The empiricism of Locke was reconciled with a belief in the natural laws of morality ('life, liberty and property'), but for Hume scepticism must be extended to everything, including science itself. Thus the knowledge that science produces is an uncertain kind of knowledge and can undermine itself. Hume thus not only rejects the deductive rationalism of Descartes, but also casts doubt on the inductive approach of Lockean empiricism. Hume argued that our knowledge derives from the actual forms of our mental perception and may not therefore correspond to an objective reality. His objection to induction was that we cannot generalize from cases of which we have experience to those which are unknown to us. In this way Hume questioned the correspondence theory of truth characteristic of much of rationalism.

Another enduring legacy of Hume was his argument that the realm of facts and the sphere of values cannot be crossed: we cannot infer values from facts. Human values, such as laws and rights, cannot be derived from reason since they are only conventions not objectively grounded facts, he claimed. Hume's scepticism was that it recognized the role of imagination and emotions as well as human freedom in shaping society. Hume's importance for the social sciences is evident in his rejection of the methodological individualism of Hobbes and in acknowledging the space of the social. Like many thinkers of the age, such as Vico in his cyclical theory of history or Montesquieu in his quest for the 'spirit of the laws', or Rousseau who demonstrated that equality is social and not natural, Hume offered an essentially social view of human action, which cannot be reduced to Hobbes's methodological individualism and its model of self-interest. His approach can be contrasted to the epistemological individualism of Locke and Descartes for whom nothing social enters questions concerning the nature of knowledge (Manicas, 1987: 11–12). Hume's social view of human beings was reflected in his attempt to find general laws of human nature which demonstrate that society is more than the sum of its parts and that freedom is possible. For all his scepticism, Hume was a conservative thinker for whom the separation of facts and values ultimately preserved the latter from any strong criticism other than what 'common sense' dictates.

The objectivity of the social was more extensively appreciated by Hume's contemporary, Adam Smith, who wrote *An Inquiry into the Nature and Causes of the Wealth of Nations* [1776], a work which exhibited the experimental and empiricism advocated by Hume and became a classic of the new 'moral sciences'. Smith and other Scottish thinkers, such as John Millar and Francis Hutchinson, demolished the prevailing notions of the social contract with a more social scientific account of what he called 'conventions' that could not be explained by 'contracts'.

Scotland played a leading role in the formation of modern social science, which flourished in the secular universities. In France the Enlightenment emerged out of the court society and developed in the rapidly developing civil society which provided new spaces for public discourse to form. The rationalism of the Enlightenment was characterized by a strong attack on religion, with the *philosophes* such as Voltaire and D'Holbach and the *Encylopèdistes* such as Diderot engaging in empiricist tirades against theology. While many of these salon intellectuals took the individual as the cornerstone of knowledge, others began from the perspective of society. From a positivistic outlook, the physiocrats, who were a group of political economists, including Francois Quesnay, represented the view that society is determined by laws similar to those operative in nature.

Rousseau and Montesquieu had a stronger concept of society as the object of study *sui generis*. Rousseau was one of the first to use the word 'society', as in *The Social Contract* [1762], though one of the first uses of the word goes back to Thomas More's *Utopia* [1516]. With the Enlightenment intellectuals, society as 'civil society' is seen as a sovereign domain autonomous of the state, which was still absolutist. It was fateful for the subsequent history of social science that this sense of society as a domain against the state was subordinated to a conception of science which reflected a statist view of science. 'Social science' was a term that was coined by Condorcet in the initial stages of the French Revolution and introduced to the English language via his writings (Heilbron, 1995: 110). Social science, which replaced the older idea of moral science, became rapidly conceived as an area of state reform policy, associated with the reform politics of Turgot, and was institutionally modelled on the natural sciences, in particular mathematics. As a positivistic inquiry, social science first developed in France during the Restoration after the fall of Napoleon, who had supported the natural sciences, and it was very much in the spirit of the natural sciences that the social sciences became institutionalized as a state-centred knowledge culture in France. Positivism became associated with 'useful' or technically exploitable knowledge for the purpose of social engineering by the administrators of the state. This was the sense in which Comte used it as the methodology of 'sociology', a term he coined, to describe the science of industrial society. The social preconditions of social science as positivistic inquiry was the administrative modern state, which required the systematization and coding of knowledge. Social science as a positivistic institution thus became tied to policy-making and state administration. Moreover, the beginnings of national differences in the conception of science begins to emerge from the 1790s onwards.

Against this tradition which equated scientific knowledge with natural science and the need of the state for a form of knowledge to be used in social administration, the intellectuals of the Enlightenment stood for a more radical kind of knowledge that could be used in programmes of social reconstruction. This conception of science can be seen as the continuation of the original ambitions of the New Learning and had a major role to play in the formation of social science. The Enlightenment writers did not simply glorify science for its own sake but were critical of the intolerance of the French state and its knowledge politics. During the revolutionary period there was the possibility that an emancipatory new science of social reconstruction might emerge, but this hope was shattered by the aftermath of the Revolution with the formation of the modern French state. Both under the absolute Ancien Regime and the modern post-Revolutionary state, the Enlightenment was isolated from institutionalized science, which was forced to retreat from a political role, and was thereby compelled to take up an oppositional position. This oppositional role had a major role in the formation of social science as a form of normative and critical reflection on society. Thus, from the beginning of the modern period, social science was divided between occupying an institutional role as part of the state apparatus or being an extra-institutional discourse. Until social science became institutionalized in the universities from the late nineteenth century it remained bifurcated between intellectual critical culture and expert systems. The former largely existed in the literary public sphere and the latter within the institutions of the state.

This bifurcation was not always an impediment to the formation of a mature social science. Lepenies (1988) writes of the borrowing of social science, in particular sociology, from literature which in the Enlightenment period had a social role. Balzac, for instance, first intended to call his work, not *Comèdie Humaine* but *Etudes Sociales*, Zola spoke of a '*sociologie pratique*', and with Flaubert literature and social critique were indistinguishable. According to Lepenies, sociology emerged as a 'third culture' between natural science, on the one side, and on the other literature and the humanities. Isolated from the official expert culture fostered by the state, sociology found itself with not only natural science as a rival but also literature. Fearing that the association with literature might ruin its aspiration to scientific status, sociology preferred to model itself on the natural sciences rather than on literature and the humanities from which it distanced itself. This was exacerbated by the fact that on the whole the counter-Enlightenment was allied on the side of a literary social science, with reactionary and Romantic thinkers looking more to literature than science for an orientation for social science. In England, where since the Restoration the educational establishment lay greater stress on literature than on science, social science was often equated with literature, as is evidenced by the literary-social scientific writings of Mathew Arnold, H. G. Wells, D. H. Lawrence and Julian Huxley. In Germany, the circle around the poet Stefan George had an important role in the shaping of sociology. Georg Simmel, for instance, was a mediator between science and literature, and Max Weber was influenced by the Romantics, but was critical of the Romantic quests of poets to aspire to scientific knowledge. Even American empirical sociology was not untouched by literature: Robert Lynd, one of the principal figures of the Chicago School, was influenced by the writings of D. H. Lawrence, whose theme also was the impact of modern industrialism on traditional communities (Lepenies, 1988: 186).

The foundation of the modern university system in the nineteenth century opened up new possibilities for social science to develop as a competing form of knowledge to both natural science and literature.

The Emergence of Nineteenth-Century Positivism

The classic proponent of positivism was Auguste Comte, who also coined the word 'sociology', meaning science of society. In his *Course of Positive Philosophy* [1830–1842] he outlined the basic ideas of positivism. For Comte 'positive' science was certain knowledge and a contrast to imaginary knowledge in its reliance on empirical methodology. In contrast to the Enlightenment intellectuals, the *philosophes* and others, it was positive as opposed to negative critique. Thus, from its inception in the restoration period, positivism was a project conceived in opposition to critique and in recognition of the objectivity of something called 'society'. With Comte empiricism in the tradition from Locke to Hume is transformed from pure epistemology to the actual practice of empirical methodology. Knowledge no longer has to prove itself merely through a critique of sensory perception, but must submit itself before methodological investigation: there can be no truth without observation. The empirical henceforth refers to the domain of objectively existing facts and science is the observation of those facts. With the identification of the empirical with the factual, rationality too shifts from the epistemological to the scientific and becomes equated with methodology. In this way Comtean positivism inherited the traditions of empiricism and rationalism, and established a distinction between the intellectual and the expert: positivism was to be a form of knowledge based on scientific expertise. While for Condorcet social science was modelled on mathematics, for Comte it was to be modelled on physics; it was to be a value free, explanatory, descriptive and a comparative science of general social laws. The themes with defined social science were those of stability and change: 'statics' was the study of social stability and 'dynamics' the study of change or evolution. This concern with stability and change can be seen in the context of the aftermath of the French Revolution and the overthrow of the Bourbon monarchy in 1830, events which shaped Comte's thought. As a reformer, Comte was like most liberals not a revolutionary and feared social disorder, but did not stand for Restoration reactionism. This experience with crisis led him to believe that social order was the natural condition of society. For sociology this had the consequence that it became more concerned with the question of order than of change. Although positivism was to become associated with a conservative and affirmative view of science, it was originally an attempt to free science from speculative thought and from the authority of received wisdom.

Social science or 'social physics' thus began its uncertain career in the mirror image of natural science and came to be the expression of modernity itself. The doctrine of positivism was outlined in the context of a philosophy of history which Comte, under the influence of the industrial utopianism of Saint-Simon, developed from Turgot. The basic idea was that the evolution of human society through the ages culminated in the modern epoch of positivism in which science was itself the secular spiritualism of industrial society. In this Comtean worldview, positivism was the highest expression of scientism: the idea that science, which alone has access to true and objective knowledge, can provide political and moral leadership for society.

In Britain positivism was reflected in the writings of the Victorian utilitarians, such as J. S. Mill, and in the rise of social evolutionism as represented in the thought of Herbert Spencer. Mill, however, was greatly influenced by Comte, about whom he wrote a book in 1865. In his *A System of Logic* [1843] he defended empiricism as an inductive science of general causal laws. While recognizing differences between the study of nature and the study of society, he stood for the unity of the scientific method. Mill was very critical of the idea of a scientific politics and stood for a model of useful knowledge. The principal difference between French and British positivism was that in Britain science was not itself seen as capable of providing political leadership. This was a reflection of the fact that while England had taken the lead in science in the seventeenth century, the centre of gravity shifted to France, as was to be the case in the following century when it once again shifted to Germany. The Victorians tended to link science to the idea of moral improvement and social reform within the limits of the liberal polity. Sociology was from the beginning caught in the bind between the positivistic heritage of moralistic reformism and administrative knowledge.

For Mill all explanations have the same logical structure and society can be explained by the laws governing nature. More important for social science was Spencer who helped to popularize the word 'sociology' in England as a new science of society based on the method of the natural sciences. While Comtean positivism tied social science to physics, Spencer took biology as the paradigmatic science. Under the influence of Darwin, Spencer developed a functionalist-evolutionary social science which had considerable impact on the subsequent history of the social sciences. The basic ideas of this approach are that social structures are explained in terms of the functions they perform and social change is the result of functional adaptation. His *Social Statics* [1850] clearly shows the influence of Comte and a concern typical of Victorian social thought with social order. Spencer also linked theory construction to empirical analysis, compiling vast quantities of data for the building of general theory. Darwin himself was influenced by Spencer, who formulated the notion of 'the survival of the fittest', a term which found its most famous expression in the *Origin of Species* [1859].

Comte's influence in shaping the positivistic self-understanding of the social sciences extended largely through Spencer in England and Émile Durkheim in France, who both established the foundations of modern empirical sociology and functionalist theory. Durkheim's conception of social sciences was set out in 1895 in the *Rules for the Sociological Method* which argued for a model of social science very much based on natural science, but one that discarded the philosophy of history. His approach was also opposed to psychologism, the attempt to explain society by reference to the consciousness of the individual. Society for Durkheim is a reality in itself and sociology is a realist and inductive science of social facts. The object domain of social science is a reality which is composed of facts and laws between those facts. All of social reality can be broken down into facts and analysed in specific case studies of which Durkheim was the first major modern exponent. His approach was an anti-naturalist realism since he held that social facts were different from natural facts. Social facts differ from natural facts in that they are social representations, but they are nonetheless facts and can be examined without recourse to prior theoretical constructions. While facts are the raw data, the aim of social science is the search for causal laws. Theory for Durkheim is subsequent to observation which proceeds inductively from facts to hypotheses to general causal laws. These general laws are conceived in terms of their functions: social phenomena are explained by their social functions. Durkheim insisted on the priority of causality as the proper subject matter of sociology.

Politically a liberal reformer and a believer in modern moral individualism, Durkheim was no radical and feared the breakdown of French society, which was threatened not only by the spectre of the Paris Commune and the Dreyfus Affair, but also by German aggression, as witnessed by the Franco-Prussian War. His conception of social science was a conservative one in that it stressed social cohesion through cultural consensus as the normal condition of society and social change was identified with disorder or dysfunctions. The role of the social scientist was confined to that of a neutral observer of an objectively existing reality over which they had no control.

Functionalism combined with empirical social science had its most important success in North American universities where social science as a profession was established rapidly from the late nineteenth century onwards, culminating in the Chicago School, which was the leading school in sociology in the 1920s. While the research of the Chicago School went beyond positivism, embracing, for instance, under the influence of Georg Simmel, social interactionism, its self-understanding was radical social criticism. Pragmatism was an important influence in the Chicago School (Joas, 1993). Works such as John Dewey's *The Public and its Problems* [1927] were important in mediating empirical research with theory. One of Dewey's concerns was the link between democracy and knowledge, a relationship he believed must be rescued by a policy-oriented science. American pragmatism exemplified a tradition of social science which was characterized by the priority of positivistic empirical research with theory serving an applied role. Thus empirical micro-case studies using statistical methodology became the hallmark of American sociology. However, what guided research was more government policy and social administration than intellectual critique. The influence of pragmatism in time declined.

Existing somewhat uneasily alongside empirical sociology was the more theoretical sociology of Talcott Parsons and Thomas Merton, but which had also inherited the positivistic conception of social science as value-free inquiry. The Parsonian conception of social science can be seen as the expression of the core values of America society – liberal democratic consensus within the egalitarian market structures of capitalism – and as an historical alternative to European fascism and communism. Functionalism and positivism became closely linked in the combination of quantitative empirical research within an evolutionary conception of society based on modernization and functionalist theory. Paul F. Lazarsfeld's sociology is an example of the use of a mathematically based empirical social science, which co-operated with the functionalism of Parsons and Merton.

The Emergence of Neo-Positivism

The positivistic conception of science, I have suggested, has traditionally been linked to liberal reformism, if not radicalism, reacting to historical crisis. The great historical crises that marked the path of modern positivistic and rationalistic science were the 'general crisis' of the seventeenth century, the French Revolution and its aftermath, and the First World War and the rise of fascism. The latter provided the context for a new kind of positivism in the 1920s, when many intellectuals of a liberal and left disposition (such as Ernst Mach, Moritz Schlick, Carl Hempel, Otto Neurath) reacted to the anarchy of ideology as well as obscurantist metaphysics which were creeping into academia in the period preceding and following the war. The 'logical positivism' of the Vienna Circle demanded a conception of science based on the natural sciences, in particular physics which was to be the model for all the sciences.

Logical positivism was inspired by the new developments in physics, such as Einstein's theory of relativity and quantum mechanics, and stood for the ideal of a unified science based on the certain knowledge of mathematical logic. German idealism was also one of their targets, since it had become an ideology that had failed to separate science from the domain of belief.

One of the key features of logical positivism – the basis of neo-positivism – was that there are only two kinds of knowledge, empirical knowledge (knowledge derived from experience) and logical knowledge (which is derived from logical analysis). Mach offered one of the classic formulations of logical positivism as the methodological objectification of reality in the analysis of laws governing facts. Carnap's *The Logical Structure of the World* [1927] became one of the enduring treatises of logical positivism. Undoubtedly the most famous statement of the school was Ludwig Wittgenstein's correspondence theory of truth in the *Tractatus Logico-philosophicus* [1921], a work which Wittgenstein later refuted when he moved towards a relationist theory of truth. Logical positivism radicalized this view by proposing that the only valid kind of knowledge is observable and verifiable knowledge.

A second and major influence on neo-positivism was linguistics and the analytical philosophy of language. This school was very influential in Anglo-American conceptions of science, such as the realist and analytical traditions associated with Russell, Ayer, Nagel, Ryle and Quine. The rise of the new science of linguistics led several proponents of logical positivism, in particular Wittgenstein and Carnap, to see science in terms of a form of language. In opposition to positivism and the empirical, experimental method with its concern with facts or things, neo-positivism emerged around a concern with the language with which things were described. Where everyday language is imprecise, neo-positivism was driven by the ideal of a pure scientific semantics, the chief characteristic of which was the logical relation of words, not of words and things. Thus was born the idea of a scientific language in which the logical structure of the world could be described without recourse to the language of the world. Preserving the aspiration for a pure foundation of knowledge that has always been a feature of positivism, neo-positivism rejected presuppositionless inquiry.

Logical positivism imposed a heavy burden on science, and especially the social sciences, since it denied the validity of any form of language other than a pure logical system. However, once logical positivism moved beyond philosophy a broader neo-positivism gained influence in the philosophy of science in the post-1945 period in the United States as a result of the migration there of German and central European philosophers fleeing from the Nazis. Gradually, the possibility of reconciling the deductive bias and logical semantics with inductive inquiry allowing for testing and verification was accepted if science were to be possible at all. Quite simply, science had to be able to explain reality and to do this it had to move beyond the limits of a purely logical analysis constrained by a pure semantics. In sum, an empirical, as opposed to a formal, turn in neo-positivism became evident with the recognition that a key feature of science is explanation.

Two major examples of this empirically inclined neo-positivism were Carl Hempel and Ernst Nagel, who advocated a nomological deductive method for all the sciences, including the social sciences. In his *The Structure of Science* [1961] Ernst Nagel argued that the objective of scientific investigation is the search for behavioural regularities. As with the earlier logical positivists, he was strongly opposed to any inclusion within science of intentional meaning and argued that science must be explanatory. Neo-positivists hold that science must be able to make generalizations on the basis of observable regularities. In this view, the social sciences, such as sociology, must be able to do this if they want to become genuine sciences. Clearly this favoured quantitative analysis of large-scale data. This was also the position of the Carl Hempel who strongly advocated nomological (or the search for laws) analysis within a broadly deductive framework. Hempel was particularly influential in the philosophy of the social sciences which he wanted to establish as part of a unified science. He believed that the search for general historical laws could be used for predictions: explanations must have the power of prediction. Others such as Otto Neurath, who was politically Marxist, believed that a neo-positivist approach in social science would provide a universal language by which the social world could be objectively analysed.

The Break-Up of Positivism: Popper and Kuhn

In the inter-war years positivism appeared to be the dominant influence in the philosophy of science. Logical positivism and professional empirical social science were in ascendancy since the death of Durkheim and it seemed that only Weberian sociology (to be considered in the next chapter) was capable of offering an alternative.

The critique of positivism can be viewed from two angles. One angle is to trace the revolt of the social sciences against the hegemony of the natural sciences. This involves looking at the hermeneutical-interpretative revolt from the neo-Kantians to Weber and modern hermeneutics (the subject of the next chapter), and the Marxist and critical theory revolt from Marx to the Frankfurt School to neo-Marxism and Habermas (the subject of Chapter 3). The other angle is to look at the internal undermining of positivism from such developments as the neo-positivist departure, Quine's critique, to the revival of Science and Technology Studies (STS) and the Sociology of Scientific Knowledge (SSK). This will involve shifting the perspective to the philosophy of science more generally for positivism has not been merely attacked by social science: it has been far more pervasively and effectively criticized by post-positivistic conceptions of natural science itself which have sought to rescue realism from positivism. Ironically, then, the result is that many positivists operating in the social sciences hold to a conception of science that has been abandoned by modern natural science itself.

One of the most important early developments in the internal breakdown of positivism was the Duhem-Quine thesis of the underdetermination of scientific theories by evidence. Quine had established a relationist theory of truth and the indeterminacy of reference, which undermined the inductionist and foundationalist basis of classical positivism by showing that evidence neither confirms nor refutes a theory or hypothesis. With this, Quine demolished one of the major assumptions of positivism in all its forms. For Quine, truth is a function of the relationship between words (including whole theoretical systems), and not of the correspondence between words and reality. The idea of theory-dependency in observation was confirmed in work as diverse as Poincaré, Einstein, Popper, Kuhn and Toulmin (1953).

In addition to these developments, there emerged an entirely new kind of philosophy of language after the publication of Wittgenstein's *Philosophical Investigations* [1953], which was a total abandonment of the earlier philosophy of language in terms of a formal semantics for one that was based on the analysis of 'language games'. This was also evident in the philosophy of the influential British philosopher Alfred Ayer who introduced the idea that meaning and truth is dependent in part on the way words are used. These developments in the direction of a pragmatics of language that recognized the reality of common sense within the language of science gave a philosophical basis for a new departure for social science beyond positivism.

In the remainder of this chapter, I shall confine the discussion to two important critics of positivism who wrote from the perspective of the philosophy of science, namely Karl Popper and Thomas Kuhn. Although not specifically concerned with the social sciences, they had a huge impact on the way we think of the scientific endeavour.

Popper's theory of science can be viewed as a critique of positivism, in particular of logical positivism, which he aimed to refute; but his was a critique which did not abandon all aspects of positivism. For critics of positivism as a methodology of science, positivism in its inductive empiricist form is unable to explain the principled rejection of evidence. In *The Logic of Scientific Discovery* ([1934] 1959) Popper outlined the basic tenets of the method he advocated, critical rationalism. The main thesis in this revolutionary work in the philosophy of science is that the principle of verification must be replaced by the principle of falsification, sometimes called the hypothetico-deductive method. The logic of science, he argued, does not proceed inductively as in Baconism, that is, from the observation of data to the construction of theories or hypotheses. Science does not prove anything by conducting experiments, no matter how numerous, for the very reason that no matter how often a theory is tested there is always the possibility that it can be falsified. Popper's argument against verification, or justificationism, is illustrated by his famous example that 'no matter how many instances of white swans we may have observed, this does not justify the conclusion that *all* swans are white' (1959: 27). Popper instead proposes the principle of falsification, or the 'trial and error' theory. Instead of proceeding inductively, science progresses deductively through attempts to falsify the results of previous theories. Rather than proceeding from the particular to universal, Popper argues science proceeds from the universal (that is, scientific hypotheses) to the particular, but from hypotheses.

Popper thus demolished one of the axioms of positivism, namely that science proceeds from the observation of data by means of experiments which when repeated are verified allowing us to infer general laws about the nature of reality. Popper shows that the logic of science is determined not by a path to absolute verifiable knowledge, but by attempts to falsify the results of other theories and therefore the theories science provides are only ones which have withstood falsification. The scientist does not gather facts or data in order to construct a theory, rather they accumulate data to falsify prevailing theories: 'Knowledge does not start from perception or observations or the collection of data or facts, but it starts, rather, from *problems*' (Popper, 1976: 88). The result is that scientific knowledge is uncertain knowledge, but is nevertheless the most certain kind of knowledge human beings can aspire to: its certainty consists of its falsifiability. The objectivity of science is the objectivity of its method and this is all that separates science from non-science. The theories of science are ultimately only tentative conjectures to solve problems and cannot be verified by empirical evidence, no matter how weighty it may be. Scientific statements are then statements that are in principle open to falsification, ones whose truth content can be tested empirically. Scientific truths can only be 'corroborated'; they cannot be verified. Tautological or metaphorical statements cannot therefore be scientific since they cannot be falsified. Popper believed this also applied to Marxism which he regard as historicist (i.e. a metaphysical philosophy of history) and based on the positivist illusion of historical laws.

Marxists, he argued, always stressed the evidence in favour of their theories while ignoring evidence which could falsify them.

Critical rationalism breaks certain defining tenets of positivism. It rejects the naive inductionist notion that the scientist observes reality without theoretical predispositions, for the scientist always operates from a theory which has withstood attempts to falsify it. Science, Popper contends, does not criticize reality. In this sense it is value free for the scientist may not make judgements on the subject matter of science. The critical task refers entirely to the scientific method which, Popper argues against scientistic positivism, must reflect on itself for science is fallibilistic, always potentially in need of improvement and correction: the best theory is always the best tested one. While up-holding the unity of the scientific method for all the sciences, Popper concedes that the subject matter of the social sciences differs from that of the natural sciences. The nature of causality in society cannot be compared with natural causality, where it is always invariable while in society it is contingent. Moreover, it is the aim of the natural sciences to make prediction possible, while in the social sciences predictions can be self-fulfilling prophecies and thus do not met the criterion of falsifiability. Yet, Popper stands ultimately in the empiricist tradition of Hume in the recognition that absolute certainty, which Cartesian rationalism strove for, is not possible while admitting that knowledge of reality is possible however imperfect it may be. He believed in the unity of the scientific knowledge, arguing that the principle of falsification also applies to the social sciences. While severely criticizing naive scientism, he nevertheless stood for a scientistic concept of science as the bearer of the most perfect form of knowledge. Thus, Popper stands in the Platonic tradition that separates knowledge (*logos*) from opinion (*doxa*).

In sum, the importance of Popper's critical rationalism is that he rejects the naturalistic fallacy of positivism not just in social science but primarily in natural science. In striking a major blow against the positivistic conception of natural science as a theory of how natural science operates, Popper undermined the possibility of a positivistic social science which has always required the alibi of positivism in the natural sciences. Popper, it must be mentioned, was not the only critic of induction. Other leading critics, were Nagel, who wrote *The Structure of Science* [1961]; Zetterberg, who wrote *On Theory and Verification in Sociology* [1966]; and Hempel and Oppenheim, who advanced an 'deductive nomological' approach.

Popper's theory of science has been the subject of great controversy, and Popper himself modified some of his earlier extreme and somewhat simple claims. It will suffice to mention here that the most important revision he made in face of massive criticism was that the logic of science does not only depend on the principle of falsfiability, for a theory is discarded not once it has been falsified but only when a new theory is there to replace it and, moreover, a degree of verification is possible if a theory withstands numerous attempts at falsification.

At this point we can consider the work of Thomas Kuhn, whose place in the history of the philosophy of science is as revolutionary as the importance he accords to the logic of scientific innovation itself. Like Popper, he accepted the unity of the scientific method of theory testing, but went beyond him in recognizing the intrusion into science of what philosophers from Plato to Popper banned, namely opinion. With Kuhn the republic of science becomes a community of scientists united in the errors of the ways they have come to accept.

Kuhn in his classic work *The Structure of Scientific Revolution* ([1962] 1970) has offered the most sophisticated alternative to Popper. His main thesis is that science proceeds neither inductively as positivists maintained (from observation to theory) nor by the falsification of theory. The most important factor in science is the shift from normal science to revolutionary science. He claimed, with many of Popper's critics, that scientific progress is not dependent on falsification to bring about a change in a paradigm. Scientists, he firmly believed, do not learn from mistakes, particularly if these errors are going to have very far-reaching consequences for the way science is conducted. Kuhn in effect reduces Popper's principle of falsifiablity to problem-solving within normal science. In the course of 'normal science' scientists attempt to resolve problems or puzzles whose solutions are contained within the paradigm they operate, for paradigms also influence the questions as well as the answers. Kuhn argued normal science does not look for anomalies for it is content to remain with the problems the paradigm is capable of solving. However, when an anomaly occurs, this 'puzzle solving' may not be enough as the limits of the paradigm may be challenged. In general scientists, Kuhn argues, are reluctant to break from a paradigm which offers them security. Scientists in the course of normal science do not look for anomalies and use the paradigm to impose the prevailing consensus. Thus the concept of truth that prevails is more one of consensus than correspondence. Very often it takes a new generation to make the break as it may require a fundamental shift in cultural values. If an anomaly persists it may lead to a period of crisis in which 'extraordinary science' occurs which is characterized by a plurality of views and debate on the fundamentals of the paradigm begins. A new paradigm is then ready to emerge in order to solve the anomaly. The new paradigm subsequently comes to be accepted as normal science and a new consensus is established. However, a paradigm is rejected only when a new one is available, for without a paradigm there can be no meaningful science. This may take a considerable length of time (so extraordinary science may be more 'normal' than 'normal science').

Kuhn maintained Popper's break with positivism was incomplete for his principle of falsification only applied to normal science and could not explain the great scientific innovations. In normal science researchers are not in fact trying to refute a theory, but merely looking for a solution to a puzzle, rather like a chess player who is not normally questioning the rules of the game. He also finally refuted positivism on the grounds that verification may be possible within one paradigm, but the same set of facts could imply a different outcome in a different paradigm: evidence can be used in different ways depending on one's paradigm. Where Popper saw science as a process of ongoing critique of itself, Kuhn saw science as the rule of the paradigm, wherein a degree of progress might be possible. In contrast for Popper progress entailed by necessity a 'revolution', but if this led to an overgeneralization of revolutions, Kuhn was ultimately in the camp of the closed society of the 'normal' science of the paradigm where learning occurred from the authority rather than from errors.

Kuhn's importance in the post-empiricist conception of science consists of his demonstration that progress in science does not depend on induction or on deduction, but on revolutionary breakdowns in paradigms: observation does not lead to theory. His starting point is not reality but scientific constructions (Trigg, 1985: 14). Neither the accumulation of evidence nor the ability to falsify a theory explains how science works for these criteria fail to take account of the role of revolutions in science. These revolutions involve the intrusion into science of non-scientific elements, such as cultural values which make some scientists blind to the implications of an anomaly and open the eyes of others. By admitting the role of a 'revolutionary transformation of vision' in the logic of science and the importance of historical and social context, Kuhn contributed to demolishing the scientistic self-confidence of positivism in its identification of science with the holistic discourse of perfect knowledge, and, moreover, casts doubt on the role of progress in science in so far as this was cumulative. Scientific paradigms cannot be judged because they are themselves the basis of judgement: science as a cognitive system is ultimately shaped by the institution of science.

Nevertheless Kuhn was not a relativist and believed in scientific progress, despite having demonstrated its ultimate limits. While the incommensurablity thesis claimed that paradigms are frequently incommensurable, progress may still be possible in one paradigm but not necessarily across paradigms. Since Kuhn rejects not only absolute proof but also the principle of falsification, the only criterion left in his model is the prevailing consensus. In this sense Kuhn remained ultimately in the positivist camp since he denied the possibility of critical and rational consensus (Bernstein, 1979: 93). It was a view of science that was unable to explain change. However, one of the most important consequences of Kuhn's work derived from the importance he gave to the role of the 'scientific community' in the construction of science. Kuhn revitalized the empirical study of science in the turn away from an ideal methodology to the study of science by scientific means; moreover, his work was followed by the naturalization of epistemology a wide-ranging movement today, the core of which is neo-empiricist, conventionalistic and naturalistic study of scientific practice. In the present context, it may be said that Kuhn hastened the demise of positivism which was breaking down internally and criticized from without in various ways by a whole new generation of science studies and post-positivist philosophies (see Rorty, 1979; Fuller, 1993). The significance of Kuhn is that he established a discontinuous view of science as marked by ruptures. This challenged the prevailing idea that goes back to the Enlightenment of science as a continuous process.

It would not be possible here to enter into a discussion on the debates to which Kuhn has given rise. I shall merely comment on Lakatos's critique, which is generally considered the most important attempt to place the post-empiricist theory of science somewhere between Popper and Kuhn, briefly introduce Feyerabend's anarchistic theory and finally discuss the implications of Kuhn specifically for social science. Again, the point is to show that the context for post-positivistic philosophy of social science are these developments discussed here within all of science.

Lakatos's critique of Kuhn revolves around the central critical argument made against Kuhn, namely that his concept of a revolution is irrationalist and too general as is the notion of a single dominating paradigm governing normal science. Instead, Lakatos (1970, 1978) proposes that normal science be considered more as a research programme which survives falsification for reasons of its general acceptability. This situation cannot be regarded as a paradigm since it does not have the general status that Kuhn attributed to it. The transition from one research programme to another is not always revolutionary in the irrational manner implied by Kuhn, but the product of rational exploration of rival methodologies. The situational logic, such as cultural values and historical milieu, is thus less important than Kuhn believed. The result of Lakatos's intervention was a levelling of Kuhnian theory down to critical rationalism. However, he goes beyond Popper in arguing that the progress of science does not occur merely through attempts to falsify theory by new evidence, but in Kuhnian terms whole research programmes can be falsified. He modified Popper's principle of falsification to what he called 'sophisticated falsificationism': it is not single theories that are falsified but entire programmes and this occurs only when there is an alternative available. In other words, refutation does not automatically lead to rejection. Moreover, he tried to accommodate a degree of confirmation of theories. The history of science is the process by which increasingly more progressive programmes replace less adequate ones, but all of which, including programmes subsequently proven to be false, are important in the progress of science.

Paul Feyerabend, in *Against Method* (1975), represents one of the final figures in the relativization of science. His 'anarchistic theory of knowledge' argued for a pluralistic view of science which did not elevate science above other kinds of human knowledge, such as religion. Feyerabend generalized Kuhn's extraordinary science to be nature of all of science and argues, in Wittgensteinian manner, that the meaning of science derives from its social application. The result of Feyerabend's critique is radical relativism. Feyerabend was a controversial and provocative figure who believed that science should be organized so as to enhance the possibility of a democratic society. In *Science in a Free Society* (1978) he argued for the disestablishment of science in society, demanding it be reduced to the status of just one belief-system among others. Science, in his view, should not be supported by the state since state-sponsored science is undemocratic and is mostly conducted without the consultation of the public (see Chapter 8).

The implications of post-empiricism in the theory of science for the social sciences have been ambivalent. On the one side, Kuhn succeeded in demolishing the scientistic self-understanding of positivism in the history of the natural sciences and therefore struck a blow against positivism in the social sciences. On the other side, his theory of science is primarily a theory of natural science and cannot be applied so easily to social science, which is characterized more by a multi-paradigm status. The Kuhnian paradigms, even when reduced to Lakatos's research programmes, seem more like disciplines themselves in the social and human sciences. Social scientists are too divided to accept paradigms and it is therefore questionable if something like 'normal science' characterizes the social sciences where there is a plurality of competing paradigms available. There is also another problem with the reception of Kuhn in social science. The consensus theory of science that Kuhn proposed has had an oddly conservative reception, often confirming positivism rather than undermining it. Kuhn himself rejected most of the radical implications of his breakthrough and denies the possibility of an external critical rationality that is independent of the epistemic practices of the time (Fuller, 1992: 251). The idea of a cognitive consensus model within the scientific community had more appeal to conservative positivists than to more radical and critical conceptions of social science (Martins, 1972: 52). Indeed, the actual empirical conducting of positivistic social science is not in fact challenged by the Kuhnian approach which primarily emphasizes the role of revolutions in the breakdown of paradigms.

Steve Fuller in a major assessment of his work has shown that where the orthodox view of Kuhn's work, *The Structure of Scientific Revolutions*, was that it heralded the revolutionary impulses of the 1960s; in fact it reflected the conservative preoccupations of the Cold War and provided an enduring myth of the 'end of ideology' thesis which limited the cognitive horizons of science (Fuller, 2000a). Fuller presents Kuhn as the champion of paradigms, who, despite the potentially innovating concessions to methodological relativism, sought to anchor science in problem solving activities where there are no major theoretical or methodological disputes. In this way, according to Fuller, Kuhn gave to science a history that made it safe from the criticisms that were beginning to be voiced against 'Big Science'. In other words, Kuhn ultimately divested science of its radical elements, making it both free from and for democracy.

Conclusion: After Positivism

In order to take the post-empiricist critique of positivism to its conclusion a consideration of other positions which would be appropriate: these positions fall into two broad groups, namely realism and constructivism. The former is principally represented by the critical realism of Roy Bhaskar, who rejects positivism in favour of an emancipatory theory of science which is both explanatory and interpretative. This critical realism seeks to rescue the sciences from relativism. One of the aims of realism is to retain the claims of science to objectivity and truth without conceding anything to scientism and the absolute unity of the scientific method. Critical realism can be seen as a way of rescuing realism and the emancipatory promises of science from positivism and from relativism. Constructivism, on the other hand, is a more diffuse term to describe different post-empiricist approaches. In their most sophisticated forms, constructivist schools are best represented by the reconstructive-pragmatic social science of Habermas and Apel, postmodernism, various other positions such as interventionism, feminist epistemology, utilization research and Bourdieu's critical practice. However, to enter into a discussion on the critical realism and constructivist schools would be to jump ahead. These developments will be discussed in later chapters. In the next chapter the main historical alternative to positivism within the social sciences is discussed: the hermeneutic and interpretative approaches. While the aim of the present chapter has been to show that positivism underwent major internal transformation arising out of developments relating to neo-positivism, the next chapter will look at fundamentally non-positivistic approaches within the philosophy of the social sciences, but which had their origin in the humanities as opposed to the experimental sciences as was the case with positivism.

2 Hermeneutics and Interpretation: The Search for Meaning

Introduction: Defining the Hermeneutical Approach

In the previous chapter the critique of positivism was looked at from a point which broadly accepted the unity of the scientific method, even though it saw the subject matter of social science as being different from that of the natural sciences. Positivism evolved from its origins in radical liberalism to become the dominant form the institution of science took in modern society. Although positivism took many forms, underlying them was a belief that the purpose of science was to explain reality. With the institutionalization of science under state control, the radical challenge to positivism was mostly represented by Marxism (which along with the critical tradition will be looked at in the next chapter). In this chapter the hermeneutical tradition, predominantly associated with nineteenth-century German thought, is examined from its origins in the counter-Enlightenment of Vico and Rousseau, to eighteenth-century philology to the neo-Kantian school, phenomenology and its evolution into the interpretative social science of Weber and the psychoanalysis of Freud. Finally, modern hermeneutical approaches are briefly considered in order to provide a full picture of the anti-positivist tradition in terms of the understanding versus explanation controversy.

While a discourse of realism pervades positivism, a discourse of constructivism runs through the hermeneutical tradition: social reality is seen as a meaningful construction and not as an objective reality. The hermeneutical tradition entered the social sciences with Max Weber and was based on the fundamental insight that the prevailing positivistic orientation in positivism was limited not only in explaining social and cultural phenomena but also in understanding the social world. The hermeneutical approach is characterized by the following dominant tendencies:

Interpretation Hermeneutics, which means interpretation, stands for the subordination of explanation and description to interpretation, which cannot be reduced to mere observation. The structure of social reality, which consists of objectifications of human meaning is too complex for observation to provide us with a realistic representation. Therefore the scientist must interpret in order to reach the deeper levels of reality.

Anti-scientism The proponents of the hermeneutical approach argue for a strong separation of the social and the human sciences from the natural sciences in both the method and the subject matter of science. Underlying this is a strong claim for the separation of facts from values.

Value-freedom While being a major departure from positivism, the hermeneutical approach has generally been conceived of as value-free and ultimately implies relativism. In other words, the scientist does not enter into a critique of the subject matter. In this respect, hermeneutical social science is not a departure from positivistic social science. Yet, this sense of value-freedom is in conflict with the orientation of hermeneutical knowledge towards the improvement in self-understanding. This is what makes it ultimately different from positivism.

Humanism The proponents of the hermeneutical approach generally presuppose the unity of human nature which makes interpretation possible. Thus, while different cultures and historical periods may have different values, there is an underlying human nature which remains constant: the belief that the world cannot be meaningless.

Linguistic constructivism Most hermeneutical approaches emphasize the importance of language as the basic structure of society. Society is seen as a linguistically and meaningfully constituted. In this respect the hermeneutical approach involves a fundamental departure from positivism and its methodological individualism.

Intersubjectivity Hermeneutical interpretation differs from positivism in that it implies an intersubjective relationship between science and its object. The hermeneutical conception of science is not then a passive one, but one that implies an element of cultural construction and which can lead to self-understanding or world-disclosure.

The hermeneutical tradition has in general been associated with a conservative ideology, particularly its twentieth-century exponents. This is a contrast to the positivist tradition, which notwithstanding its absorption into the state, has been more associated with a liberal view of society. While positivism emerged in the context of the rise of modern consciousness in the revolt against the authority of tradition and political absolutism, the hermeneutical tradition has been more a product of a conservative attitude to culture. Its origins lie later in the Romantic critique of the rationalistic Enlightenment. With its emphasis on subjectivity, cultural essentialism and the production of meaning as the enduring embodiments of humanity, the hermeneutical tradition fostered an uncritical attitude to society. The role of power in shaping meaning tends to be ignored and a consensual rather than conflict model of society is presupposed. Subjectivity is seen as static rather than as self-transformative. The social or contextual conditions which give rise to particular systems of meaning are not emphasized.

The hermeneutical approach represents the communitarian strand in the consciousness of modernity and can be contrasted to the instrumentalizing logic of positivism. Positivism, with its belief in the unity of the scientific method, represented the rationalistic dimension of modernity. The hermeneutical tradition, on the other hand, was equally modern in its belief in the unity of the subject and its idea that the world is ultimately meaningful. It should also be mentioned that the hermeneutical tradition within social science was not opposed to explanation as the aim of science, but was opposed to the exclusive preoccupation with a narrow conception of explanation in favour of a broader interpretative dimension.

From the late nineteenth century we can distinguish two strands within the hermeneutical tradition. First, the tradition of hermeneutics leading from neo-Kantianism and the German Historical School to Weber's sociology and Freud's psychoanalysis. This school of thought is characterized by its objectivism: the scientific study of human meaning can aspire to objectivity. Second, the tradition of the philosophy of language stemming from Heidegger's critique of Husserl's phenomenology and Wittgenstein. This school of thought, which has been more characteristic of the philosophy of the human sciences than the social sciences, is characterized by subjectivism: the denial of the objectivity of science which, it is held, cannot transcend its cultural context. A further characteristic is its strong emphasis on the importance of language in the construction of the social. Leading figures in this more philosophical version of hermeneutics were Ernst Cassirer and Maurice Merlau-Ponty and, more recently, Peter Winch, Hans-Georg Gadamer and Charles Taylor.

Developing out of these traditions, which we can call following Gadamer philosophical hermeneutics, modern sociological hermeneutics emerged. In this context, three approaches can be identified. The first is represented by phenomenological hermeneutics, which is best associated with Alfred Schutz, who stands between Weber's objective hermeneutics, on the one hand, and on the other the philosophy of language of Wittgenstein and Heidegger. A second tradition can be found in the ethnomethodological and ethnographic approaches, such as those of Harold Garfinkel, Erving Goffman and Clifford Geertz. Finally, Paul Ricoeur, Habermas and Karl-Otto Apel, who bring hermeneutics in the direction of 'critical hermeneutics'.

Before outlining these schools and their modern critics, I begin with a brief account of the rise of the hermeneutical idea.

The Origin of Hermeneutics

The word hermeneutics derives from Greek myths in which Hermes was the messenger of the gods. The word therefore suggests the interpretative process of communication. Hermeneutics as a methodological concept first arose in seventeenth-century German philology in the context of biblical interpretation. With the rise of Protestant theology and the reaction against papal authoritarianism, the question of the interpretation of the scriptures became important. This model of a form of textual interpretation that did not require priestly authority continued to guide the hermeneutic tradition, which continued to regard society as a text. The aim of hermeneutics is to get at the hidden meanings embedded in texts.

While not being a major part of the Enlightenment, of which it was in many ways a departure, it was greatly influenced by the culture of the rationalist philosophers who sought to de-mystify religion. With the Enlightenment, hermeneutics shifts from biblical exegesis to philology more generally and became the science of textual interpretation. Friedrich Schleiermacher in the nineteenth century has been credited with establishing hermeneutics as a science of human meaning. For him hermeneutics, as the interpretation of meaning, could be applied to all forms of human communication.

Hermeneutics evolved from an analysis of texts to the study of culture, in particular the question of how one culture can understand another removed in time. The hermeneutical method, the 'hermeneutical circle', was based on the structure of dialogue. Interpretation involves the ability to understand the intentions of another human being; it is the ability to penetrate to the hidden meanings of utterances or the concrete forms they might take. In order to achieve a complete understanding, the interpreter must proceed by relating the whole to the parts. Units of meaning are possible only in a wider context. The hermeneutical task is to reconstruct the relationship of individual units of meaning to a meaningful context. To do this observation is not enough since meaning cannot be subject to simple explanation and description, which characterizes positivism. Hermeneutic interpretation must also be intuitive and sensitive to the multilayered realities of meaning.

Early hermeneutics was characterized by a strong psychologism. Schleiermacher distinguished between grammatical and psychological interpretation. The former referred to language and is comparative while the latter refers to the creative act in which meaning is generated and is intuitive. The essence of the hermeneutical method was for the reader/interpreter to enter the mind of the author/speaker. This entailed psychologism since the hermeneutic approach was initially seen as a dialogical relationship in which the reader had to identify with the author. The hermeneutic method also became known as the method of empathetic understanding, or interpretative understanding.

Hermeneutics was closely linked with the study of history and culture, reflecting a view that is often called historicism. Historicism entails the view that there is a fundamental difference between the natural and the human sciences which is due to the fact that the laws of society are different from those of nature and human history is the unfolding of these laws: only human beings have a history. Historicism maintains that these laws can be scientifically studied. Giambattista Vico was an earlier exponent of a hermeneutical consciousness within a historicist framework. In his *New Science* [1725], Vico argued that the laws of history, while being very different from the laws of nature, have objective characteristics. The 'new science' was the science of history: the study of the laws of historical evolution which Vico believed had a cyclical nature. His hermeneutical approach is evident in his emphasis on the relativity of human cultures and the belief that science can transgress historical time. The historian, he believed, can understand earlier cultures through empathetic understanding and historical awareness. The importance of Vico is that he was one of the first to argue for a radical separation of the human and the social sciences.

Herder reflected a similar concern with an interpretative approach to the study of history and culture. In stressing cultural differences as natural to human society, Herder argued for an interpretative approach which had a major impact on German Romanticism, which reacted to the Enlightenment cult of reason with the cult of feeling. The idea that there are homogeneous cultures separated from each other by essentialistic traits and that science can overcome these divides was a very influential view, inspiring Europeans to study 'primitive' and 'exotic' societies. The Romantic conception of different cultural worlds, to which science could gain access, inspired anthropology as the study of 'primitive' peoples and Orientalism as the study of 'exotic' peoples. Critiques of anthropology and Orientalism, such as Edward Said's (1979), have established the argument that these nineteenth-century conceptions of social science were not in fact dialogical but imperialistic. The interpreter and interpreted were not on equal footing, for the European social scientist was not only interpreting an alien culture, but was also constructing it for the purpose of intellectual mastery: the fusion of horizons was ultimately a hegemonic enterprise.

These considerations reveal that the interpretative approach involves more than understanding: the interpreter in trying to understand another culture or social actor is also consciously or unconsciously drawing upon a background of prejudices, which shapes the act of interpretation bringing into question the neutrality that hermeneuticists attribute to it.

Finally, something must be said about the institutionalization of the humanities with respect to the hermeneutical conception of science. In the previous chapter it was argued that positivism became the dominant institutionalized form science took in England and France. In Germany the institutionalization of science took a slightly different form. In the nineteenth century the universities played a leading role in institutionalizing the human sciences into which the social sciences were subsumed. The professionalized ethos of culture in the universities was an important part of German cultural identity, for in Germany, unlike Britain and France, the state tradition had not succeeded in establishing a national identity.

The Neo-Kantians, Weber and Freud

One of the most influential schools of hermeneutic thought was the German Historical School, or neo-Kantianism. While neo-Kantianism can refer merely to any group or individual who had recourse to Kant's philosophy in the nineteenth century (Köhnke, 1991), in the more specific sense used here it refers to a movement associated with a turn to historical thought in Heidelberg and Marburg from the 1860s to the end of the century. The neo-Kantians, whose line extends from Dilthey through Windelband and Rickert to Weber, reacted both to the idealist implications of Kant's philosophy and to the prevailing positivism in German intellectual circles in the second half of the nineteenth century. The debate on the methodological foundations of the social sciences, the *Methodenstreit* (or 'the dispute on method'), coincided with the debate between the Historical School of economics in Germany led by Gustav Schmoller, who reacted against the liberal tradition and argued for an institutional and socio-historical approach, and the Austria School of economics, led by Carl Menger, who promoted a positivistic economics. The idea of understanding an author better than they understood themself is fundamental to the hermeneutical approach, which combines interpretative sensitivity with the quest for objective knowledge. Before exploring the neo-Kantian idea of science, we need an account of the Kant's theory of knowledge.

Kant's critical idealist transcendental philosophy was an attempt to mediate between idealism and rationalism. The basic idea underlying Kant's philosophy in his great work *The Critique of Pure Reason* [1781] was that empirical knowledge, as knowledge of external objective reality, presupposes that reality has a structure which can be known, but this external structure is imposed by the internal forms of our mind, for the perception of reality is not passive. Space and time are the *a priori* or innate forms with which reality is perceived and are independent of reality itself. In order not to concede too much to Hume's sceptical empiricism, Kant tried to preserve a link with rationalism. He argued that while our perception of reality is structured for us by the *a priori* forms of our mind, it is also 'synthetic', which means that it can tell us something about objective reality, but what it can tell us has to be assumed, not known: objective reality exists, but philosophy can only tell us how knowledge is possible and what appears to us. In other words, knowledge must be restricted to the realm of phenomena, or that which appears to consciousness – this was the lesson of Kant's critical philosophy.

Empiricists such as Locke and Hume argued against metaphysics, claiming that knowledge comes from what we experience and is not derived from absolute principles. Kant's problem was to reconcile this view, which he supported, with the rationalist view that knowledge can be objective. In Kant's view the rationalist alternative to metaphysics was too simple: in claiming that certain knowledge can be acquired it was assuming that reality had a knowable form. Empiricism, on the other hand, is too sceptical and cannot therefore provide science with the assurance of objectivity. Kant believed that certain concepts, such as causal necessity, are not merely products of the *a priori* or innate structures of the mind (in the way space and time are) but also tell us something about objective nature, even though such concepts cannot tell us the nature of reality in itself which must remain unknowable. His method was 'transcendental idealism', meaning a critique of the limits of knowledge: knowledge of phenomena is knowledge of only that which appears to us. The 'critique of pure reason' was a critique of reason in its attempt to overstep the limits of knowledge. The conclusion of Kant's philosophy is that objective reality exists and it is rational to believe that we can gain knowledge of it not as it is 'in itself' (the unknowable 'noumena') but only as it can be known by the structures of our mind, the world of 'phenomena'. Pure Reason is reflection on the world beyond phenomena (the abstract ideas of god, immortality, freedom), while scientific knowledge is knowledge of phenomena.

The neo-Kantians were unhappy with Kant, whose philosophy was too much based on the natural sciences and had very little to say on the human sciences. Kant's moral philosophy defended the idea of the autonomy of moral reason, his political philosophy proposed a cosmopolitan political order and his aesthetic philosophy argued for the autonomy of the aesthetic. Yet, his critical philosophy did not result in a theory of the human sciences. The neo-Kantians can be seen as radicalizing Kant's concept of the 'critique of pure reason' to the 'critique of historical reason'. While Kant argued that scientific knowledge is possible within the limits of a critique of the conditions of the possibility of knowledge, the neo-Kantians argued for a science of the conditions of possibility of cultural knowledge. The defining tenet of neo-Kantianism is the demand for a separation of the human sciences from the natural sciences.

Underlying neo-Kantian thought is a certain kind of humanism: the assumption that there is a common human nature. Without this underlying belief in the unity of the human condition, interpretation would not be possible. Although the neo-Kantians rejected Romanticism, the dualism of nature and spirit as well as the dualism of nature and morality is to be found in their division of the sciences. A predominantly German tradition, an English version of neo-Kantianism can be found in R. G. Collingwood and C. P. Snow's ([1959] 1993) famous thesis of the 'two cultures', and in the United States Peter Berger defended this humanist vision of sociology in his book *Invitation to Sociology* ([1963] 1966). Benedetto Croce in Italy can also be mentioned in this context.

One of the most important of the neo-Kantians was Wilhelm Dilthey, who established the foundation of the human sciences as a domain distinct from the natural sciences. In his *Introduction to the Human Sciences* [1883], he argued that the human sciences are based on a descriptive psychology of the changing forms of human subjectivity or consciousness. The forms 'mental life' embodied were to be the subject matter for the human sciences. In opposition to positivism, Dilthey argued against causal explanation, claiming that the structure of mental life is meaning which cannot be causally explained. While the human sciences sought understanding (or *Verstehen*), the natural sciences seek causal explanation.

A central idea in his work was the notion of *Erlebnis*, or 'lived experience', which he believed was the distinctive subject matter of the human sciences. In other words, the subject matter of the human sciences is already meaningfully constituted. *Erlebnis* refers to the world of social meaning, which is embodied in history and is prereflective, for it is rooted in the hermeneutics of everyday life.

This sense of the emotional and unreflective dimension of human action reflects the tradition of Rousseau, Vico, Humbolt and Herder and can be contrasted to the rationalistic and empiricist traditions from Descartes through Locke to Kant. He proposed a method of objective understanding as the universal method for the human sciences. Though his own concern was primarily with history, objective understanding was to be based on psychology, which was for him the model science and which he combined with Husserl's phenomenology to provide a theory of historical meaning. Thus biography was the paradigmatic example of how objective understanding operates. His thought, however, slowly moved from a concern with psychologism to a more sociological sense of the hermeneutic interpretation of entire cultures (Outhwaite, 1975: 26).

Dilthey occupies an important place in the history of the philosophy of science. His importance undoubtedly consists of his systematic defence of the autonomy of the human sciences from the natural sciences. However, he also bequeathed an enduring conception of the natural sciences as being positivistic, a view that has survived in the work of Habermas. One of the arguments I am proposing in this book is that it is no longer possible to have a positivistic conception of natural science while arguing for an anti-positivistic social science: positivism is itself a questionable perspective, especially if we take seriously developments that have occurred within the experimental sciences themselves.

Before concluding this discussion on neo-Kantianism, it is important to mention two prominent figures who have been influential in the philosophy of the human sciences, Rickert and Windelband. The principal contribution of Rickert and Windelband was the argument that the difference between the natural and human sciences lay less in their subject matter, as Dilthey had argued, than in the methodology of the sciences. They therefore emphasized epistemological and methodological rather than ontological issues in the demarcation between the sciences. Richert and Windelband were, like Dilthey, reacting to the growing influence of the natural sciences in the human sciences, in particular in the study of history. Unlike Dilthey, they did not conceive the historical method in psychologistic terms.

In general it can be said that the neo-Kantian debate did not revolve centrally around the social sciences. History, psychology and economics were the principal sciences at stake and the overall conception was one of the human sciences confronting the natural sciences. Rickert, however, insisted on the exclusion of psychology from what he preferred to call the cultural sciences. It was not until Max Weber that social science began to acquire a special identity of its own.

Weber stood in the neo-Kantian tradition but broke from it in one crucial respect. Weber, who was strongly influenced by Rickert, believed that the social sciences must combine explanation and understanding. The neo-Kantian tendency had been to argue that explanation is characteristic only of natural science while the human sciences rely on understanding. By combining explanation and understanding into a unitary methodology, Weber broke the link with the classical hermeneutic tradition. His sociology can be more accurately described as interpretative sociology, in order to distinguish it from the older hermeneutic tradition. Nevertheless, it must be said that Weber upheld the neo-Kantian separation of the sciences, while establishing the autonomy of social science. The distinction between the human sciences and the social sciences is best illustrated in the rise of sociology as a profession distinct from its competitor disciplines, history, jurisprudence and psychology. Weber was decisive in severing the connection between sociology and psychology, providing a separate methodological foundation for the former. For Weber, social science differs from natural science in that it is focused on history and culture, which are the carriers of social meaning.

Weber marks the concrete transition from pure humanistic hermeneutics to interpretative social science in that as a social scientist he was interested in the study of social action and not in the interpretation of texts or indeed also psychologistic interpretation. It is important to appreciate that Weber sought to unify the scientific method by combining explanation with understanding (*Verstehen*). Weber's social science can be discussed under three categories: (1) the theory of explanatory understanding; (2) ideal types; and (3) the ethical neutrality of science.

(1) Meaning, for Weber, could be a subject of social scientific study if the hermeneutic approach is radicalized by combining it with explanatory models. Weber distinguished between two kinds of understanding. The first kind includes rational understanding and emphatic understanding. The second kind involves direct understanding and explanatory understanding. Weber's sociology was mostly an investigation of the latter kind of understanding which concerns the motivations (that is, the causes) leading to

action. This was the methodological idea underlying his famous work, *The Protestant Ethic and the Spirit of Capitalism* [1904–5]. Social science was ultimately an explanatory science of meaningful human action. The core of the explanatory-understanding conception of sociology is the search for motivations to explain social action. He thus gave methodological primacy to purposive-rational action: an explanation depends on relating goals to motives. Despite conceiving of social action as social, Weber nevertheless operated with a model of methodological individualism to the extent that understanding was always the understanding of the actions of an ideal individual (Outhwaite, 1983: 126). Weberian analysis strongly emphasized the identification of motivations, in contrast to Durkheimian sociology which stressed the external controls on social action, the so-called 'social facts'. Moreover, Weberian analysis looked to the wider cultural and also civilizational presuppositions of social action in order to make possible comparison of different cultural worlds.

(2) In Weber's view the social world of meaning is too complex to be directly observed. Therefore, and in opposition to positivist approaches, he favoured the use of 'idealization', or ideal types. Ideal types have the function of simplifying reality, in particular its causal structure, in order to aid the construction of theories. His understanding-explanatory social science involved the construction of ideal typical models of rational-meaningful action in order to be applied in particular contexts. The aim of explanation is causal explanation of motivating meaning. Weber believed that the use of ideal types was specifically characteristic of the social sciences. In this it should be noted he was clearly mistaken for natural science also involves such idealization.

(3) Weber also believed strongly in the ethical neutrality of science. In a famous speech given at the University of Munich in 1918, 'Science as a Profession', Weber ([1919] 1970) defended a value-free social science with the argument which pervaded his entire writings: modernity entails the differentiation of rationality into three cognitive spheres: science, law and aesthetics. Today, it was Weber's firm conviction, science can only be a professional activity, it cannot reverse what he called the 'disenchantment' of the modern age, that is, it cannot enchant people by providing them with meaning. Science cannot answer the question of 'which of the warring gods should we serve' since science is only one cognitive sphere. For Weber (1970: 147–8) the burden of science as a profession was to

accept that 'the various value spheres of the world stand in irreconcilable conflict with each other' and that 'different gods struggle with one another, now for all time to come'. The cultural pessimism of Weber's generation, and the influence of Nietzsche and Schopenhauer, was reflected in his vision of scientific disenchantment, which in essence confined science to explaining meaning, not providing it: 'The fate of our times is characterized by rationalization and intellectualization and, above all, by the "disenchantment of the world." Precisely the ultimate values and most sublime values have retreated from public life either into the transcendental realm of mystic life or into the brotherliness of direct and personal human relations' (1970: 155).

Weber demanded of the social scientist to make an 'intellectual sacrifice' and not expect science to offer meaning. The discourse of science is a disenchanted one in which only 'intellectual integrity' can play a role: science has become a profession. However, in his reference to the 'vocation' of science, there is the suggestion of a higher mission.

In this outline of the hermeneutical tradition in social science mention must be made of Sigmund Freud and his first major work, *The Interpretation of Dreams* [1900]. Psychoanalysis is an important expression of the new interpretative method which claimed the status of scientific objectivity. While Dilthey took biography as the starting point for his theory of understanding, Freud conceived *The Interpretation of Dreams* after the hermeneutic model of philological research (Habermas, 1978: 214–15). The hermeneutical approach was based on the necessity for interpretation because meaning and memory can be unreliable. This approach was reflected in psychoanalysis which also sought to make unintelligible meanings objective. While the neo-Kantians and Weber worked with a notion of conscious intentionality, Freud worked with the idea of the unconsciousness. Instead of historical or biographical memory, psychoanalysis is addressed to the distorted structures of the unconsciousness. Instead of the text as the subject matter, Freud's depth hermeneutics was addressed to the dream. The dream is like a text, a set of meanings that have to be interpreted.

Psychoanalysis entails a different kind of hermeneutics to that favoured by the cultural sciences: instead of leading to mere understanding, it leads to self-reflection and enlightenment about the mechanism of repression. In this way psychoanalysis is a therapeutic science involving an emancipatory moment denied by the neo-Kantians. Despite the fact that Freud himself moved towards a more positivistic conception of psychoanalysis, which he saw as a unified science capable of universal explanation, his basic insights had a huge impact on the self-understanding of the social sciences.

Heidegger and Wittgenstein: The Linguistic Turn and Philosophical Hermeneutics

The hermeneutical tradition discussed in the previous section was characterized by a sense of objectivity: hermeneutical interpretation aims at objective understanding. In this section, I examine another tradition in hermeneutics in which the emphasis is more on the subjective dimension, or context-bound interpretation. Interpretation does not require the transcending of cultural contexts for interpretation is more like a dialogue. This tradition of what can be called philosophical hermeneutics begins with Heidegger's critique of Husserl's phenomenology and continues in the mature philosophy of Wittgenstein to form the basis of modern hermeneutics, whose representatives include Peter Winch, Hans-Georg Gadamer and Charles Taylor. With the rise of subjective hermeneutics the philosophy of consciousness is replaced by the philosophy of language. The neo-Kantians from Dilthey to Weber presupposed a model of consciousness whose reference point was historical individuality. Even in Freud, the reference point of consciousness was the unconsciousness, which was seen as a distorted version of consciousness. But for subjective hermeneutics, consciousness must be replaced by language for reality is mediated by the symbolic structures of language. Against objective hermeneutics, it is argued, consciousness cannot be understood in its pure form; against positivism, there can be no neutral scientific language.

Heidegger was the originator of subjective hermeneutics and marked the turn to language, which was also taken up by Ludwig Wittgenstein. Heidegger's approach emerged in the context of a critique of the phenomenological approach of Edmund Husser. Phenomenology belongs to the tradition of objective hermeneutics and entails the view that objective or 'pure understanding' is possible. According to Husserl, everyday knowledge is naturalistic. Science, in contrast, aims at pure understanding which it achieves by bracketing out everyday naive knowledge in order to arrive at pure knowledge. However, Husserl's phenomenological approach, which he termed 'transcendental phenomenology', was far from positivism and entailed a critique of scientism. For Husserl all knowledge begins with consciousness and this cannot be derived from the methods of the natural sciences. This is because the natural sciences – and Husserl was particularly aiming his attack on the new science of psychology – are not sufficiently reflective of the life-world of which they are a part.

For Heidegger the problem with phenomenology was that it failed to see that reality was constituted by language and therefore scientific knowledge must be mediated by language. Unlike Husserl, Heidegger regarding understanding as constitutive of the life-world itself and was not something that could be arrived at only through 'pure understanding'. In other words, Heidegger, wanted to rescue the 'naturalistic attitude' which Husserl sought to demarcate from science. With Heidegger understanding becomes part of 'Being' itself: method and ontology are collapsed into each other. Fundamental to all earlier kinds of philosophy – rationalism, empiricism, positivism, hermeneutics – was the assumption that method was distinct from ontology. Heidegger tried to argue that understanding is the fundamental ontological characteristic of the life-world and is embodied in language. Interpretation can never transcend the life-world context for consciousness is not independent of language. The function of science is 'world-disclosure'. Heidegger made the point of transition from epistemology to ontology: questions of method were now to be settled by reflections on ontology. Ontology, which means the nature of reality, for Heidegger in *Being and Time* [1927], was the context in which understanding arises. Understanding as an ontological activity refers to pre-cognitive knowledge.

Although operating within a very abstract philosophical hermeneutics, Heidegger had an important impact on the philosophy of the social sciences in two respects. First, he established the importance of language in the self-understanding of science which can no longer operate within the philosophy of consciousness. The idea of the linguistic constitution of the social is fundamental to many kinds of modern social science ranging from symbolic interactionism (Mead), the sociology of knowledge (Mannheim), neo-Weberianism (Winch), to poststructuralism (Derrida) and post-modernism and governmentality (Foucault), to constructivism and realism. Second, more contentiously, Heidegger's philosophy resulted in a conservative conception of science for ever constrained by its social context. Subjective hermeneutics was opposed both to objective explanatory knowledge and to the critique of society. Thus both relativism and historicity were the enduring traits of philosophical hermeneutics.

Heidegger developed his subjective hermeneutics via a critique of the objective hermeneutics of the neo-Kantians and Husserl's phenomenology. Ludwig Wittgenstein, in his critique of positivism, argued for a similar conception of science. In his early work the *Tractatus* [1921], he defended a theory of universal scientific language, which he later rejected in favour of a theory of language based on 'forms of life'. In his *Philosophical Investigations* [1953], Wittgenstein provided a theory of the linguistification of the social. In arguing that the limits of language are the limits of the world, he established the foundation of linguistic hermeneutics. This conception of science argues that all of reality is linguistic and representations of reality by science are themselves 'language games'. By means of the concept of a 'language game' Wittgenstein demonstrated how language is defined by its use and how all reality is ultimately shaped by language. Reality is mediated by language according to Wittgenstein: reality is a linguistic construction. But the meaning of language is defined by its use: meaning is pragmatic not essentialistic.

The importance of Wittgenstein consists of his contribution to the critique of the philosophy of consciousness, which was presupposed by positivism. Heidegger and Wittgenstein established the foundations for contemporary subjective hermeneutics. Their contribution to the critique of the philosophy of consciousness from the perspective of language was reflected in the writings of Gadamer and Winch, who have made significant contributions to debates on the self-understanding of social science. Gadamer is one of the principal representatives of hermeneutics conceived of as subjective and linguistic; he is also noteworthy in having brought linguistic hermeneutics in a historical direction.

In *Truth and Method* ([1960] 1979) Gadamer opposed the neo-Kantian model of hermeneutics, which aimed to arrive at objective understanding. The problem for Gadamer was the relationship between truth and method. His argument – which was directed against the rationalist and hermeneutical traditions which, despite their differences, subordinated truth to method – was that truth is prior to method and resides in the ontological structure of understanding. Gadamer, from a neo-Heideggerian perspective, argued, furthermore, that the act of understanding is always tied to the cultural situation of the interpreter and there will always be a bridge between the world of the interpreter and world of the interpreted. While the aim of hermeneutics is to bridge that gap, the 'fusion of horizons' will be more a matter of mediation in the sense of a translation than perfect understanding. In other words, for Gadamer there will always be a residue of untranslated subjectivity for interpretation can never be complete. Gadamer rejects the aspiration to understand the author better than they understood themself: we can never entirely understand the intentionality of another person. We can never fully penetrate the mind of another person, but we can, however, enter into dialogue and bring about a 'fusion of horizons'. It is for this reason that Gadamer is critical of the older hermeneutical tradition, which in his view had not fully broken from naturalism.

For Gadamer there are two kinds of hermeneutics. There is the hermeneutics of everyday life, the acts of understanding which are embedded in everyday language, and there is the scientific method of understanding. The latter is the interpretation of interpretations. This process has been described by Anthony Giddens as the 'double hermeneutic' (1976: 162). Since science is rooted in first order of linguistic interpretations, it itself must be a part of the historicity of understanding. Science is itself a historical project embedded in history and culture. Interpretation involves the reliving of tradition which can never be transcended, but can be translated.

The British philosopher Peter Winch made one of the most often discussed defences of a hermeneutic methodology for the social sciences. In his influential *The Idea of a Social Science and its Relation to Philosophy* (1958) Winch combined Wittgenstein's philosophy of language with Weber's interpretative sociology to produce a critique of the prevailing orthodoxy of positivism. His main argument was that the social sciences should be more allied to philosophy than to the natural sciences. Winch's target was the positivistic conception of social science held by Durkheim, Mill and Pareto as well as Wittgenstein's own attempt to separate science and philosophy.

Winch based his position on the argument that conceptually and logically the social sciences are different from the natural sciences. The difference is both methodological as well as ontological for society and nature are two quite different entities. In particular Winch opposed the importance of causal explanations in the social sciences and proposed an interpretative approach based on a re-reading of Weber. Weber's approach offered an alternative to positivism in its stress on interpretative understanding of social action. But the problem with Weber, in Winch's view, was that Weber failed to see that social action is primarily defined by language: it is rule determined, not causally determined. Against Weber's methodological individualism, Winch argued meaningful social action can be understood only if social action is linked to the system of rules in language. Drawing on Wittgenstein's concept of a 'form of life' and the thesis that meaning is created in 'language games', he argued that social action is 'rule-following' within a concrete form of life: 'our language and our social relations are just two different sides of the same coin' (1958: 123). In this way he opposed both causal explanation and empirical sociology in favour of a philosophical sociology. The role of social science is to investigate the different forms of life. Against positivism in social science, Winch opposed the position that scientific concepts are fundamentally different from those which are to be found in everyday life. He argued that the social scientific concepts, unlike those in the natural sciences, are rooted in everyday life and therefore an external position cannot be taken.

The implication of Winch's contribution to the philosophy of social science was relativism. Winch followed Wittgenstein with the notion that reality is structured by language, a position which entailed relativism since linguistic rule systems were seen as specific to concrete forms of life. As with Gadamer, his conception of social science was rooted in a conservative view of the interpretative capacity of social science which was for ever context-bound. However, the importance of Winch is that he opened up the question of language to social science. While his view that the social sciences must be allied more to philosophy than to the natural sciences is a contentious issue, he firmly established the importance of a hermeneutic approach in the social sciences. Moreover, his conceptualization of the natural sciences as positivistic is also a position that has been challenged by more recent theories of science.

Philosophical hermeneutics can be associated with a broad spectrum of approaches, and which are largely confined to the humanities. Ernest Cassirer, a German neo-Kantian, developed a theory of symbolic forms, which can be located in this tradition. The French philosopher Maurice Merleau-Ponty was important in bringing the social sciences, especially sociology, closer to philosophy. Mention, too, can be made of the Canadian philosopher Charles Taylor, who wrote an influential essay on the 'hermeneutical sciences of man' (Taylor, 1971).

Towards Sociological Hermeneutics

By sociological hermeneutics is meant the rise of a distinctively hermeneutical approach within the social sciences, distinct from philosophical hermeneutics. This was originally the basic intention of Weber, but it was not until the philosophical hermeneutics developed the theory of language that a methodologically coherent sociological hermeneutics could emerge.

This development is most evident in the work of Alfred Schutz, who proposed a phenomenological hermeneutics which was based on Weber and Husserl, and to a lesser extent Heidegger. Schutz rejected positivism and argued, following Husserl, that the concepts of social science are rooted in the life-world of everyday life. In this sense his approach is phenomenological, but is firmly located within a broadly conceived sociological hermeneutics. His conceptualization of social science goes beyond Husserl in combining elements from Heidegger and Weber, thereby avoiding the imminent solipsism of Husserl, though it is generally accepted that he failed to do full justice to the ontology of the social. The central methodological idea in Schutz is subjective interpretation. As with Weber this entails the interpretation of the subjective meaning held by social actors themselves in various contexts, but unlike Weber this is something intersubjectively conceived. Like Winch, he insists on the importance that social scientific concepts refer to those which social actors hold. But social science operates also at a higher level. Like Weber, he emphasizes the importance of ideal-typical constructs to explain social reality. The objectivity of interpretation consists of the adequacy of the ideal-typical constructions of the social scientist. Language is the most important social tool in the construction of meaningful social action. Social action is always intersubjective and mediated by language. The aim of theoretical models in social science is to explain subjective interpretations. His hermeneutical approach was uncompromisingly value-free, for social science must be objective and explanatory as well as being verifiable. One of his central concepts in methodology was the distinction he drew between 'first-order' and 'second-order' constructs. The former refer to everyday knowledge while the latter refer to scientific knowledge as a reflection on the everyday. Thus with Schutz, the goal of an explanatory social science is saved from the accusation of neo-positivistim.

Finally, as important examples of sociological hermeneutics, ethnographic and ethnomethodological approaches can be mentioned. Where neo-positivism was primarily interested in the analysis and explanation of large-scale social phenomena, sociological hermeneutics is mostly concerned with the micro-analysis of everyday life. Situationalism, in contrast to objectivism, is what is characteristic of these hermeneutically inclined approaches that have led to the social constructionism and new debates on the link between the micro and the macro levels of analysis. In this context mention can be made of the founder of ethnomethodology, Harold Garfinkel, whose *Studies in Ethnomethodology* [1967] led to an emphasis on small group situations and social interaction at a time when Parsonian structural functionalism with its typical concern with macro-analysis and the evolution of modernity was the orthodoxy within sociology. But the real evolution was less in the turn to micro-analysis than in the incorporation into the language of science the interpretations that people in everyday life made of their social worlds. Although this was partly recognized by Schutz, it was only with Garfinkel that it took on a radicalized reflexive dimension. With this comes the gradual descent of social science into the situation-boundness of everyday life.

Sociological hermeneutics was the main challenger to the dominant neo-positivist philosophies of social science that prevailed in the 1950s to 1970s, when this gradually went into abeyance. An important expression of it was frame analysis, as in Erving Goffman's pioneering work *Frame Analysis: An Essay on the Organization of Experience* [1974]. This work established the foundations of social constructionism with a conception of meaning as ordered into frames which 'construct' the social world (see Chapter 6). The interpretative approach advocated by Clifford Geertz can also be regarded a major example of sociological hermeneutics. According to Geertz in his book *The Interpretation of Cultures* [1973], cultural phenomena are primarily public and can be decoded semiotically using an approach he called 'thick interpretation', which in his view also had explanatory power. In contrast, 'thin interpretation' is all that neo-positivistic approaches can achieve simply because they are unable to reach the deeper levels of meaning. In this ethnographically oriented approach, description if hermeneutically driven is also capable of explaining human behaviour.

Conclusion: Towards Critical Hermeneutics

The hermeneutical approach has been characterized by a fundamental opposition to positivism. The social and human sciences are conceived of as methodologically distinct and with a separate subject matter from the natural sciences. While, as we have seen, there are many different conceptions of hermeneutics, ranging from subjective to objective approaches, the dominant traditions tend to presuppose an uncritical view of society. Interpretation does not involve a critique but mere understanding. Thus in the hermeneutic approach reality is left untouched. Hermeneutics has been conceived more in terms of a dialogue than an interrogation of reality. Science, it is held, cannot offer meaning and is itself a product of a form of life which it cannot transcend. Thus, theorists such as Winch and Gadamer argue from a Wittgenstein and Heideggerian background that social science cannot cross cultural boundaries and understand 'alien' cultures for interpretation is always culturally specific.

This conception of social science as a prisoner of its own time has been criticized by Paul Ricoeur, Karl-Otto Apel and Jürgen Habermas, who have argued for an approach which may be termed 'critical hermeneutics' (Thompson, 1981). Since the work of Apel and Habermas will be considered separately in Chapter 4, I shall conclude this discussion with a few remarks on Ricouer.

The French philosopher Paul Ricoeur developed the hermeneutical method in a general theory of textual interpretation. Although strictly speaking more in the tradition of philosophical hermeneutics, Ricoeur's hermeneutic approach challenges the illusion of historicity in much of hermeneutical theory and is highly pertinent to sociological hermeneutics but represents a particular approach which can be termed critical hermeneutics. Taking as his point of departure the text as the model of social action, Ricoeur argues that the meaning embodied in the text is not the same as that which the author intended. Objectivity is constituted by the text itself and is independent of subjectivity. In other words, as a result of its distantiation from its origin the text is open to a plurality of interpretations. Like Heidegger, Ricoeur operates with the concept of 'world disclosure'. For him the truth of a text is the world which it discloses. Against Gadamer, Ricoeur argues that the act of interpretation requires a degree of distance from the tradition in which the text is embedded and therefore the act of interpretation is never a 'fusion of horizons'. In other words, interpretation contains a critical moment which allows the interpreter to transcend the text. While Ricoeur is primarily interested in the interpretation of the past, the critical theory of communication proposed by Habermas is more strongly focused on the critique of communication in contemporary society.

3

The Dialectical Imagination: Marxism, Critique and Emancipation

Introduction: Defining the Dialectic

The previous two chapters looked at the classical conceptions of social science as modeled on the natural sciences or as modeled on the human sciences. The principal differences between positivism and hermeneutics concerned the question of the unity of the scientific method (causal explanation and empirical observation) and the role of values within science. In this debate the positivistic conception of social science has undoubtedly had the upper hand and to varying degrees has been the most influential in the institutionalization of social science. The hermeneutic idea has also clearly been influential but has not had the same impact as positivism in as far as the scientific status of social science is concerned. These two approaches can also be seen as mirroring the conflict between constructivism and realism, with hermeneutics as representing an emergent constructivist view of social reality, and positivism as a realist view.

Yet, for all their differences the two methodologies share a common presupposition: value-freedom in science. While some of the classical positivists such as Saint-Simon and Comte believed that scientism entailed a 'scientific politics', this has mostly been a marginal episode in the history of positivism which has stood for the ethical neutrality of science and a strict demarcation of the roles between the scientist as professional and, on the other side, the intellectual and politician.

In this chapter I examine a third tradition in social science which has offered a challenge to both positivism and to hermemeutics. Marxist social science has been one of the main opponents of positivism, and it can also be seen as a competitor to hermeneutics. Against scientism and interpretation, Marxism elevates critique to the centre of the stage. As a critique of society, Marxist social theory breaks from the belief in the ethical neutrality, or value-freedom, of positivism and hermeneutics. Instead of self-understanding, self-transformation is the issue. For Marxists social scientific knowledge must be critical knowledge for positivistic knowledge or mere understanding is an affirmation of the existing society. Critique has an internal connection to emancipation, which is denied by the proponents of positivism and hermeneutics. Marxist social science aims at the transformation of society by deepening society's consciousness of itself. Thus for Marxists the dividing line between the intellectual and the professional is a fine one since knowledge cannot be separated from political commitment and the struggle for emancipation. Science is not just an institution but is also a cognitive system. Critique and emancipation are dialectically linked in the Marxist method. Dialectics refers to the process by which the contradictions in society are resolved through the raising of consciousness. The dialectical method involves the linking of theory with practice. The ultimate test of knowledge is its transformative power in a historical process of emancipation. In this sense the discourse of radical constructivism really begins anew with Marx, who can be seen as having taken up the earlier ideas of social reconstruction, which were suppressed in the early modern period.

To summarize and to provide a working definition, the following four characteristics typify Marxist social science. It is to be emphasized that these are highly simplified characterizations and should be seen as points of reference.

Critique Science does not aim to explain or understand society for its own sake. Knowledge is inherently critical of the prevailing order and seeks to reveal the system of domination. Marxism can be compatible with positivism and hermeneutics in so far as it uses the methods of explanation and understanding in a critical manner.

Emancipation As a critical theory of society, a central problem for Marxism is the question of normative foundations. The normative foundations of critique cannot be derived from science but form the political commitment to emancipation. Marxist social science is therefore intended to be an emancipatory practice concerned with social change.

Dialectics Unlike hermeneutics and positivism, Marxism does not presuppose the unity of the interpreting subject or the unity of method. Science proceeds dialectically in relation to its object, constituting it and being at the same time constituted by it. Theory and practice are mutually interwoven.

Historicism and determinism One of the most contentious issues in Marxist theory is the question of whether there are historical laws deriving from economic determinism. Marxism entails the notion of historical materialism, the idea that economic forces are the most important forces in history. Historical materialism is often labelled historicism, meaning a deterministic philosophy of history.

I begin by outlining the origin of the idea of critique in Kant and Hegel. The main sections of the chapter deal with Marx's conception of social science as a 'critique of political economy' leading onto neo-Marxist arguments, in particular the critical theory of the Frankfurt School which transformed the 'critique of political economy' into a 'critique of ideology' and with Habermas (to be discussed in the next chapter) a critique of distorted communication.

From Hegel to Marx

The concept of critique is very much linked to the ideas of contradiction, crisis and conflict. For Marx critique referred to the dialectical process by which contradictions in society are raised to the level of crisis and resolved through conflict. The idea of critique received its first major formulation in the philosophy of Kant, though the Enlightenment intellectual Pierre Bayle was an earlier and important representative of the idea. It will be recalled from Chapter 1 that Kant's classic work, the *Critique of Pure Reason* [1781], demanded a separation of 'pure reason' from science: reason cannot provide empirical knowledge of the objective world. Only science can do this and if reason is employed as science the result will be 'antimonies' and 'contradictions'. Reason for Kant must be confined to knowledge of abstract ideas, such as freedom, god, mortality. To use reason to acquire empirical knowledge is a contradiction. Therefore the critique of reason for Kant was a critique of the false application of reason in science. Hegel reacted to the formalism of the Kantian concept of critique and above all the idea that critique must avoid contradictions.

For Hegel critique refers to the historical process of self-reflection. History is itself the manifestation of reason, which cannot be confined to the speculative domain. By means of the concepts of the dialectic, Hegel hoped to avoid the dualism in Kant's thought. Reason, as the sphere of absolute knowledge, and science, as the sphere of cognitive knowledge of the empirical objective world, were opposites for Kant and could not be reconciled without contradiction. Hegel's departure from Kant amounted in effect to an attempt to historicize reason. In order to do this, Hegel argued reality is essentially contradictory and that change occurs through the overcoming or resolution of contradictions. The central idea of the dialectical conception of history was that of the negation of reality by the forces within it and the progress to a higher level of being. The guiding motif in Hegel's thought was the idea of world constitution. Human history can be seen as a process, which Hegel called phenomenological, by which reason becomes manifest in the world. This constitution of reason expresses itself in different historical forms but the ultimate realization of reason occurs in the domain of absolute spirit, or pure thought. Hegel was decidedly ambiguous as to whether human history was a process of self-realization or a medium for the expression of a higher spirit. The ultimate unity of subject and object occurs in pure thought contemplating reality. Thus the self-reflection of reason referred to reason itself and not society in which reason only externalized itself. For Hegel knowledge does not itself change reality: knowledge is purely reflective. In a famous passage in the preface to the *Philosophy of Right* [1821], Hegel compares knowledge to the Owl of Minerva, the Roman symbol of knowledge:

> One more word about giving instruction as to what the world ought to be. Philosophy in any case always comes on the scene too late to give it. As the thought of the world it appears only when actuality is already there cut and dried, after its process of formation has been completed ... when philosophy paints grey in grey, then has a shape

> of life grown old. By philosophy's grey in grey, it cannot be rejuvenated but only understood. The Owl of Minerva spreads its wings only with the falling of the dusk.

Hegel's concept of knowledge was one which emphasized its totalizing nature. As the interpretation of an age, philosophy comes too late to contribute to the forces of social change. This question of the relation of knowledge to its object, society, has never ceased to trouble modern social science.

Karl Marx belonged to a group of left-wing followers of Hegel, known as the 'Young Hegelians', who criticized the abstract and conservative nature of Hegel's thought. The aim of theory for Marx was not to conceive the world in the sphere of pure thought but to change it; as he wrote in the *Theses on Feuerbach* [1856]: 'Up to now the philosophers have only interpreted the world, the point now is to change it'. In other words, intellectual criticism is insufficient. Hegel's philosophy was an idealist philosophy of history which viewed human history as the progressive manifestation of reason in the world. Marx's philosophy of history, the historical materialist conception of history, must be seen in the context of Hegel's philosophy of which Marx was very critical. Influenced by the left-Hegelian Ludwig Feuerbach, Marx argued history cannot be explained in terms of the manifestation of an idea, but must be seen in its real material context. The problem for Marx with Hegel was that he had not gone far enough in historicizing Kant's philosophy. Hegel had simply applied Kant's concept of reason to history, which was still interpreted from the perspective of an absolute principle realizing itself in human history. This was what Marx and Engels called the 'German ideology', the ideology of the German idealist philosophers. Thus, for instance, the idealist philosophers interpreted the French Revolution as a great liberating moment but, fearful of its consequences, drew conservative conclusions from it. The Revolution was seen as the embodiment of Reason and not as something that its participants themselves could fully understand.

The materialist conception of history, sometimes called 'dialectical materialism' (though this is a term Marx himself did not use), must be seen as a radicalization of Hegel, and not as a theory of economic determinism. In his early writings *The Paris Manuscripts* [1844], Marx outlined the theory of historical materialism in terms of a notion of 'praxis'. Historical materialism does not refer to materialism in the conventional sense of the word, but to the practical world of human labour and self-realization. The notion of 'labour' had a wider significance for Marx, for whom it encompassed a spiritual dimension, signifying self-constitution. Labour and praxis were closely connected ideas and which can be seen as the material embodiments of Hegel's notion of reason. Thus, for Marx, instead of reason realizing itself in the world, it is a question of seeing how human labour realizes itself in praxis. Related to the notion of praxis was the concept of alienation. While Hegel had reduced alienation to the abstract problem of the separation of subject and object, reason and society, Marx saw alienation as the real condition of society. Alienation arises when the products of labour are separated from agency and confront agency as external objectivations. Alienation results from exploitation in the class system. The goal of praxis was the overcoming of alienation in the raising of a radical class consciousness. Praxis is also a political concept referring to the transformative powers of human agency, something which Hegel denied. In calling for the 'end of philosophy', Marx demanded a more politically committed kind of theory which was not merely interpretative but which would also be transformative. Hegel claimed philosophy can only interpret the world; Marx argued for a form of knowledge which would be part of the process of social change.

The importance of Hegel to Marx was two-fold. First, and most importantly, Hegel's concept of the dialectic provided the basis for a social scientific methodology. While the dialectic ultimately for Hegel referred to the movement of thought, for Marx it suggested a way of conceiving of history as a real and material process. Second, with its emphasis on history, Hegel's philosophy pointed a way out of speculative metaphysics. Although Hegel did not succeed in breaking from metaphysics, he had made a decisive intellectual break. Thus history itself for Marx could be seen in terms of the notion of world constitution. In Marx's philosophy the world is constituted in the rise of consciousness. Consciousness in the historical materialist conception of history refers not to the self-reflection of reason but to the raising of class consciousness and the ultimate realization of reason was the ideal of communism.

Social Science as the Critique of Political Economy

Marx's mature conception of social science can be described in his own terms as a 'critique of political economy'. Along with Weber's interpretative social science and Durkheim's positivistic social science, Marx's critique of political economy belongs to the classical foundations in modern social science. In what follows I shall give a brief sketch of the principal ideas underlying it.

The key ideas underlying Marx's social science are the movement from *contradiction* to *crisis* to *conflict* to *social change*. The starting point is the notion of contradiction. Applying the Hegelian concept of dialectics to the social structure, Marx demonstrated how industrial capitalist society is organized around fundamental contradictions. These contradictions derive from the class structure which is based on the exploitation of labour. The contradictory nature of capitalism consists of the fact that the workers in exchanging their capacity for labour, that is, their labour power which is measured in terms of labour time, receive only a wage while the capitalists, the employers, use the labour of the workers to produce commodities, which generate profit or 'surplus value' when they are sold on the market. The resulting inequality is a structural inequality since there are two classes, those who work for wages and those who live from profit. The former own only their labour (which capitalism reduces to mere labour time), while the latter own the means of production. This inequality is responsible for alienation since the products of labour are reduced to externalized commodities and the pursuit of profit becomes the dominating force in society shaping all aspects of life to its laws. Marx believed capitalism is based on a structural contradiction. It was his view that all societies were based on contradictions of different kinds, but in modern capitalism the contradiction has become more acute and concentrated in the class structure and that this exists as an endemic structure. In capitalism the surplus is extracted not by the state, as in the feudal mode of production, but by the class system which has institutionalized economic exploitation. In his economic theory Marx explored further contradictions within the capitalism, such as the falling rate of profit. It will suffice here to stress the fact that for Marx social reality is by virtue of its very structures contradictory and that these contradictions relate to the relationship between different kinds of social agency.

The implication of contradiction is crisis. In Marxist social science, a crisis is a stage beyond a contradiction and refers to the deepening of a contradiction to the point where the structures sustaining the contradiction undergo a severe strain. A crisis, however, does not necessarily amount to a point of transition. According to Marx, capitalism as a result of its class contradiction was perpetually in a state of potential crisis. In order to prevent contradictions from reaching the point of crisis, capitalism produces ideology. The role of ideology is to construct social reality in a way that the underlying contradictions are not fully transparent. Ideology is a function of class power which is rendered naturalistic or opaque. When Marx argued that the economic forces of capitalism, which he called the 'substructure', determined the form of the 'superstructure' (religion, law, culture and other social institutions such as family and education), he was not claiming that everything is reducible to economic forces and always takes an ideological form. Marx was making two claims concerning economic causality. First was a strong thesis of materialism. It is crucial to see that this was formulated as a critique of idealist intellectual systems, such as the still influential Hegelian philosophy, which attempted to explain everything in terms of ideas. In opposition to Hegel, Marx tried to show that there were powerful material forces shaping the world of ideas, be they those of philosophy, religion or culture in general. Consequently human history cannot be explained by reference to idealistic constructions, which are mere ideologies. Many critics of Marx have failed to note that his critique of ideology was mostly developed in the context of a critique of idealist philosophy and have therefore, in taking it out of its intellectual context, attributed to it the thesis of economic determinism. Second, a weaker thesis of economic causality was present in his writings. This consists of the claim that historical change is primarily brought about by changes in modes of production when the forces of production reach a point of maturity that they can no longer be contained in the existing society. It was Marx's conviction that capitalist society had created a form of production which was for ever challenging its own very limits. Thus capitalism was a crisis prone system.

The crisis ridden nature of capitalism leads to conflict. Marx believed that the mechanisms of repression and ideology control were not so powerful that they could prevent class conflict from emerging and challenging the system of domination. Central to the theory of class conflict was an implicit notion of consciousness. In Marx's social theory consciousness was something that was class specific, or existed in a heightened form in the identity of the working class. The normative foundations of Marxist social science resided in a belief in the already existing normative framework of the working class whose social interests were to be the reference points for the ideal society. A certain conception of subjectivity is therefore presupposed as the political address of social science. One of the assumptions is that the Marxist subjectivity is only in need of leadership and science must provide an emancipatory role in facilitating the revolutionary goal.

Conflict leads to social change. Marx seems to have conceived social change as revolutionary, a total change in the organization of society. Proletarian revolution was different from mere reform which did not touch the basis social structures themselves. The concept of social change in Marx had strong resonances of utopianism for the communist society of the future was seen as ideal society and one that could be reached only by a fundamental break with the existing society.

The general conclusion to be drawn from this with respect to the cognitive status of Marxist social science is that the role of social science is one of emancipation. As an emancipatory practice, social science must be materialist and critical. Materialist in the sense of being anti-obscurantist and drawing attention to the role of material forces in the shaping of ideas; critical in the sense of revealing the mechanisms of domination that operate in different forms of social organization.

Marxism differs, then, very much from hermeneutics and positivism. In opposition to the hermeneutical approach, which aims at mere understanding and is often supposed to be value-free, the Marxist approach is more explanatory than interpretative. Language and cultural objectivations are more likely to be seen as ideological or derivative of substructual determinants. Rather than focusing exclusively on culture, Marxism is much more concerned with the relationship between agency and structure. Thus the aim of social science is less the interpretation of culture than the critical transformation of social structures through the setting free of agency. The hermeneutical approach, while recognizing the fact that society differs from nature in that society undergoes change, reduces change to the cultural dimension, thus neglecting the role of agency in bringing about change and at the same time the shaping of agency by structure. Marxism thus offers a dialectical approach which attempts to link agency, structure and culture together. The dialectical approach recognizes that the subject matter of society is constantly in a state of change or potential change. The role of science is to be able to express that very state of change and by doing so to hasten the process of change.

Marxist social science also departs company from positivism, which like hermeneutics argues for the value-freedom of science. Marxists do not see science as standing outside society but as an integral part of society. The Marxist conception of science does not transcend society but seeks to transform it by identifying with the most historically advanced form of consciousness. In this sense Marxism implies radical constructivism. The role of the intellectual and that of the professional cannot be so neatly separated as in positivism and hermeneutics where the scientists stand outside their subject matter. For Marxists every observation and interpretation is itself a kind of world constitution, for in observing and interpreting we are also transforming reality. For this reason we can say that the dialectical conception of history involves both realism and constructivism.

A further difference between Marxism, on the one hand, and on the other positivism and hermeneutics is in the relationship between society and nature. For Marx nature is not a domain outside society confronting it as an external object waiting to be mastered by society and by contemplative science. Nature and society are part of a dialectical movement which unfolds through praxis. Labour, as the transformative power of agency, is the link between nature and society. For positivists, on the other hand, nature is something to be dominated by science while the proponents of the hermeneutical approach argue for the strict separation of nature and society.

The relation between Marxism and positivism is less clear on the question of causation. The much discussed question of Marx's positivism, 'scientific Marxism', concerns the relation of economic causality and social change. Some interpreters, both critics, such as Popper, and followers, such as Althusser, have claimed that Marx favoured a deterministic view of history (the doctrine of 'historicism'), claiming that the laws of history demonstrate a succession of modes of production leading to the supercession of capitalism by socialism and eventually to communism. As I have suggested above, these arguments, while having some basis in Marx's writings, depend on a highly selective reading of certain polemical arguments Marx made in criticizing the idealist philosophers or in support of radical movements. Yet, it is clear that Marx, as most thinkers of his age, did adhere to a linear conception of history conceived of in terms of a progressive movement in stages. Charles Darwin's *Origin of the Species* was published in 1859, the same year as Marx's *Critique of Political Economy*. Historical materialism can be viewed in the context of evolutionary theories of history and utopian socialism.

One of the enduring debates that Marx gave rise to is the question of the priority of structure or agency. A conventional view is that the early 'philosophical' Marx of the *Paris Manuscripts* in the 1840s held to the priority of agency while the later 'sociological' Marx moved towards a model of structural determinism. There is indeed some ambiguity as to whether Marx in the mature writings believed that structural changes within the economy bring about social change or whether social agency itself is the primary cause of change. Clearly Marx believed structure and agency were dialectically related from the point of view of theory, but ontologically he seemed to have laid greater stress on structure. It is in this sense that Marx was a realist, but in so far as his realism was expressed in a dialectical form it necessarily embodied constructivism.

A second debate on Marx's work concerns the role of culture in relation to agency and culture. Beyond criticizing the essentialistic and idealistic constructions of culture in German philosophy in his time, Marx was not particularly interested in questions of culture. It was the unfortunate fate of his work that twentieth-century Marxists chose to operate with a materialist conception of culture, a position which, as I have argued, cannot be seriously credited to Marx himself. It was against this kind of materialistic Marxism that the Frankfurt School reacted to in proposing a new kind of Marxism, known as critical theory, the defining characteristic of which was the transformation of the critique of political economy into the critique of ideology.

A final issue to be considered is the question of the normative foundations of critique. For positivists the normative foundation of science was the doctrine of scientism, the identification of knowledge with science. For Marx, the normative foundations of science ultimately lay not in science itself but in the consciousness of the proletariat. Ideology was seen as obscuring the real interests of the proletariat and it was the function of social science to break through the mechanisms of reification. As I have already argued, this position implies constructivism. Secure in its identity as an emancipatory practice, Marxist social science did not have to question its normative foundations too closely. Marxist epistemology always assumed that science as a cognitive system was in possession of truth and that this truth corresponded in some way to the revolutionary and constructivist potential in the consciousness of the proletariat. Ideology was thus a 'false consciousness', while science was true consciousness.

Underlying the question of the normative foundations of critique lay a theory of human needs. Marx assumed that capitalism was incapable of satisfying human needs and that it would be replaced by a system that was capable of satisfying human needs. But the problem, which has perplexed much of neo-Marxism, is that human needs are not self-evident, waiting to be realized from social structures from they are alienated, and social science therefore cannot so self-confidently assume that it is the interpreter of human needs.

Critical Theory and the Critique of Ideology

The school of social thought known as 'critical theory', or in its more narrow definition the 'Frankfurt School', was above all concerned to reconsider the question of the normative foundations of Marxist social science. With critical theory Marxism shifts from being a critique of political economy to the critique of ideology. The restructuring of Marxist social theory was as a result of the failure of emancipation under the conditions of advanced capitalism. Drawing heavily on the sociology of Weber, which emphasized the disenchantment of culture, and the cultural pessimism of philosophers such as Nietzsche, the Frankfurt School stressed the importance of ideology, which in the age of the 'culture industry' can no longer be seen as incidental to capitalism, a representation of reality. With the growth of new forms of power, ideology in the view of Theodor Adorno and Max Horkheimer had become a form of reality in itself. Therefore the kind of critique that is called for is a critique of ideology. With the critical theory of the Frankfurt School the idea of critique reaches its penultimate expression in a totalizing critique of modern society.

The Frankfurt School refers to a group of mostly Marxist intellectuals of Jewish background associated with the Institute for Social Research in Frankfurt in the later part of the Weimar era. With the rise of Hitler from 1933 the school moved to the United States and returned to Frankfurt in the early 1950s. By the early

1970s most members had died and a new generation of critical theorists emerged around Jürgen Habermas. The principal theorists of the Frankfurt School were Theodor Adorno and Max Horkheimer, while Herbert Marcuse was one of the famous representatives of critical theory though he was not directly related to the Frankfurt group.

The Frankfurt School writers emphasized the link between philosophy and social science, but differed from the neo-Kantian and Wittgensteinian approaches in that they came from a predominately Marxist background. Its methodological statements were elucidated by Horkheimer, Marcuse and Adorno in three classic works.

In a famous essay, 'Traditional and Critical Theory' ([1937] 1972), Horkheimer outlined the basis of critical theory as a critique of positivism. Traditional theory referred to Cartesian rationalism and the instrumentalizing logic of modern positivism, while critical theory was a critical and dialectical theory which does not accept the existing order. This essay and the *Dialectic of Enlightenment* [1947], written by Adorno and Horkheimer, were the two most influential expressions of the critical theory of the Frankfurt School.

Marcuse's *Reason and Revolution* ([1941] 1977) is also a major statement of critical theory as a critique of positivism. In this work Marcuse established the basis for a Hegelian Marxism as a radical departure from the positivism of Comte. Against Comte's belief that social facts are objective and to be merely observed, he argued the function of theory as a critique is to understand the negations and self-contradictions built into social reality. For Marcuse, as for the Frankfurt School, the problem was not merely Comtean positivism, but also Marxian positivism. In order to overcome economic materialism in the deterministic sense, Marcuse, who was heavily influenced by Heidegger and more appreciative of Mannheim than Horkheimer and Adorno, favoured a return to the more Hegelian elements in Marx's early thought.

The project of critical theory also received one of its most famous methodological statements in the book Adorno edited, *The Positivist Dispute in German Sociology* ([1969] 1976), which emanated out of an exchange between Adorno and Popper at a conference on the logic of the social sciences held by the German Sociological Association in Tübingen in 1961. The positivist dispute was in fact a misnomer, since much of the debate was in fact a confrontation between Popper and Adorno and is better described as a debate about critical theory and neo-positivism, as represented by critical rationalism. For both Popper and Adorno, critique is the essence of science, but for the latter critique is immanent. Against Popper's critical rationalism, Adorno defended critical theory as a social science of society as a totality. The essence of critical theory is the dialectical method which aims to grasp the contradictory nature of society. Popper's critical rationalism, for instance, regarded reality to be free of contradictions, which are products of our epistemological inadequacy. Adorno's criticism was that contradictions are inherent in reality and cannot be eliminated by increased scientific knowledge (1976: 108). He accused positivism of confining objectivity only to methodology and not to what is investigated (1976: 71). Positivism is thus an affirmation of the status quo, while critical theory attempts to grasp society in its totality. If this is carried out dialectically the idea of a counter-factual norm will be apparent: 'Society, the knowledge of which is ultimately the aim of sociology if it is to be more than a mere technique, can only crystallize at all around the conception of a just society. The latter, however, is not to be contrasted with the existing society in an abstract manner, simply as an ostensible value, but rather it arises from criticism, that is from society's awareness of its contradictions and its necessity' (Adorno, 1976: 118). In order to do this it is not possible to confine analysis to atomistic facts: 'Empirical social research cannot evade the fact that all given factors investigated, the subjective no less than the objective relations, are mediated through society' (Adorno, 1976: 84). Adorno, however, is not opposed to empirical research, but insists on the necessity for empirical research to be integrated into a critical theoretical framework. This kind of critical social theory was reflected in the *Authoritarian Personality* [1950], an empirical research programme supervised by Adorno and which was theoretically designed to discover authoritarian traits in the personality structure of modern society.

The attempt to reorient German sociology away from American positivistic social science, revealed considerable common ground between the antagonistic positions of Adorno and his chief protagonist in the German positivist dispute, Karl Popper, since both shared a common rejection of empiricism. However, in his desire to reject any sociology that accepted without critique the accounts of the world of people, Adorno could not develop a truly radical sociology and tended to move towards cultural criticism.

The critical theory of the Frankfurt School can be seen as an extension of the Marxism of Georg Lukacs, which emphasized the importance of alienation and reification. Like Lukacs the Frankfurt School aimed to explain the absence of revolution in modern society and the rise of totalitarianism. As an attempt to place Marxist social science on new foundations, critical theory can be seen as synthesis of Hegel, Nietzsche, Weber and Freud.

Critical theory is often called Hegelian Marxism because it tries to recover some aspects of Hegel's philosophy which Marx failed to follow through. The principal idea is the notion of the dialectic, which for Adorno is the basis of critical thinking. While Marcuse emphasized the philosophy of praxis in the more Hegelian writings of the early Marx, Adorno developed the idea of 'negative dialectics' to provide a philosophical foundation for critical social science. Critique for Adorno was an act of intellectual negation and did not have to emanate from a particular form of consciousness. Much of his work is a defence of the autonomy of critical thinking. With Marcuse, Adorno was also inclined to see history in a Hegelian manner as a struggle for recognition but one in which subjectivity is for ever imprisoned in its objectified forms. Hegelian Marxism was a constructivist reaction to what was commonly regarded a reductionism in Marx's thought. Marcuse, in reinterpreting Hegel, argued how knowledge is always a striving after that which does not yet exist. The dialectical conception of history reveals how reality is contradictory, its negation is built into it and therefore every existing condition can be seen as containing the potential for change, which is the working out of contradictions. While Hegel confined the dialectic to the world of thought, Marx reduced it too much to economic processes. The dialectical critique favoured by critical theory is one that penetrates to all dimensions of society.

The critical theory of the Frankfurt School is renowned for its pessimism. In order to appreciate this pessimism it is important to see that the origins of critical theory lay as much in German cultural pessimism as in Marxism. The tradition of Nietzsche and Weber was an important influence in early critical theory. Nietzsche's interpretation of modernity as a descent into irrationalism and nihilism and Weber's notion of the disenchantment of modernity as a result of instrumental rationalization lay behind the pessimistic argument of the *Dialectic of Enlightenment* [1947], one of the classic statements of the Frankfurt School. Weber's sociology demonstrated how modernity had become an 'iron cage', a totally administered world which had suffered a loss of meaning and a loss of freedom. For Adorno and Horkheimer, Weber's sociology provided a basis of a theory of culture, which was absent in Marx.

Mention must also be made of the importance of Freud who demonstrated that rationality and consciousness are illusions and that repression is the basis of civilization which is a struggle between the pressure principle and the reality principle. For the Frankfurt School, Freud provided a social psychological theory explaining how the masses identify with authority. In this way the repressive nature of capitalism could be understood as well as the failure of emancipatory politics. This Freudian dimension revealed that consciousness is not something uniform and coherent waiting to be realized by emancipatory politics. Indeed, the very struggle for emancipation can led to repressive identification in what Erich Fromm called the 'fear of freedom'.

With its theoretical foundations in Hegelian Marxism supplemented by Weberian cultural pessimism and Freudian theory, the critical theorists aimed to explain how capitalism both expands and at the same time negates opposition. Their theme was the fate of critical thought in a century dominated by the three great repressive and integrating forces of fascism, Stalinism and the culture industry of advanced capitalism. These events typified the rationalizing and homogenizing logic of modernity in its instrumentalization of culture. The Frankfurt School believed that there was no essential difference between fascism and Stalinism, both being products of modern totalitarian state capitalism, and the culture industry of the post-wars decades was the continuation of the instrumentalizing logic of modernity. With the culture industry and organized mass entertainment, ideology penetrates into the cultural sphere and ceases to be an illusion or a 'false consciousness'. One of the central arguments of the Frankfurt School was that the effectiveness of ideology as a system of control lies not so much in its false messages, but in its sheer ability to be able to remove the desire for change from society and its negation of critical thinking: reality is itself an ideology. In this way critical theory sees reality as the ultimate construction.

Alienation is given a new significance in critical theory which no longer locates alienation in the sphere of labour but in the 'system of needs' itself. Marcuse argued how 'social control is anchored in the new system of needs' and as a result Marxism cannot claim to speak in the name of an unfulfilled human need. Therefore, the only conclusion is that 'confronted with the total character of the achievements of advanced industrial capitalism, critical theory is left without the rationale for transcending this society'.

The conclusions of the Frankfurt School were that the working class can no longer be seen as the revolutionary subject. With the rise of the 'totally administered society' and the commodification of culture, emancipation cannot come from labour. Hence the need for ideology critique and cultural criticism. But the Frankfurt School largely reduced critique to a totalizing critique and ultimately appealed to the autonomy of the aesthetic sphere which was the last refuge for negative or critical thinking. In the age of what Marcuse called 'one-dimensional man' only 'autonomous art' – high art which resists commodification with the help of its formalistic and uncompromising nature – can be genuinely free from mass consumption. The critical theory of the Frankfurt School ultimately amounts to intellectual elitism since it argues that opposition can only be conducted by the solitary intellectual or high art confronting social reality in an act of defiance.

Conclusion: The Institutionalization of Marxism

The Frankfurt School has been one of the most influential traditions in neo-Marxism and has greatly shaped conceptions of social science as critical practice. Probably the most important contribution it has made has been in the critical theory of culture and communication. In this regard the movement played a key role in the cultural turn in the social and human sciences. While there are few today who would defend the classical theories of the Frankfurt School, the implications of their writings with respect to the normative foundations of critique are far-reaching. The most basic question is what is the normative foundation of a conception of social science which proclaims itself to be emancipatory.

The history of Marxist social science in the twentieth century can be seen as a series of crises for its emancipatory endeavour. In the conflict between emancipation and critique, Marxism has mostly opted for critique. Indeed, much of Marxism critique has been a kind of self-critique and by the 1970s became an institutionalized methodology in university departments throughout the western world. With the professionalization of opposition, Marxist social scientists have on the whole tended to view Marxism more as a form of critique than an emancipatory practice. Secure in the knowledge that social revolution would not disturb the tranquility of academia where Marxism was nourished, Marxist inclined social scientists condemned social democracy and middle class society as a necessary illusion. The proliferation of Marxist sociology in the 1970s had more to do with the quest for tenure than the search for the scattered traces of revolutionary consciousness.

In 1990 Marxism entered its final crisis as an all-encompassing critique of western society. The collapse of communism in Eastern Europe and the break-up of the USSR brought to a conclusion the illusion of radical subjectivity which had sustained the Marxist project for over one hundred years.

At about this time Marxism in social science was internally divided between realism and constructivism. On the one side, there were the realists who held onto the more traditional tenets of the Marxist faith such as the deterministic emphasis on structure and, on the other side, the constructivists who emphasized culture and ideology. Agency remained under-theorized, with the result that no Marxist school was able to understand the direction social change was taking by 1989.

4

Communication and Pragmatism: Habermas, Apel and the Renewal of Critical Social Science

Introduction: Social Science and Discourses of Modernity

The positivist dispute can be characterized as having three major interventions. The first was the turn to a post-empiricist science from a point within natural science and which broadly accepted the framework of positivism conceived of as a methodology. The most important representative of this was Popper whose critical rationalism set the terms for a post-empiricist philosophy of science, but one which preserved the unity of science while rejecting the unity of its subject matter: social and natural facts were two separate domains and science can be only methodologically critical but not socially critical. The second rupture was the interpretative turn from its origins in the hermeneutical and neo-Kantian tradition from Dilthey to Weber, which argued for a separation of the human sciences from the natural sciences. Weber sought to combine explanation and understanding into a unified interpretative but value free social science. The third was the recovery of critique by neo-Marxism but especially critical theory from Adorno and Horkheimer to Marcuse, who argued for a normative or emancipatory social science. These three discourses on social sciences – explanation and description, understanding and interpretation, and critique and emancipation – were in their unique ways discourses of modernity and took as their cognitive foundations the cultural pillars of modernity, which were respectively: the unity of science, the unity of the interpreting subject and the unity of the project of emancipation.

To these discourses corresponded the great ideological narratives of modernity: liberalism, conservatism and socialism. Positivism was largely an ideology of liberalism and expressed a great faith in the unity of science, its rationalistic and explanatory aspiration for intellectual mastery, planning and control. The hermeneutic-interpretative tradition was reflected in a predominantly conservative and communitarian view of society with its emphasis on language, society as an objectivation of meaning and value neutrality on questions of culture. The critical tradition reflected a belief in the emancipatory power of modernity and of the demystifying role of science in the universal quest for emancipation. It was primarily an ideology of socialism.

What in fact happened was that 'the sociological discourse fell apart', to use Peter Wagner's (1994: 109) apt phrase: classical social science failed to integrate its diverse components into a unified discourse. While social science had almost reached the point of being accepted by the intellectual and political elites as the interpreter of modernity by the beginning of the twentieth century, it was unable to maintain this role for long and split into separate spheres. Max Weber, for instance, had been instrumental in drafting the ill-fated constitution of the Weimar Republic. But today the age of the political influence of intellectuals and professionals has passed. Empirical social research and social policy research of a predominantly positivistic nature flourished in the United States and in Britain, while the heritage of classical sociology became absorbed into either philosophy or Marxism in Western Europe.

Classical positivism in the Durkheimian sense lost its faith in the liberal ideology, which in its classical form collapsed with the democratization of society and the subsequent rise of fascism. The hermeneutical tradition failed to sustain a professional sociological discourse and became absorbed into philosophy, as is evidenced by figures such as Winch, Gadamer and Ricoeur. Finally, the radical tradition of Marxist thought provided a credible alternative to philosophical sociology and to empirical policy research, but was never able to reconcile the normative contradiction between acceptance of social democracy and social revolution.

The three traditions were never, of course, quite separate from each other. In the United States Parsons's grand theory, which purported to be a systematic theory of the evolution of societies and in the classical tradition of Weber, existed uneasily along side empirical social research. American pragmatism, the tradition of John Dewey, G. H. Mead and Charles Peirce, too, preserved an important distinctive theoretical tradition. Elsewhere the classical tradition was preserved through Marxist or critical social research (in the United States by the Frankfurt School in exile). Many leading American sociologists, such as Robert Lynd, co-author of the classic works of Chicago School *Middletown* [1929] and *Middletown in Transition* [1937], retained a broader vision of the task of sociology in a changing world. Lynd's two central questions were how is community possible in the wake of rapid industrial change and what is the public role of sociology in the age of the professions (Aronwitz 1988: viii–ix). His *Knowledge for What?*, written in 1939 under the influence of social science's embracing of the New Deal, anticipated, from the perspective of American pragmatism, the writings of Jürgen Habermas in the 1970s in calling for a normative link between knowledge and social interests. In his view the professionalization of social science has resulted in the betrayal of the intentions of the founders for whom professional knowledge had an emancipatory function. It is therefore interesting that we can speak of the betrayal of sociology from a point within American empirical social research.

Post-empiricist social science was internally divided between these traditions – the positivist, the hermeneutical and the critical – until the positivist dispute in German sociology culminated in the very similar attempts of Karl-Otto Apel (1980, 1984a) and Jürgen Habermas (1978, 1988) to resolve the three social sciences into a unified vision in which Weber's mediation of explanation and understanding was reworked into a critical hermeneutical communication theory. The central ideas of this approach revolve around the linking of knowledge to cognitive 'interests'. Habermas argues that different kinds of scientific knowledge rest on different interests, the characteristic of social science being its interest in emancipation. Habermas's conception of social science is a synthesis of hermeneutical understanding of communication, causal explanation of structures of domination, and critique. With this new synthesis Habermas believes he could rescue critical theory from the fate of the negative dialectics of the Frankfurt School's totalizing critique. Habermas's critical theory thus shifts the normative foundations of critique from the self-denying critique of ideology to the hermeneutic critique and reconstruction of human communication. His approach can be seen as a radical constructivism since it is centrally concerned with an attempt to link knowledge to cognitive interests on the basis of a pragmatic theory of communication.

The remainder of this book will be concerned with outlining the different interpretations of post-empiricist social science. This chapter looks at the most ambitious and far-reaching philosophy of social science, the critical hermeneutic or 'reconstructive' approach of Habermas and Apel. My aim will be to show that while the projects of Habermas and Apel offered the most promising prospects in the 1970s for a comprehensive synthesis of the three classical methodologies of social science, their attempts have largely failed and new approaches must be found in order to finalize this project. Subsequent chapters will examine other approaches, ranging from deconstructionism to standpoint epistemology and new debates on constructivism and realism.

Habermas on Critique and Communication

Habermas's philosophy of the social sciences was developed in the context of three debates: (1) the critique of positivism in the early 1960s, a debate which in fact was more a critique of Popper's particular brand of neo-positivism, namely critical rationalism; (2) a critique of Gadamer's philosophical hermeneutics; and (3) a critique of the critical theory of the Frankfurt School and more broadly of Western Marxism. I shall examine each of these in turn, before proceeding to his principal methodological work, *Knowledge and Human Interests* ([1968] 1978).

The publication of the *Positivist Dispute in German Sociology* in 1969 was a turning point in debates on the philosophical and methodological foundations in the social sciences. The importance of the debate is that it marked the emergence of different conceptions of post-empiricist social science. In this dispute 'positivism' was in fact a misnomer since none of the participants were representing positivism as such (Keat, 1981: 23). In the previous chapter I commented on Adorno's debate with Popper, showing how the debate emerged between critical rationalism and critical theory. The former is a development within neo-positivism and is deeply opposed to some of the traditional assumptions of positivism, such as induction (the construction of theory from the observation of data). Adorno's attack was not then positivism, but critical rationalism which the proponents of critical theory maintained had not broken from positivism. Adorno and Habermas were primarily criticizing the idea of value-freedom in critical rationalism.

Habermas entered the debate on behalf of Adorno, accusing Popper of decisionism. According to Habermas social science differs from natural science not only in its subject matter but also in its methodology. In social science the scientist cannot be normatively separated from the object of research in the way Popper attempted. Social science involves a critical engagement with its subject matter. The key point in his critique of Popper concerns the question of normative consensus on what is to account as an acceptable theory. Habermas accepts much of Popper's criticism of positivism to the extent that theory is not the result of the presuppositionless observation of facts and that science proceeds from theoretical problems to observation. The problem for Habermas is how theories in the social sciences are in fact normatively constructed. Accepting Popper's argument that theories involve provisional consensus within the scientific community and that the logic of science is not one of presuppositionless inquiry, Habermas claims that the normative content in consensus building cannot come solely from the scientific discourse itself but must come from the logic of communication. In excluding social content from the scientific community, Popper resorts to scientific decisionism, according to Habermas; that is, Popper sees scientific interventions and the entire logic of science to be a matter for scientists to decide (Habermas, 1976a: 151). In this early essay, originally published in 1969, the essence of Habermas's social theory was present: 'Research is an institution composed of people who act together and communicate with one another; as such it determines, through the communication of the researches, that which can theoretically lay claim to validity' (1976a: 152). Habermas accuses Popper of falling to the illusion of pure theory and neglecting the pre-scientific hermeneutical dimension involved in social science which cannot separate itself from 'knowledge-guiding interests'. The idea that knowledge is guided by social interests is fundamental to Habermas's conception of social science. Popper, Habermas argues, can ignore the social interests underlying the constitution of knowledge only by recourse to the ideology of value-freedom.

Drawing on the Marxist notion of dialectics, Habermas argues social science has a dialectical relationship to its object; science is not separate from the social world in the way Popper believed. But in order to develop the dialectical method, it is necessary to go beyond dialectical materialism and embrace hermeneutics. The relevance of hermeneutics, in particular in the linguistic tradition, is that it offers a perspective on the pre-scientific constitution of science. This forms the background to Habermas's debate with Gadamer, whose *Truth and Method* was published in 1960, a few years before the positivist dispute began. Habermas attaches great importance to the hermeneutical tradition but is also very critical of its conservative bias. His aim is to rescue what is valuable from this tradition in order to build a critical hermeneutical theory of social science. The value of the hermeneutical tradition in Habermas's estimation is that it established a clear demarcation between the natural and human sciences both in methodology and ontology. In particular, a hermeneutical approach offers what is also absent from Marxism and the critical theory of the Frankfurt School, namely a concept of the self-reflection of science. The essence of this self-reflection, as was argued in Chapter 2, was the linguistic constitution of society and science. Gadamer's Heideggerian philosophical methodology stressed the role of language in interpretation and the dialectical relationship of science to its subject matter. Habermas (1988: 117) acknowledges the significance of the linguistic turn in philosophy: 'Today the problem of language has taken the place of the traditional problem of consciousness: the transcendental critique of language takes the place of the critique of consciousness'.

Where Habermas differs from Gadamer is in the political and normative conception of methodology. The method suggested by philosophical hermeneutics indicates a commitment to relativism in the sense of a failure to address political practice. One of Gadamer's basic suppositions, which is also reflected in much of communitarian philosophy, is that science cannot transcend cultural contexts. In other words, for Gadamer social science in interpreting social meaning merely provides 'understanding'. This means for Habermas that hermeneutics does not have an emancipatory moment for this would require evaluation and evaluation entails critique. Gadamer's concept of understanding is based on a notion of consensus derived from the acceptance of tradition, whereas Habermas's concept of consensus is one that is discursively formed. Thus instead of understanding the past, Habermas speaks of 'consensus oriented towards reaching an understanding'. This debate on the relation of critique to hermeneutics centred around a discussion on the significance of tradition and authority. For Gadamer interpretation in the social and human sciences involves the interpretation of tradition whose authority is not something for modernity to be too preoccupied with transcending. The present can only be reconstructed out of its past. Gadamer does not see the authority of tradition as something regressive or dogmatic to be transcended by an emancipatory critical theory. This is the kernel of the difference with Habermas for whom an emancipatory moment in the interpretative process is essential. What for Gadamer is a 'fusion of horizons' is for Habermas a critique of ideologically distorted communication: reflection cannot be confined to the model of translation or dialogue for language can be a medium of domination. Hermeneutical reflection must be radicalized by bringing it in a critical direction.

At this point the third debate can be introduced, the critique of critical theory. Habermas's writings are an on-going debate with his former mentor Theodor Adorno and the heritage of the Frankfurt School. The idea of a critical theory of society is the essence of his social theory and his philosophy of the social sciences is an attempt to establish the normative foundations of critique. He departs fundamentally from the conception of critique held by the Frankfurt School in several respects. First, critique is not a totalizing critique of modern society but a reconstructive one. While Adorno and Horkheimer rejected the prospect of emancipation as real possibility, and therefore held to a pessimistic critique of modernity as a closed system of domination, Habermas's aim is to reconstruct the emancipatory potentials in modern society. Therefore he rejects the idea of a 'negative dialectic' in favour of a 'critical hermeneutical' science. Second, from the vantage point of a theory of communicative action, social science must break from the philosophy of history, which the Frankfurt School was entrapped in. Third, the dialectical method must be developed from the perspective of the philosophy of language. A critical hermeneutical theory of society seeks to rescue communication from ideology. If communication is taken as the starting point and not instrumental domination, social science must in principle admit of the possibility of emancipation.

Habermas accepts the Frankfurt School's thesis that there is no longer a revolutionary subject in modern society. The collapse of the historical subject is in fact to be seen as a liberating development for it opens the prospect of a wider concept of social transformation. The failing of Marxism, including the critical theory of the Frankfurt School, was that it operated with a notion of consciousness, which Habermas argues must be replaced by communication. Shifting the focus onto communication allows us to see that the normative foundations of social science cannot rest on something like the 'consciousness of the proletariat' or Marcuse's new subjectivity. If the lesson of modern philosophy has been that consciousness is constituted in language, then the task of science is to see how the communicative potential for social change can be reconstructed out of existing forms of communication. With this insight Habermas's social theory shifts the foundations of critique from the critique of ideology to the critique of 'distorted communication'. It is no longer a question of seeing how ideology disguises real human needs or even manufactures new ones, but a matter of examining the conditions under which rational communication, that is communication unconstrained by power, is possible.

Towards a Reconstructive Social Science

Habermas outlined his conception of a critical hermeneutical social science in two works, *On the Logic of the Social Sciences* ([1967/1970] 1988) and his major work *Knowledge and Human Interests* ([1968] 1978), as well as the collection of papers, *Theory and Practice* (1977). His approach is based on linking knowledge with its social interests, on the one side, and on the other subjecting knowledge to self-reflection and critique.

Habermas's starting point is the problem of the normative foundations of critique in Marxism. While agreeing with Marx's critique of Hegel (that is, the 'materialization' of the theory of knowledge, or the shift from epistemology to social theory), he argues Marx created a different kind of normative problem: 'Marx never explicitly discussed the specific meaning of a science of man elaborated as a critique ideology and distinct from the instrumental meaning of natural science' (1978: 45). In Habermas's view, then, Marx held onto a positivistic conception of critique, frequently comparing his critique of political economy to the methods of the natural sciences. This methodological approach was reflected in his normative theory which tied emancipation to the instrumental-technical level of work, thus ignoring the communicative dimension of society. In order to transcend the positivist bias in Marxism, Habermas argues for a restructured Marxism which will require integrating the hermeneutical tradition of the neo-Kantians and the modern philosophy of language as represented by American pragmatism (in particular Charles Peirce), and Freudian psychoanalysis. The result was a critical hermeneutical theory of social science.

In his schema there are three kinds of knowledge, which correspond closely to the three sciences (natural, human and social sciences): Habermas refers to these as 'cognitive' interests, which means 'knowledge' interests. 'The approach of the empirical-analytical sciences incorporates a technical cognitive interest; that of the historical-hermeneutic sciences incorporates a practical one; and the approach of critically oriented sciences incorporates the emancipatory cognitive interest' (1978: 308). The importance of interests with respect to science is that they determine the social context of science. If science is based on interests, then pure science or scientism is untenable. In Habermas's view the interests underlying scientific knowledge are linked to specific dimensions of social action: 'knowledge-constitutive interests take form in the medium of work, language and power' (1978: 313). The interest in prediction and control is related to the world of work, which Habermas terms instrumental action. Hermeneutical knowledge aimed at understanding is linked to communicative interaction or language. Critical emancipatory knowledge is linked to the experience of power.

In Habermas's framework there is a firm distinction between the positivistic and hermeneutical sciences, and the interests underlying them. This distinction corresponds closely to the neo-Kantian dualism of explanation, as characteristic of natural positivistic science, and understanding as characteristic of the hermeneutical human sciences. Habermas is primarily concerned with the methodology of the social sciences and, following Max Weber's synthesis of explanation and understanding in an interpretative sociology, he argues that the social sciences involve both explanation and understanding. However, he departs from Weber in demanding that social science is a critical science of society. Drawing on the Marxist heritage of the Frankfurt School and the psychoanalytical theory of Freud, Habermas demonstrates how social science is to be seen as a critical-reflective science with an emancipatory interest. Thus, the social sciences employ the explanatory or analytical and empirical methodologies as well as those of the historical and cultural sciences. Neither approach alone is sufficient, and together they must be deepened into a critical approach.

By viewing social science as rooted in emancipatory interests and combining explanatory and hermeneutical methodologies, Habermas believed he succeeded in providing a comprehensive philosophy of science. His synthesis was aimed at finding a solution to the problem of the conflict between the three methodologies of explanation, understanding and critique and thereby overcome the respective illusions of scientism, relativism and emancipation. His approach resists the tendency to conflate social science with philosophy as much as it opposes positivism.

Since the publication of *Knowledge and Human Interests* in 1968, Habermas developed his philosophy of social science further, establishing what he has called 'reconstructive' social science. This turn in his thought reflected his growing concern with social theory, and in particular with the social foundations of critical communication. Before commenting on the significance of reconstructive social science, some clarification of his social theory is necessary.

Even prior to his methodological works of the 1960 and 1970s, Habermas in his first work, *The Structural Transformation of the Public Sphere* ([1962] 1989a), undertook a reconstruction of the various structural forms of public opinion, which was for him an empirical manifestation of rational and self-reflective critique. This early work was written as an implicit critique of the pessimistic ideas of Adorno and Horkheimer, which reduced modernity to processes of instrumental rationalization. Habermas's social theory, in contrast, aimed to show that communicative action is distinct from instrumental action. Thus, by taking the example of the critical function of public opinion in the critique of power, he demonstrates how communication had an important role to play in modern society. In *Legitimation Crisis* ([1973] 1976b), he developed this thesis by arguing that even in the conditions of late capitalism, systems of domination cannot dispense with the need for legitimation. Fundamental to his social theory is the thesis that power can be challenged by communicative reason. His social theory is thus an attempt to examine the social conditions of protest and the critical questioning of power. In this way Habermas broke from the critical theory of the Frankfurt School, for legitimation cannot be reduced to ideology. For Habermas, ideology is never total enough to destroy the need for active legitimation. In the two-volume *Theory of Communicative Action* ([1981] 1984, 1987) Habermas outlines a theory of modernity which does not exclude the possibility of social learning. Modernity has an emancipatory dimension which consists of its communicative potentials, which are based on the 'universal pragmatics' of human communication. We cannot go into the details of this now, other than to note theory rests on a formal theory of communication which holds that all of human communication is based on the presupposition of consensual agreement as an in principle possibility. The universal pragmatic structures of communication are conditions of the possibility, as opposed to the specific institutional form, of all social relations and of democracy.

The theme of Habermas's book is the conflict between the communicatively integrated structures of the life-world and the functionally integrated structures of the system. In the conclusion of this major work in constructivist social theory, Habermas argued the future task of critical social science lay in establishing a new relation to society: 'the development of society must *itself* give rise to the problem situations that *objectively* afford contemporaries a privileged access to the general structures of the lifeworld' (1987: 403). The perspective of a social theory based on a theory of communicative action and the incomplete project of modernity offers the philosophy of the social sciences new insights. In *Knowledge and Human Interests* Habermas demonstrated the basis of social science in the cognitive interest emanicipatory but did not demonstrate how this cognitive interest itself was constituted. His work concluded with an analysis of Freudian psychoanalysis, which offered a means of conceiving of social scientific self-reflection along the lines of a therapeutic critique. Habermas's mature social theory of communication demonstrates how emancipatory interests are constituted in the critique of 'distorted communication'. In this way the Marxist critique of ideology as a critique of 'false consciousness' is finally reconstructed into a critique of distorted communication. Reconstruction for Habermas refers both to theory-building and to the practice of theory. In the *Reconstruction of Historical Materialism* (published in English as *Communication and the Evolution of Society* [1976], 1979), he defended the basic relevance of the Marxist approach to society, but insists that it must be 'reconstructed' in light of developments in hermeneutical theory and, above all, in the theory of communication: reconstruction means 'taking a theory apart and putting it back together again in a new form in order to attain more fully the goal it has set for itself' (1979: 95). Whereas the earlier theory of cognitive interests tried to link science and social interests too closely, the communicative turn suggested a more nuanced way of establishing the connection between science and society. Responding to the new social movements of the 1970s, Habermas now began to see science and especially social science as based on communicative currents rather than merely on cognitive interests as such. Although he did not jettison the notion of cognitive interests, he moved critical theory in the direction of a theory of communicative action.

At a deeper level, Habermas's conception of critical hermeneutical social science is reconstructive in the sense that it aims to uncover the distorted forms of communication and thereby reveal the emancipatory potentials in communication. Social science must reconstruct the rational and critical norms inherent in human communication in order to show how domination can be challenged. The theory of communicative action has tended to stress less the investigation of distorted communication than the conditions of social transformation and the possibility of universalistic morality around discursive democracy. A concern with discursive democracy has become the focal point of his work since *Between Facts and Norms: Contributions to a Discursive Theory of Law and Democracy* ([1992] 1996a). For Habermas democracy must be above all a discursive process and cannot be reduced to morality or to formalistic decision-making. In this work his aim is to connect democracy to both communication and to law, for radical democracy, in Habermas's view, must have a connection with both communicative structures of the life-world and the legal structures of the state if social change is to be brought about.

Habermas's mature position is that social change can only be brought about by institutionalizing critical public discourse. As I shall argue in the final two chapters, the contemporary conception of social science is moving towards this notion of discursive democracy which provides science as a cognitive system with a new institutional system capable of enhancing the democratization of knowledge. Habermas's work did not make this connection between science and democracy, but went close to it. Since the theory of communicative action, Habermas has not dealt in depth with the philosophy of the social science, aside from a brief return to it in a later work, *Truth and Justification* [1999], where he attempts to extend the communicative approach to incorporate insights from pragmatism and realism.

Apel and the Critical Hermeneutical Theory of Science

Essential to Habermas's conception of science is that knowledge involves a relation to a socially constituted normative order. In his early methodological works he was satisfied to outline this in terms of a model of cognitive interests of which the interest in emancipation was fundamental to social sciences. Concentrating on a social theory driven by the theory of communicative action and led by discursive democracy, Habermas did not develop some of the implications of his early methodology. In this respect it is instructive to consider the work of Habermas's contemporary, Karl-Otto Apel, who had been influential in shaping Habermas's own position and had himself developed a more advanced philosophy of social science.

The concept of cognitive interests underlying science is also fundamental to Apel's (1979a, 1979b, 1980, 1984b) philosophy of social science. However, Apel's conception of a post-empiricist philosophy of science is more finely worked out than Habermas's, who is primarily interested in social theory. While Habermas tied social science to types of cognitive interest, Apel goes further in developing a theory of the ethical foundations of science. His philosophy of science is written at a high level of philosophical abstraction, with his substantive theses outlined only by critical comparison with other philosophical positions, in particular Kant, Wittgenstein and C. S. Peirce, rather than by reference to research programmes or specific research problems. This is a tendency shared with many philosophers of science, who do not explicitly substantiate their arguments but develop them immanently through the critique of other theories. For instance, Apel, like Habermas, constantly uses the expression 'transcendental' or 'transcendental pragmatic' to describe his approach. In this instance a transcendental approach does not mean 'transcendent' but refers to the Kantian method of investigating preconditions, or the conditions of necessity for knowledge. Apel's approach derives from linking Kant's transcendental approach (explicating the necessary preconditions for scientific knowledge) with Peirce's pragmatism (which stresses the role of the community of scientists and knowledge as mediated in language) and the philosophy of language (as represented by Wittgenstein and Heidegger). One of Apel's most important ideas is that the preconditions of scientific knowledge is communication. It is through communication that the objects of knowledge are constituted. Apel thus locates himself in the Kantian and Hegelian tradition with a view of the objects of knowledge constituted in the actual process of knowledge. His transcendental-pragmatic philosophy of social science aims to include the constitutive dimension of knowledge, that is the process by which science itself constructs the objects of knowledge.

Apel's most significant contribution to post-empiricist science is the threefold thesis that science rests on consensus, that this consensus can be achieved only through communication, and that the consensual communication in science rests on a commitment to a political ethics. In his view the normative foundations of all science cannot be divorced from ethical concerns. Therefore most of his arguments are outlined as a critique of scientistic conceptions of positivism (the identification of science with valid knowledge) and the idea of value-freedom or the ethical neutrality of science. From a political-ethical perspective, Apel is arguing for the recognition of the public role of science. In this context, a central question for Apel is the relation of science to societal responsibility (Apel, 1978a).

Apel's argument that science, and in particular social science, rests on a form of consensus which can only be communicatively outlined by means of a critique of positivism and hermeneutics which created the illusions of scientism and relativism. Against positivistic theories of science, Apel proposes the model of cognitive interests. He identifies three primary ones: the technical interest in controlling an objectified environmental world, interest in understanding and interpretation, and the interest in critical self-reflection (1979b: 8–9). The first is characteristic of natural science, the second which is modeled on the Aristotelian notion of 'praxis' is characteristic of the human and cultural sciences, and the third relates to the goal of bringing about change and is characteristic of the social sciences. Apel, however, it must be stressed, does not see the division in cognitive interests between the sciences in exclusive terms. In his view the social sciences themselves provide a particularly favourable field of demonstration for the application of cognitive interests which can be complementary. Thus, the social sciences can involve all three cognitive interests depending on the particular subject areas. History and philology, for instance, are more likely to be based on interpretative understanding than on the critique of ideology, which is more characteristic of sociology. Apel then proceeds to argue that the social sciences differ from the natural sciences in that they are constituted partly by their object, which is language. Social scientific knowledge involves a bridging of two language games, that of the theorist and that of research object. But, in contrast to the neo-Kantian hermeneutical tradition, Apel argues for the need for a critique of ideology. A hermeneutical or interpretative approach is limited by its acceptance of existing forms of consensus and becomes just as normatively blind as positivism or Marxism. A critical approach, on the other hand, argues less for mere self-understanding than transformation. Explanation and understanding culminates in the critique of ideology conceptualized in terms of a model of universal communication (Apel, 1980: 72, 125). By 'universal communication' Apel means communication (and claims to scientific expertise) that can be said to be valid or legitimate. Validity is determined not by recourse to author or first principles but by discursively mediated agreement.

In this respect Apel and Habermas are not too far apart. The main difference is that Apel applies more coherently the theory of communication to science, whereas Habermas is more concerned with developing a wider communicative theory of democracy. Both Apel and Habermas operate with a consensus theory of truth, though it would be more accurate to term it a discursive theory of truth since their conception of consensus differs fundamentally from hermeneutical and communitarian models. Consensus does not refer to the existing concrete forms of consensus, but to a 'regulative principle'. Consensus is presupposed in all forms of communication by virtue of the use of language. The 'scientific community' is a product of the life-world to the extent that it is also a 'communication community' and cannot dispense with language even within science. The model of consensus Apel argues for is one that stresses its normative role as a regulator of a discourse directed towards agreement. Thus consensus serves the critical function of a counterfactual norm, which is at the same time embedded in the real contexts of communication, be they those of science or everyday life. Taking up in a critical manner Wittgenstein's notion of a 'language game', Apel argues every real language-games presupposes an ideal one which can be used to overcome the irrational limits of communication in existing forms of life: 'This goal of a hermeneutic enlightenment that does not leave everything as it is, cannot, of course, be achieved without the inclusion of the critique of ideology which must also be entrusted with the task of engaging in a critique of whole forms of life and their official language games' (Apel, 1980: 172). Apel's defence of a communication theory of social science is intended to overcome the dangers of scientism, dogmatism and relativism, for which positivism, Marxism and hermeneutics are respectively responsible.

The uniqueness of Apel's philosophy of science consists in his thesis that science as a communication community cannot abdicate itself of societal responsibility. The ethical-political role of science ultimately rests on the task of realizing the 'ideal communication community' in the 'real communication community'. In this Apel appears to hold to a stronger sense of closure than Habermas's, whose notion of the 'ideal speech situation' is more indeterminate (Apel, 1997). Apel rejects B. F. Skinner's scientistic argument that only scientists can save humanity from a threatening global catastrophe. Apel claims, in contrast, that '[o]bjective science and subjective freedom and responsibility of scientists reciprocally presuppose each other, they stand and fall together' (1978b: 91–2). Rather than eliminating responsibility from the domain of science or reducing responsibility to technocratic scientism, the 'objective must be to rescue freedom and responsibility from the domain of irrational decision and from the impotence of manipulable privacy and to mobilize their potential for collective freedom' (1978b: 92). Apel concludes his most important work with the argument that the sciences 'derive their regulative principle through the postulate of the realization of the ideal communication community in the methodological and in the ethical normative sense of a non-subjective arbitrary grounding of value judgments. Consequently, they serve an empirical and normative reconstruction of the historical situation and, therefore, they serve the "formation" of public opinion' (1980: 284). In his view the social sciences, in particular sociology, have the task of bearing the burden of emancipation in so far as this can be achieved on the level of 'reflexive self-understanding'.

Although Apel emphasizes the critical, reconstructive role of social science, this kind of social science is only one. His framework recognizes the differentiated nature of social science, which includes in addition to critical social science 'quasi-nomological behavioural science', which concerns quantitative analysis and has explanation and prediction as its objective; 'quasi-biologistic functionalist systems theory' dealing with nature and with self-organizing systems; 'hermeneutical sciences of communicative understanding'.

The Limits of Habermas and Apel

One of the central arguments of this short book is that the identity of social science can no longer be formulated as a critique of positivism. While one of the most promising developments in the philosophy of social science was the model of a critical hermeneutical social science proposed by Habermas and Apel in the 1970s, this conception is no longer tenable for a number of reasons. The exemplary achievement of Habermas and Apel was to combine the challenges to positivism stemming from the hermeneutical tradition and the Marxist tradition of critical theory. The synthesis they aimed to bring about failed for a number of reasons. I would like to suggest two reasons why Habermas and Apel's conception needs to be taken in a new direction, which will involve looking at new developments revolving around realism and constructivism, on the one side, and on the other a consideration of the divided legacy of pragmatism.

The first problem with Habermas and Apel's critique of positivism lies not so much in their model of critical hermeneutics as with their assumptions about the nature of positivism in natural science. They make the fatal mistake of falsely attributing to the natural sciences a model of positivism which is to be rejected by the social sciences. This is a position which is now increasingly recognized as no longer tenable. In particular Habermas, as has been frequently pointed out, failed to resolve the problem of the place of nature in his philosophy of the social sciences. Nature is portrayed as something outside society and the appropriate form of science for dealing with it is natural science, which Habermas assumes is based on a technical cognitive interest. While social science is based on an emancipatory cognitive interest, natural science in his view sees nature as something objective. Meaningful frames of reference apply not only to the social and human sciences but also to the natural sciences.

The critical hermeneutical view of science has been undermined by developments within natural science itself which suggest that nature is not an unchanging entity existing objectively outside society and confronting science as something to be mastered. I would go so far as to argue that positivism has in fact been more undermined by natural science itself than by the successive waves of attack social scientists have launched against it in the name of critique, hermeneutics, deconstructionism and emancipatory politics. The problem is that the model of positivism held by the proponents of critical hermeneutics can be seriously questioned as a characterization of the natural sciences. If positivism is not applicable to the natural sciences, the whole framework of cognitive interests is called into question. It is now increasingly being recognized that positivism is not merely a false conception of social science, but it is an anachronism in the natural sciences (Bernstein, 1979; Keat, 1981: 73). The experimental sciences no longer correspond to this model of science. For instance, it can be argued that nature is not an objectively existing entity outside human constitution but is socially constructed. In the age of the new social movements, the thesis that nature is something to be technically mastered is no longer a tenable position.

Thomas Kuhn (1970) demolished the positivistic myth of science as based on methodological induction and demonstrated that profoundly irrational forces are involved in the progress of science. Since Einstein, the Newtonian idea of nature has collapsed with natural scientists increasingly tending to see nature not as a reality existing in itself and inherently unchanging, but as a self-generating system. The new philosophy of nature is increasingly appealing to the idea of constructivism, which only recently has made an impact on sociology though it has been for long a central concept in biology. Nature as a self-generating system is often referred to as 'autopoesis' (this will be discussed further in Chapter 7). Moreover, hermeneutics is also relevant to the natural sciences, as Richard Rorty has argued (Baert, 2004).

The implications that these developments have for the philosophy of the social sciences are difficult to specify at the moment, but they do suggest that the hitherto terms of debate on the philosophical foundations of the social sciences will have to be rethought. A post-empiricist or anti-foundationalist philosophy of social science cannot simply appeal to the neo-Kantian separation of the human and the natural sciences, with social science allied more to the former than the latter: it no longer possible to assume that natural science is addressed to nature as an objectively given reality. With this insight – nature as autopoesis – the idea of society, too, as a domain existing outside social scientific discourse must also be abandoned for constructivism reaches into the social domain. The upshot of this is that a non-positivistic model of realism is possible (Outhwaite, 1987).

The second criticism I wish to make against the adequacy of

critical hermeneutics relates to the concept of emancipation. Although it is a position Habermas has not entirely renounced despite clearly moving beyond it, the implications of his discourse theory (Habermas, 1993, 1996a, 1996b) suggest that emancipation is no longer the normative basis of social science. The problem is that emancipation is not the unproblematic thing that Habermas assumed in the 1960s in the heat of the student movement and the critical German educational reforms. Emancipation today in the age of identity politics has itself given rise to new kinds of problems. Certainly, his notion of critique of distorted communication and the subsequent development of the theory of communicative action, was an improvement of the earlier notion of a critical social science based on emancipation; however, as previously argued, this did not quite solve the problem of the normative foundations of critique. Apel's philosophy clearly problematized this to a greater extent, arguing that science is based on ethical foundations, which can be understood only in communicative terms. The implications of this are that the shape of a future philosophy of science will have to radicalize the communicative foundations of science. In order to do this a model of cognitive interests will be unnecessary. The cognitive framework of science is moving beyond science itself to embrace critical public discourse.

A final point may be mentioned concerning the relationship between theory and empirical research, on the one hand, and on the other the relationship between intellectual and professional cultures. These are issues which do not invalidate the project of critical hermeneutics but call for consideration on its usefulness as a framework which could be of greater benefit to the actual practice of social science. Habermas's social theory and philosophy of social science has had a great impact on social science providing it with a new theoretical framework and sense of purpose. But the indications now are that this has reached its limits and a new intervention is needed.

The philosophies of social science espoused by Habermas and Apel are among the last of the great synthesizing attempts to ground social sciences in a grand social theory of modernity. These attempts ultimately failed quite simply because they were just one approach and, moreover, ran against the rising tide of post-modernist scepticism of the promises of modernist thought, which Habermas and Apel believed was still relevant to the current time. Indeed, one of the major dimensions of their philosophy of social science – pragmatism – was revived in an entirely different context and provided an unexpected link with postmodernism, which proved to be more enduring.

Pragmatism: From Peirce to Rorty

Pragmatism has been alluded several times in this chapter. Both Habermas and Apel have been influenced by this movement within American social and political thought. Habermas's universal pragmatics and Apel's owe a lot to the work of C. S. Peirce, Josiah Royce, Charles Morris and John Dewey. In particular, the view that knowledge is mediated by signs and is part of language more generally lent itself to the critical hermeneutics of the German philosophers for whom it was also part of a cognitive anthropology. But pragmatism had wider implications, as will now be briefly outlined.

As the word indicates, pragmatism refers to action and thus suggests a conception of science as a practical engagement with the world. For the pragmaticist, knowledge is neither speculative nor observational, but has a practical role to play in improving social life. In John Dewey's terms, knowledge must be tied to democracy. This is a position can be contrasted to the dominant rationalistic view of knowledge since Plato as disinterested speculation and superior to the naive forms of knowledge associated with *doxa*, or opinion. Since its inception, in the writings of Peirce, who used the term 'pragmaticism', pragmatism was opposed to the dualism of subject and object, seeing both as connected, but not in the sense of Hegelian Marxism. Indeed, pragmatism was an alternative to the prevailing Hegelian idealism in early twentieth-century American philosophy for many, such as Dewey. Pragmatic knowledge is a situated knowledge that unfolds in attempts to solve problems creatively. Unlike Marxism, it is not driven by a dialectic of conflict entailing the transformation of modernity and its structures of consciousness.

The core idea in pragmatism is that knowledge must be translatable into action. The resulting notion of practice has resonances in the notion of the public utility of science with which Dewey has been strongly associated. Pragmatists have tended to avoid the more strongly Marxist driven political practice in favour of a stance that stresses the role of the public but strongly supported the attempt to link theory and practice, philosophy and social inquiry, concept formation and empirical research. Where Dewey tended towards a somewhat instrumentalized conception of the utility of knowledge, Peirce held to a more mediated view of knowledge that while having an end is closer to a guide for action. It is in this sense of a transcendental orientation that Apel and Habermas noted and to which can also be related more recent notions of discursive democracy and the deliberative organization of society (see Aboulafia et al., 2001).

Pragmatism as a philosophy of social research was strongly opposed to positivism in so far advocated a view of social reality as intersubjective. Rather than see the subject matter of social science as objectively given 'facts', pragmatists saw as the object of social research social issues or problems. In that sense, then, a social fact had to be theoretically constituted and this in turn necessitated a practical view, such as public relevance.

One of the most important of the American pragmatists was Charles Morris. Originally associated with logical positivism in so far as that movement was concerned with the creation of a universal scientific language, Morris developed a pragmatic philosophy of language which, unlike neo-positivistic conceptions of a pure semantics was a semiotics in which meaning was defined by use. In his major works, such as *Foundation of the Theory of Signs* [1938] and *Signs, Language and Behaviour* [1946], he established himself as a forerunner of semiotics, the theory of signs.

Pragmatism has been very influential, having an impact on logical positivism, empirical social research in the United States, the symbolic interactionism of G. W. Mead, Habermas's universal pragmatics, Apel's transcendental pragmatics, and more recently the neo-pragmatism of Richard Bernstein and Richard Rorty. The latter movement has brought about a revival of pragmatism which has been reinterpreted as anti-foundational philosophy. In *Praxis and Action* [1971], *The Restructuring of Social and Political Theory* [1976], *Beyond Objectivism and Relativism* [1983] and the *New Constellation* [1991], Bernstein reintroduced the relevance of pragmatism in the context of critical readings of the new generation of social and political theorists, including Habermas. In essence, the position he has advocated is one that sees pragmatism as compatible with non-dogmatic critical theory, postmodern multiplicity and a hermeneutic sensibility.

Richard Rorty, too, advanced such an anti-foundationalist pragmatism, since his first major work, *Philosophy and the Mirror of Nature* [1980] and in others such as *The Consequences of Pragmatism* [1982] and *Objectivity, Relativism and Truth* [1991]. For Rorty, unlike Habermas, an inherent relativism pervades science in at least two ways. Firstly, science is only one way of knowing the world, no better than other ways. Secondly, scientific truths are merely valid in so far as the pragmatically workable. Although Habermas's post-metaphysical philosophy is not too distant from Rorty's postmodern pragmatism with its typical emphasis on anti-foundationalism, the latter displays a stronger disdain for universalism, including the limited universalism of the theory of communicative action. Rorty does not see the pragmatics of communication as a basis to ground truth, as is the case with Habermas and Apel; it is instead a perpetual scepticism.

Conclusion: Pragmatism, Critique and Creativity

The upshot of the previous discussion is that one of the central assumptions of Habermas and Apel's reorientation of critical social science has proved to be deeply problematic, namely the notion that communication has a primarily rational foundation. Rorty drew attention to the non-foundationalist dimension of pragmatism, taking this further than Bernstein. Although Rorty has not been influential in the philosophy of the social sciences, his impact being largely confined to the humanities, the implications of his work have been far-reaching, not least in popularizing an idiosyncratic kind of pragmatism that has been able to accommodate more successfully developments associated with postmodernism and a wide variety of other contemporary concerns (see Baert and Turner, 2004). But beyond this, pragmatism has not produced a coherent philosophy of social science, despite having made an important contribution to rethinking some of the epistemological assumptions of science.

It might be suggested in conclusion that one of the important developments that the encounter of the critical and pragmatic traditions has opened up is the question of the creativity of action, which Hans Joas has highlighted as an important legacy of pragmatism (Joas, 1993, 1996). As we have seen in this chapter, the theme of action is also what connects the critical theory tradition with pragmatism. Although the place of critique in this is not evident and it would appear that it has been somewhat displaced by recent developments, it still remains an important challenge for the philosophy of social science.

5

Deconstructionism and Postmodernism: Implications of the Cultural Turn

Introduction: The Postmodernist Alternative

In the previous chapter I argued that reconstructive critical hermeneutics was an attempt to provide a synthesis between the competing approaches of Marxist critical theory and hermeneutics. In the 1960s and 1970s the debate on the philosophical foundations of the social sciences was primarily formed around positivism and the understanding/explanation controversy. Habermas and Apel argued, as we have seen in the previous chapter, that neither an exclusively Marxist critical theory nor a hermeneutical-interpretative approach was an alternative to positivism and its modern neo-positivist successors, such as Popper's critical rationalism. While these debates were mostly conducted in Germany and circles in North American universities with strong links with German thought, at about the same a new post-positivist debate was emerging in France which quickly spread to Francophile universities in North America and also had a major impact on British theorists. This new philosophy goes by various names – post-structuralism, deconstructionism, postmodernism – and is not merely an attack on positivism but argues for the abandonment of the entire intellectual culture of modernity, and in particular of Marxism.

Deconstructionism, qua post-structuralism, emerged in the context of a crisis of French intellectuals with Marxism after 1968 and, in the guise of postmodernism, has gained further ground in the aftermath of the general crisis of the left since 1989. There are now indications, however, that the movement has passed its zenith, with postmodernism becoming more a reflexive look at modernity than a break from it and as far as the philosophy of the social sciences is concerned and has been superseded by other approaches, such as standpoint epistemology and varieties of constructivism.

Postmodernism drew attention not only to the significance of cultural innovation but also emphasized the indeterminacy of knowledge. For postmodernists, culture is not a closed system of meaning, but is an open system of linguistic codifications. The production of culture and the production of knowledge are not separate, for knowledge is part of the cultural system. The proponents of deconstructionism no longer see the problem of methodology to lie in the illusions of positivism, for hermeneutics is also the object of critique. What they complain about is the false promises of emancipation and the illusions of the philosophy of the subject which presupposes the possibility of meaning as in hermeneutics or explanation as in positivistic social science. Thus deconstruction is a deconstructive rather than a reconstructive methodology, which recognizes the indeterminacy of knowledge, which cannot be based on fixed reference points. Its aim is not to reconstruct emancipatiory potentials, but to deconstruct the illusions of universality itself. For the deconstructionists the search for normative foundations must be rejected since the very idea of a foundation is a form of self-delusion. Methodology must accept modern scepticism and indeterminacy without accepting the illusion of the unity of the interpreting subject.

In this chapter I shall outline the various stages of the development of deconstructionism. The first stage is French post-structuralism, which was a movement in French philosophy associated with Barthes and Derrida, in the late 1960s and 1970s and had a major impact on literary criticism in Anglo-American intellectual circles from the late 1970s. Foucault's historical studies of power are very much a part of this. The second phase of postmodernism can be related to the so-called cultural turn in the social and human sciences in the 1980s. Jameson and Lyotard have been the most influential figures in promoting the idea of postmodernism, which entered the social sciences via literary criticism and cultural studies. A third and contemporary phase in the 1990s is the confluence of postmodernism and the new culturalist-emancipationist sociology of globalization and post-colonialism. The overall impact of postmodernism was to shift the explanation/understanding debate on to new issues, which while not being resolved by postmodernism, established the context for subsequent approaches.

From Structuralism to Post-Structuralism

It is helpful to begin by distinguishing postmodernism, deconstructionism and post-structuralism from each other. Deconstructionism refers to the methodology associated with post-structuralism and postmodernism, which are best described as anti-foundational philosophical positions involving extreme constructivism. Before looking at postmodernism, it is necessary to begin with post-structuralism.

Post-structuralism emerged in French philosophy in the late 1960s as a response to structuralism, from which it gets its name. Structuralism emerged out of the unlikely confluence of structural linguistics (de Saussure) and structural anthropology (Lévi-Strauss). In his *Course in General Linguistics*, given in Geneva between 1906 and 1911, Ferdinand de Saussure established the foundations with a theory of the linguistic constitution of social reality. In this theory all of social reality was based on fundamental linguistic structures. Language has only an arbitrary relation to reality and even constructs reality. Language is made up of a system of signs which can be analysed in terms of the signified and the signifier, which are not naturalistically related. This view of language had the implication that identity emerges out of difference in the interplay between signs. For post-structuralists Saussure gave a firm basis to a non-realist or anti-foundationalist theory of society. Where hermeneutics stressed the primacy of the interpreting subjects, structural linguistics emphasized the determining power of language, which is the exclusive reality. The pragmatist view of language along with the hermeneutic approach was fundamentally rejected in favour of a purely structural approach to language.

Structuralism linguistics had an impact in many fields of inquiry, the most notable being anthropology. The French anthropologist Claude Lévi-Strauss applied structural linguistics, which he encountered through the work of the Russian formalist Jakobson, in several works on primitive systems of classification. In effect, social systems of classification were thus conceived of in terms of linguistic codes. In this development Lévi-Strauss moved beyond de Saussure in one key respect, linguistic systems of classification are characterized by a certain determinacy. Lévi-Strauss argued that 'primitive societies' have arbitrary systems of thought based on logical structures and that these structures, which are indeterminate, were common to all societies. He claimed that all systems of classification were primarily linguistic and based on binary opposites (good/bad, raw/cooked, god/man) and ensure consensus in values, which in turn makes social classification and stratification possible. For structural anthropology these binary linguistic structures were fixed and were simply re-enacted by all societies, albeit in indeterminate ways. Thus modern and primitive societies were simply variations of each other and based on different combinations of the binary codes which are constitutive of all human culture. For Lévi-Strauss agency was ultimately a product of structure. Structural anthropology was reflected in sociological and philosophical thinking by the French Marxist Louis Althusser, whose writings dominated British Marxist thinking in the 1970s. Lévi-Strauss was a very influential figure, shaping the work of many French thinkers. Pierre Bourdieu, for instance, who was originally an anthropologist, operated under the influence of Lévi-Strauss into the 1960s, when he too gradually went his own way. The influence of Lévi-Strauss on Michel Foucault is also evident, especially in his early explicitly structural phase (see below).

While this is a simplistic sketch, it will suffice to set the scene for the emergence of post-structuralism, which rejected certain aspects of structuralism; it rejected the assumption of the universality of human nature, but more importantly, it questioned the notion of universally fixed codes or structures. Post-structuralism in fact was a revolt against the idea of established systems of classification. It should also be pointed out that post-structuralism was a response to two other developments. One was the crisis of Marxism for French intellectuals after 1968 when it became apparent that there was no historical challenge to capitalism. Post-structuralism can be seen as an expression of cynicism with regard to emancipatory struggles. A second point of departure was the rejection of existentialism, which had been influential in France in the 1950s and 1960s. Writers such as Claude Merleau-Ponty and Jean-Paul Sartre were not only the leading proponents of existentialism but were also associated with Marxism. Post-structuralists objected to the idea of history having a meaning and the notion of a historical Self, ideas that were fundamental to both existentialism and Marxism. Post-structuralists, while being critical of structuralists, were clearly influenced by structuralist ideas in their rejection of Marxist and existentialist methodologies which rested too much on the primacy of agency. Structuralism had the advantage that it demonstrated that agency was an effect of structure. It shared with its post-structuralist successor what it called 'anti-humanism', the notion of a founding subjectivity. Moreover, there was a certain continuity in the two movements in that post-structuralism was a radicalized version of the basic insight of structural linguistics and structural anthropology that all social systems of classification are arbitrary linguistic arrangements.

Post-structuralism took the deconstruction of agency, or the philosophy of the subject, one step further. Rejecting an approach that almost exclusively concentrated on structure, post-structuralists looked to alternatives within the field of cultural discourses. What was to emerge out of this was a notion of what was variously called desire, excess, resistance. In order to understand post-structuralism, we need to look at an important source of its inspiration. Post-structuralism was inspired not only by developments in linguistic theory, but also by the post-Freudian psychoanalysis of Lacan. Like critical hermeneutics in Germany, post-structuralism was characterized by a disenchantment with Marxism and by the turn from the philosophy of consciousness to the philosophy of language. But the implications of the linguistic turn were quite different for the French intellectuals and their Anglo-American followers. In Germany, as I outlined in Chapter 2, the philosophy of language culminated in the hermeneutical-interpretative conception of social science, while in France the philosophy of language culminated in the semiotic conception of literary interpretation, which replaced the hermeneutic idea of self-understanding with a notion of the destruction of the subject.

Jacques Lacan, a French theorist of psychoanalysis was a major representative and influential figure in early post-structuralism. The basic idea underlying his post-Freudian psychoanalysis is that consciousness is constructed by language. Lacan rejected what Freud took for granted, namely the idea that the Self could be conceived independently of language. Freud, who had not taken on board the philosophy of language, argued that the identity of the self is formed in the synthesis of the id and the superego in order to cope with reality. Identity for Lacan is something that is constantly deferred and is composed out of 'difference'. His theme is the movement from identity to difference. The outcome of this is the replacement of Freud's analysis of consciousness and unconsciousness by the analysis of language. The whole of the unconsciousness, he argued, can be examined as a system of language and the very identity of the self is made up of the constantly shifting interplay of metaphors and signs.

Roland Barthes and Jacques Derrida were the two most influential figures in French post-structuralism. With Derrida post-structuralism becomes a form of 'textuality'. According to Derrida, society and culture can be read like a text. For him there is no correct reading of a text; all readings are equally valid. The search for a correct reading is like a search for a lost totality and is always foundationalist. The philosophical hero of this way of thinking is Nietzsche, who recognized the 'loss of the centre'. For Derrida there can only be interpretations of interpretations.

Derrida's writings are generally seen as a major critique of modernity and the idea of identity, which he dismisses as metaphysical illusions because they are based on the idea of a 'centre'. Truth, reality, science are not objective but products of language and are therefore relative. For Derrida the problem is what he calls 'logocentricism', which is inherent in Western culture: the idea that there is a truth to be uncovered by science, humanism or religion and that history contains a narrative. Derrida argues against this way of thinking by saying that for every fixed idea there is also an 'absent' idea: identity requires non-identity; the self needs an other. In this way Derrida argues that ethnocentrism and racism are deeply embedded in Western culture. However, the attraction of Derrida did not lie in the critical implications of his thought, but in his attempt to reverse the priority of speaking over writing. In arguing for the centrality of writing, the 'text' became the normative reference point for many intellectuals for whom speech was 'logocentric'. This venture was connected to the decentring of the subject.

Deconstruction is the deconstruction of fixed ideas and the attempt to show that our preconceived ideas rest on the exclusion of something, on difference. Deconstruction reveals the way in which the sign is made up of an arbitrary relationship of signified and signifier. The implication of Derrida's approach is relativism, for deconstructionism can offer only deconstructions; the quest for a reconstruction must be abandoned.

Roland Barthes's early book *Mythologies* ([1957] 1973) was also a key work in popularizing post-structuralism, leading to the emergence of cultural studies. In this work Barthes analysed aspects of French popular culture (advertising, images of everyday life, tourism, cooking, and so on) in terms of a theory of signs, developed from Saussure's linguistic theory. Everyday life came to be perceived as system of shifting signifiers which constructs reality. Signs get their meaning from their relationship to other signs and not by reference to reality (which is just another sign). Reality ultimately disappears in the systems of signs.

The writings of Derrida and Barthes had a major impact on social science in the 1980s, and it was not until the late 1990s that there was evidence of a decline in the appeal of post-structuralist ideas. Derrida's writings were firstly received in literary criticism in the theory-bereft Anglo-American schools and rapidly became one of the dominant paradigms in the interpretation of the such modernists as Joyce, Beckett and Pound, for it also had a resonance with the rise of the postmodern novel. Having secured a foothold in literary criticism, deconstructionism went on to make in-roads in the relatively new discipline of cultural studies which emerged initially from literary departments in Britain. With cultural studies on the rise in the 1980s, deconstructionism began to have an impact on the social sciences, in particular in sociology, which was experiencing a culturalist turn.

Michel Foucault: Beyond Hermeneutics and Positivism

The writings of Michel Foucault have also been central to deconstructionism. However, Foucault's position is somewhat complicated since he wrote primarily on aspects of power in the shaping of modern society since the eighteenth century. Despite recent attempts to popularize his historical works as the basis of a sociology of contemporary society, he in fact wrote relatively little on the twentieth century. The postmodernization of Foucault as a theorist of the contemporary world has mostly been achieved through illuminating interviews, short essays and lectures. The evocative power of his historical studies on power have provided for many an enduring fascination and have been pivotal works in shaping what has become known as the cultural turn in the human and social science, that is growing interest in the area of culture in sociology, history and political science, an interest that has been closely linked to a rethinking of the past. In this respect Foucault can be placed alongside Kuhn as one of the most influential figures in the rewriting of the history of the sciences in a way that, while not being explicitly postmodernist, especially in the case of Kuhn, played a major role in creating the conditions for the emergence of postmodernism.

As one of the most important thinkers of the twentieth century, it is hard to sum up his central importance. For the history and philosophy of the social sciences there can be little doubt that the true legacy of Foucault is in providing the intellectual justification for 'anti-science'. Foucault established a new way of looking at modern forms of knowledge from the perspective of power. For the history of medicine, this was to entail a shift in perspective: where the received view was to look at medical science from the perspective of the doctor, Foucault put the perspective of the patient at the centre of analysis.

Foucault wrote two major methodological works on the social sciences, *The Order of Things* ([1966], 1970) and *The Archaeology of Knowledge* [1969], in which he outlined what he called the 'genealogical' methodology. In *The Order of Things* Foucault had set out most of his systematic theoretical ideas, which have undermined not only positivism but also hermeneutics and Marxism. One of its most famous arguments was that modernity as a discourse of power was also a discourse of Man (which replaced the classical discourse of representation, which was ultimately one of God): 'It is comforting, however, and a source of profound relief to think that man is only a recent invention, a figure not yet two centuries old, a wrinkle in our knowledge, and that he will disappear again as soon as that knowledge has discovered a new form' (Foucault, 1970: xxiii). By 'Man' is meant the discourse of the Enlightenment or Modernity: the idea that modern man can gain mastery over nature and society; or that human subjectivity is the measure of all things. Under the influence of Nietzsche, Foucault argues that this belief in a founding subjectivity, so central to both Marxism and hermeneutics, is a product of an intellectual system of thought that must be questioned.

In *The Archaeology of Knowledge* he outlined his theory of discourse, which develops the deconstructive approach. In the modern age all spheres of life are subject to investigation, regulation and surveillance by means of discourse. Discourses are 'language games' in which power is circulated. There is no pure subjectivity outside these systems of thought. Discourses can be compared to Kuhn's paradigms; they structure the field of knowledge and like Kuhn, Foucault was concerned with identifying ruptures in and between discourses. In all of Foucault's books we find a pervasive image of subjectivity being the product of a power game in which the rules are never revealed or understood by the players. The idea of power can be explained as a synthesis of truth (as a reference point, a founding principle), discourse (as a system of intellectual organization based on knowledge) and power (as the diffusion of discourse in society through institutions). In these works, Foucault used the metaphor 'archaeology' to characterize his approach to deconstruction. As the term indicates, it is a method designed to reveal the structures of discourse in society and their conditions of existence. Clearly, the influence of Lévi-Strauss is evident, but where Foucault departs from the structural method is to uncover the ruptures and discontinuities.

For Foucault where there is power there is also resistance; power is not simply domination and can be resisted. In his major writings, Foucault does not explore how people resist power, but in his fragmentary essays and interviews, he frequently comments on the idea that power also involves resistance. This emphasis on resistance became more pronounced in his later writings, in which Foucault used the terms 'genealogy' or 'genealogical critique' to highlight, following Nietzsche, from whom the terms derive, struggles and resistances.

The general theme in Foucault's thought is the social construction of power in modernity. This could be called social power or 'biopower' as opposed to 'political power'. Power is more than mere domination or something that is imposed on people from outside them: power is part of the nature of the social itself, and can be compared to language. The basis of his theory is the idea that modern forms of power are constructed around what he calls a discourse of individuality or subjectivity. Modernity involves the creation of human subjectivity as individualism. For Foucault power is not something imposed by the state on the individual but involves the actual creation of subjectivity: the very subjectivity of the individual is a creation of power and is at the same time the means by which power is mobilized. Foucault traces the emergence of modern forms of power by documenting the proliferation of new spheres of cultural discourse which were created with modernity.

The exercise of power is conducted through 'technologies of the self' such as sexuality. Language is central to Foucault's theory of power: language is co-extensive with power, which is why 'power comes from everywhere' (1980: 93). But this is also why it can be challenged everywhere:

'Where there is power there is resistance, and yet, or rather consequently, this resistance is never in a position of exteriority in relation to power ... These points of resistance are present everywhere in the power network. hence there is no single focus of great Refusal, no soul of revolt, source of all rebellions, or pure law of the revolutionary. Instead there is a plurality of resistances' (1980: 95/6). This statement can be read as a critique of Marcuse and a reflection of the exhaustion of Marxism for French intellectuals.

Foucault's importance for social science is ambivalent. His central idea that all social acts, including the consciousness of the individual, are nothing other than the system of power relations which define them, can be criticized on many grounds: (1) it assumes a kind of functionalist logic of explanation; (2) the idea of discourse is obscure: it varies from being a product of language to being part of the social structure, it suggests that everything is a social construction and that there is no reality outside the construction; (3) Foucault left a legacy in which relativism was overgeneralized, (4) he concentrated too much on modernity in terms of technologies and institutions of total control: the asylum, the hospital, the prison, and ignored other institutions and movements, which had a greator emancipatory function; (5) for Foucault the theorist/intellectual can only 'deconstruct' identity and power by revealing how they are constructed: this tended to rule any possibility of positive or policy-relevant research. His deconstructive approach confined critique to the margins of the discourse.

Yet, it is undeniable that Foucault occupies a central position in the self-understanding of social science today. At this point we can look at postmodernism, which was the umbrella concept linking post-structuralism and deconstructionism, on the one side, and on the other the concern with resistances and discourse.

Postmodernism and Cultural Analysis

Postmodernism can be seen as a development of post-structuralism and at the same time goes beyond that movement. Postmodernism, not in itself a movement or a school of thought, emerged in response to French post-structuralism, especially the idea of decentring fixed structures and the tendency to deconstruct the received wisdom of the past and the authority of science. However, postmodernism was also a product of the cultural turn in the human and social sciences and the ideas that have animated it reflect concerns that are quite different from post-structuralism. Postmodernism was above all a product of the cultural turn in the human and social sciences that developed in the 1980s. Without the post-structuralist revolution, in particular the pivotal significance of Michel Foucault this would not have taken the course it did.

Originally postmodernism was a particular artistic style (just as modernism referred to a literary and artistic movement). Postmodern architecture, postmodern film, and the postmodern novel, for instance, are important aspects of cultural innovation, suggesting something that challenges fixed structures and is radically open. In this sense, postmodernism refers to an intellectual shift beyond the modern worldview to something indeterminate. In the social sciences postmodernism became more or less coeval with the notion of the post-industrial society, that is a postmodern society as a society in which most people are consumers or working in the services rather than producers.

It is difficult to characterize postmodernism as methodology, since it takes very diffuse forms. It would not be inaccurate to say that the central ideas of postmodernism are: (1) society can be interpreted as a text; (2) the deconstruction of agency involves a shift in emphasis from structure to culture, with the literary text becoming a cultural discourse; (3) an anti-foundationalism approach involving indeterminacy and contingency, stressing the absence of any one correct viewpoint; (4) a concern with identifying diversity and resistances.

In order to make sense of postmodernism it is necessary to distinguish between postmodernism as a method, as an interpretation of society and as a politics: that is a postmodernist approach, postmodern society, and politics. Poststructuralism largely gave postmodernism a methodological orientation – the method called deconstructionism – but did not really say what postmodern society was. It is on this distinction that postmodernism is hopelessly vague. Moreover, the idea of postmodernism as a method is closely related to postmodernist politics: methodology is itself politics. For postmodern deconstructionists, the act of deconstruction is itself a political challenge to power, even though it cannot name its normative reference points.

Postmodernism politics is opposed to the idea of totality and rejects ideology. Its emphasis is more on heterogeneity, plurality, ambiguity, ambivalence, transgression, marginality, multilinearity, indeterminacy and contingency. It rejects emancipation as total solution to social problems. The image of society is one of fluctuating signs, fragmentation and multiplicity. It implies the reversal of Marx's base-superstructure: the world of ideas – culture as text – shapes the society. Whereas critical theorists such as the Frankfurt School or Jürgen Habermas see fragmentation (Honneth, 1995) as a negative characteristic of contemporary society, postmodernists on the whole tend to see fragmentation in more positive terms as offering more choices to the individual. Postmodern society can thus be liberating. Fragmentation as a process of disorientation is seen as something positive or the basis of the postmodern condition, and not as for Habermas an obstacle to communication.

From the perspective of social sciences, the two most influential books on postmodernism have been Jean-François Lyotard's (1984) *Postmodern Condition: A Report on Knowledge* and Frederic Jameson's (1991) *Postmodernism or the Cultural Logic of Late Capitalism*. Jean Baudrillard should also be mentioned as an influential figure in postmodernism.

It was Lyotard who popularized the term in the social sciences. As a methodological approach, postmodernism is the rejection of what he calls 'grand narratives' or 'metanarratives' which are characteristic of modernity. Above all, it is the rejection of the utopia of emancipation and the notion that knowledge can be emancipatory. As a statement about the nature of society postmodernism is the recognition that society, is itself postmodern: the post-industrial society has given way to a new stage, the postmodern stage.

The postmodern society is a 'knowledge'-based society, unlike the post-industrial society (which is serviced-based); it is an extension of the information society. Lyotard's schema is something like this. Industrial society was organized around industrial work while the post-industrial society is organized around the services and a professional technical elite. The post-industrial society can be understood in terms of the information society, which is organized around information, and the postmodern society itself, which is the latest stage in the globalizing culture of experts and consumerism.

He writes of the computerization of society and claims that the new struggles will be largely about access to information and no longer merely over wealth.

Lyotard rejected the possibility of emancipation as a total endeavour, but stressed the multiple nature of resistances. Emancipation and totality can be totalitarian. One of the characteristics of modern science is the absence of unity. Lyotard sees politics as perpetually open to new choices. The politics of postmodernism is a politics of transgression (since society is no longer organized as a totality, it cannot be overthrown by revolution). With the break-up of the unitary worldview of modernity, postmodernity is the condition of plurality. The condition of postmodernity is the collapse of all critical standards: critique is thus replaced by deconstruction.

The Italian theorist Gianni Vattimo, in *The Transparent Society,* also wrote about postmodernity as the end of modernity: the end of the view that history is unilinear; the last crisis in the idea of progress in history (Vattimo, 1992). Again, the emphasis here is on the obsolescence of critique. In the postmodern society, power has become transparent and critique of false consciousness or distorted communication is unnecessary.

For Jameson, postmodernism is the latest phase of capitalism and refers to the appropriation of capitalism of culture for its reproduction. Postmodernism is the cultural logic of capitalism in its multinational dimension. Commodification has increased the fragmentation of society. For Jameson, postmodernism is not a new stage in society; it is the latest stage in the development of capitalism. He writes about the expansion of culture through economic production in corporate capitalism: the social becomes absorbed by the cultural. While the postmodern society is a class society, the politics of postmodernism cannot be class-based: postmodern politics is a micro-politics. Jameson is closer to Marxism, in particular to T. W. Adorno, than are most other postmodernists since he still holds on to the belief in emancipation from capitalism. However, Jameson locates the emancipatory moment in the political unconsciousness. This argument inspired a series of works on the politics of 'desire', namely the view that capitalism in its constant production of commodities and subjectivities is also producing an excess that cannot be contained within the limits of the system and is forever transgressing the boundaries of experience and thought.

Postmodernists generally tend to see postmodern society as something open to new possibilities and subversive: postmodern society increases the range of options to individuals. The themes that attract postmodernist analysis are: advertising, lifestyles, fashion, subcultures, gender. There is also the suggestion that the postmodern society is a post-class society. Instead of classes, there are consumer groups (Maffesoli, 1996). Culture is seen as a kind of menu from which cultural choices can be made. Postmodernism suggests something like the anaesthetization of society: the merging of art and politics.

Communication is seen from quite a different perspective by Habermas, for whom there is always the possibility of consensus as well as solidarity through rational debate driven by the need to reorganize society through the expansion of democracy. Postmodernists, in contrast, emphasis the plurality of communication, difference rather than consensus.

For Baudrillard, the image is more real than reality itself. Image and reality have become interchangeable. With the collapse in foundations, the production of culture offers new reference points but ones which can never be unified. The distinction between object and representation breaks down. Society is ultimately constructed out of images.

A further stage in the development of deconstructionism in social science has been globalization theory and post-colonialism. The culturalist turn in sociology in the 1980s resulted in the proliferation of publications on the new global age that was supposed to be emerging in a One World society. Arising out of this confluence of postmodernism and globalization theory, a position gained currency that with the alleged break-up of the nation-state new relations of power can merge between the local and the global, bringing about the phenomenon of 'glocality'. Social science in the age of globalization acquires new tasks. Since the state is held to be no longer a powerful social actor, the focus once again becomes a notion of culture that is loses its relationship to both agency and structure. The emphasis tends towards global 'flows' of information and new hyper-realities or cyberspace. Society ceases to be the object of research, since society has itself been superseded by processes of cultural change. For others, globalization suggests the importance less of postmodernist inclinations than a new cosmopolitanism.

Postmodernist deconstructive approaches in the social sciences have also been influenced by the return to literature in recent years. Post-colonialism, which was a product of post-structural literary studies, has entered social science via postmodernism in order to fulfil the promise of emancipation, which the earlier wave of post-structuralism denied under the aegis of anti-humanism. Post-structuralism has made a comeback by striking up an alliance between post-colonialism and globalization theorists. Post-colonialism – with its politicization of race, gender and class – has been a powerful post-ideological challenge to traditional social science. It is thus from a movement in literary/cultural studies that agency, banished by earlier deconstructionists, returns albeit within a culturalist-semiotic framework in a concern with marginality, 'alterity'.

Conclusion: Beyond Postmodernism

One of the central arguments of this book is that the methodological self-understanding of the social sciences can no longer be established by a critique of positivism. The problem today for a post-empiricist social science is the retreat of much of social science into a culturalist and theory-laden discourse. According to Giddens (1987: 195): 'Structuralism, and post-structuralism also, are dead systems of thought. Notwithstanding the promise they held in the fresh bloom of youth, they have ultimately failed to generate the revolution in philosophical understanding and social theory that was once their pledge'. John O'Neill (1995: 7) writes in a similar vein:

'To my mind, it is an unfortunate result that the phenomenological critique of positivism – which antedates deconstructionism and poststructuralism – later spawned a politics of subjectivity and alterity rather than a politics of inter-subjectivity and mutuality with which it had first blossomed'.

Habermas famously dismissed postmodernists are 'young conservatives' because of the tendency in postmodernism to oppose social objectives and critical normative positions by which social arrangements can be criticized. In a major critique of postmodernism, he set up a dualism of modernity versus postmodernity and defended the continued relevance of the former (Habermas, 1990).

These may be somewhat exaggerated criticisms and do not take into account changes within postmodernist thinking, but have some relevance. I would like to sum up what I think are the principal objections to postmodernism and its deconstructionist semiotic methodology.

Firstly, postmodernity signifies less a break from modernity than a continuation of it. This is particularly a point that is highlighted in the writings of Zygmunt Bauman.

Secondly, postmodernism overemphasizes cultural issues, reducing too much of the territory of social science to the interpretation of social texts. It is questionable if society can be understood entirely in terms of the model of the text. False analogies are made between the 'death of the author' and the 'death of the subject'. The result of this conflation of the social with the text, postmodernism is unable to deal with issues relating to solidarity since this is supposed to be another metaphysical illusion and a product of the foundationalist philosophy of the subject.

Thirdly, in terms of a logic of scientific methodology one of the biggest problems is that postmodernist approaches are unable to offer convincing explanations of social phenomena. Postmodernist analysis tends to be characterized by an obscurantist style of writing.

The aim of this chapter has been to show that the deconstructionist/postmodern challenge to the established approaches has been unsuccessful in establishing in new philosophy of social science. Instead, the real contribution of postmodernist approaches has been in social and cultural theory with new questions and new ways of looking at things.

When it comes to methodology and a philosophy for social science, postmodernism is limited. The value for social science of embracing vague concepts drawn from literary criticism and evocative images of power is limited. I have suggested that deconstructionism has mostly been a fashionable genre of the 1980s and is already waning. Its major failings are its inability to articulate critical normative foundation for social science on the one side and on the other it has deflected social science from the task of providing explanations for social phenomena. Moreover, if social science is to have a public function, the question of its relation to its object must reflected upon. In conclusion, postmodernism was an important experiment in radical constructivism but ultimately failed to come to terms with the indeterminism of knowledge. But one of the most important legacies of postmodernism has been in standpoint epistemology, which will be discussed in the next chapter.

6

Return of the Actor: The Reflexive Turn and Feminist Standpoint Epistemology

One of the most characteristic features of the philosophy of social sciences in recent times is the turn to the standpoint of the social actor. This move can be seen in part in the context of a gradual return to social science of the emancipatory ideas that had been central to the Hegelian-Marxist tradition. As we have seen, against the belief that social science can be emancipatory is, on the one side, the positivist and neo-positivist conception of a value-free explanatory conception of science and, on the other, the postmodernist-inclined scepticism of emancipatory struggles. Feminism, amongst other approaches to be considered in this chapter, represents a different conception of social science as an emancipatory project based on a new conception of the social actor as situated and whose experience constitutes the basic subject matter of social science. However, the return of the actor is only one aspect to standpoint epistemology, which can be seen as an expression of a more general reflexive turn in the self-understanding of social science. Reflexivity is the key to the epistemology of the standpoint of the social actor.

With reflexivity comes the idea that the perspective of the social actor must be incorporated into the discourse of social science, which cannot remain separate from the social world. Although views differ as to the relation between the methodology of science and the standpoint of society, there is a general recognition of a reflexive relation.

The reflexive turn can be seen as a renewal of the hermeneutic tradition, but with a stronger critical trust. Reflexivity was in part presupposed by both philosophical and sociological hermeneutics, as in the view associated with Alfred Schutz that the discourse of social science constitutes a second-order level of discourse related to but distinct from the first-order constructs of the life-world. The reflexive turn can characterized as a gradual embracing of common sense and the perspective of the social actor. Where postmodernism was sceptical of the standpoint of the social actor and generally stood for a deconstruction of the subject and of human experience, feminist standpoint epistemology has called for the reassertion of the voice of the social actor and the recognition of the role of experience in science. In this concern with social context there is a clear move from the 'eye' to the 'voice' and from cognition to experience.

It is possible, then, to speak of a return of the actor to social science. This will be examined in this chapter and an assessment will be made of the implications of standpoint. The central question in the controversy to be considered is whether a reflexive social science based on human experience can be objective. Can objectivity be based on criteria other than those of the scientific method? How valid is human experience as a guide to objectivity? Briefly stated, the direction of the argument is that the reconstitution of standpoint epistemology as a reflexive project enables a committed social science to be objective.

The Idea of Reflexivity and its Application to Social Science

The notion of reflexivity suggests the application of something to itself. Reflexivity is not merely self-reflection but refers to a self-transformative capacity. For this reason, it is not simply reducible subjectivity or to intersubjectivity, but arises out of the relational encounter of subjectivity with objectivity. As an idea that has a wider application beyond social scientific methodology it is relevant to various contemporary developments ranging from identity to learning and technology. Reflexive identities, for instance, refer to multiple standpoints and the capacity to take the perspective of the other. A notion of reflexivity is involved in the idea of transferable skills, that is the use of knowledge to generate further knowledge. According to Manuel Castells, the knowledge economy is based on a reflexive application of technology, whereby information technology is not merely used to generate a product but is the product produced, as well as the material used. The reflexive attitude thus entails the self-implication of means and ends.

Thus a reflexive social science is one in which the social researcher must question their own role in the research process since they are part of the object. The adoption of reflexivity as opposed to critique as such in the methodology of the social sciences can be partly explained by the existence of multiple standpoints as opposed to a single standpoint. The older idea of a critical social science was based on a single standpoint, as in Habermas's notion of a general human interest in emancipation. But when numerous standpoints present themselves, the limits of critique become evident in the need to establish a different relation to diverse social context.

A reflexive social science is nevertheless a critical one in that it aims to make social science socially relevant and articulate political alternatives. This is a reflexive as opposed to an essentially dialectical relation in that theory and practice, science and politics, are not driven by something inherent in the nature of reality, such as class conflict. Rather reflexivity is an epistemological condition that arises when the social scientist recognizes that the scientific method consists of an effort to translate different orders of knowledge.

In this respect a reflexive social science is part of the general turn towards social context that has been a feature of the social sciences in the last three decades or so. This is the view that knowledge is contextualized and social science while being a form of scientific knowledge is also part of society. The relation between these levels of knowledge – the social and the scientific – is a reflexive one as opposed to an objectifying one.

A reflexive social science is thus characterized by a concern with connections, translations, with the relational context by which social phenomena are connected.

One of the first explicit statements of a reflexive methodology was Aaron Cicourel's *Method and Measurement in Sociology* [1964], which was a critique of the positivist inclination to reduce knowledge to measurement. According to Cicourel, sociology must be able to take account of common-sense knowledge, that is the everyday knowledge of the social actor whose cognitive operations constitute a first-order level of knowledge that offers the basic structures for social scientific knowledge to be developed. A stronger argument for a reflexive sociology was set out in Alvin Gouldner's *The Coming Crisis of Western Sociology,* which attacked the 'methodological dualism' by which theory and practice were separate and knowledge viewed as information (Gouldner, 1970). His book was a plea for a radical sociology, comparable to Habermas's *Knowledge and Human Interests*, which also derived from the same period. For Gouldner a radical sociology is a reflexive one, for the aim of social science is to make the personal political. It is neither a question of measurement nor of value-free description and explanation. A reflexive sociology is not defined by the object of study or by methods of research, but by the relation of the sociologist to society. A reflexive sociology aims to transform the self-awareness of the social scientist as a social actor and is sustained by a strong sense of commitment to use that knowledge. In this sense, then, Gouldner's reflexive approach was aimed at radicalizing knowledge into a transformative practice. The key aspect of it is 'self-awareness'.

Gouldner's reflexive sociology can be contrasted to Anthony Giddens's conception of reflexivity. In *The Constitution of Society* and in later works, Giddens developed a model of reflexivity which is very different from Gouldner's radical conception (Giddens, 1984, 1990, 1991). According to Giddens, social actors are knowledgeable and this knowledge is itself reflexive, characterized by what he called 'the reflexive monitoring of action', that is the use people make of knowledge in the everyday life. One major feature of this is the appropriation of expertise in a very wide range of activities from health and personal relations to education and work. As far as social science is concerned, through the 'double hermeneutic' the first medium of interpretation (that of the social actor) is reinterpreted by social science. The double hermeneutic is a reflexive relation in that the phenomena studied by social scientists are already constituted by knowledge. So the role of the social scientist is the reflexive task of introducing new ways of looking at things. The reflexive relation is reciprocal in that social scientific knowledge, as with all expert knowledge, is fed back into everyday life. The double hermeneutic implicates science and society in each other's order of interpretation. For Giddens, then, there are only interpretations of interpretations. Reflexivity in everyday life and reflexivity within social science is reflected in societal reflexivity of the knowledge-based economy wherein the self-application of knowledge and expertise is what characterizes the contemporary shape of society.

Tim May has characterized the critical nature of reflexivity in social science in terms of an endogenous reflexivity and referential reflexivity (May, 2000). The former refers to an agent's everyday knowledge while the latter refers to the process of re-cognition in which the agent comes to understand their situation in a more adequate manner. The critical point, however, is that the movement from endogenous to referential reflexivity is one from reflexivity within actions to one upon actions: 'To that extent, the possibility for social circumstances to be otherwise is open to scrutiny in the discursive understandings of the conditions under and through which action takes place' (May 2000: 158). Referential reflexivity is a critical reflexivity aimed at identifying the effects of power on social action leading to an enhanced potential for self-transformation.

Feminist Standpoint Epistemology

The reflexive turn has made its most notable impact on feminist philosophy of social science, which will now be considered. Feminist methodology can be defined as a concern with exploring the nature of the social experience of women with a view to explaining the mechanisms through power operates in order to bring about emancipation for women. Although feminism, especially some of the earlier versions, is not necessarily entirely to be seen in terms of a notion of reflexivity, the adoption of reflexivity in feminist epistemology has opened up new conceptions of social science.

Feminist approaches are based on the central insight that social reality is a gender construction and the normative aim of social science should be both to deconstruct this and to point to an alternative. Far from being objective, science in general is ideologically laden with male values. For instance, Sandra Harding (1983, 1986, 1987, 1991) has argued how important issues such as the role of emotion have been subordinated to a view of social actors as instrumental and rational. The historical kinds of exploitation that have been emphasized are those relating to men, such as paid work. The political issues focused on refer mostly to the public sphere, thus neglecting the private realm and the kinds of power that are formed there. In general, then, it is argued that there is a gender bias in problem definition, interpretation and normative critique. Standpoint epistemology entails more than this claim concerning the traditional subject matter of social sciences; it is a transformation in the actual epistemological categories of truth, evidence and objectivity.

The aim of the feminist standpoint critique is to develop a new methodological approach based on both a new ontology and a radicalized epistemology. Like other theorists who adopt standpoint positions, feminists such as Dorothy Smith (1974, 1987) and Sandra Harding argue that scientific knowledge is constrained by the social location of the scientist. The recognition of this limitation is what characterizes the reflexivity of standpoint epistemology. Hilary Rose has argued that the social existence of women leads to quite different kinds of experience which in turn require a different cognitive approach from science (Rose, 1983).

For this reason, it can be suggested that in standpoint theory knowledge or epistemology is subordinated to ontology, that is to a particular view about the nature of reality. Moreover, science cannot dispense with the first-order concepts of social actors. The normative aim of social science is to show how the existing reality is socially constructed along gender lines and must be reconstructed to give expression to women's experiences. Feminist social science thus tries to deconstruct the existing male-centred constructions in order to realize new possibilities for women. Standpoint thus has an emancipatory purpose. According to Nancy Hartsock, who developed the notion from Marx's materialist approach concerning the standpoint of the proletariat, a 'standpoint is not simply an interested position (interpreted as bias) but is interested in the sense of being engaged. The concept of a standpoint depends on the assumption that epistemology grows in a complex and contradictory way from material reality' (Hartsock, 1983: 285).

Feminist epistemology arises out of the confluence of Marxism and postmodern deconstruction. It was from Marxism that the notion of standpoint was developed, but it was from postmodernism that a new critical edge was discovered with the notion of deconstruction. However, the deconstructive moment in feminism differs very much from other postmodern thought in that it does not dispense with the importance of solidarity and the need to be able to conceive alternative realities. In other words, feminism entails a normative critique of society which requires a closure to indeterminacy: it is constructivist rather than deconstructivist. In other words, feminist standpoint epistemology aims to transform women's social experience by creating forms of knowledge that can liberate women from patriarchic social relations.

One of the key ideas in feminist epistemology is the notion of 'situated knowledge', that is the claim that knowledge derives from a position. Positioning, according to Donna Haraway, is what needs to be critically examined since it is not about occupying a fixed location (Haraway, 1988). It is a matter of being able to see the complex web of social relations in terms of tensions, resistances, transformations.

For standpoint theorists the object of study is also the subject; the knower and the known are the same. The reflexive relation is one of self-scrutiny and questioning one's own role in the research process. Three kinds of standpoint epistemology can be identified: radical, reflexive and postmodern.

Radical epistemology tends to equate method, truth, objectivity and neutrality with masculine objectivity. Women's experience is the starting point and, moreover, only women can have knowledge of women and the aim of science is emancipation for women (Stanley and Wise, 1983). In subordinating epistemology to ontology, the implication is that gender differences are reflected in, or in some way related to, epistemological differences. In this radical formulation the reflexive moment is relatively limited to the demand that the researched must be included in the research.

In contrast to this strong conception of the standpoint of social science, reflexive standpoint argues for a weaker kind of standpoint and, concomitantly, a stronger reflexivity. Reflexive standpoint recognizes the separation of women as the subject and feminism as an approach. Moreover, objectivity is not dismissed as a masculine value. This conception of standpoint is less empiricist in its attitude to experience and more theoretical and hermeneutic. While it adheres to the basic notion that a reflexive methodology is one in which the researcher questions their role in the research process, it extends this to the epistemological level in terms of a notion of situated knowledge that is both objective and critical.

Finally, postmodern standpoint rejects all attempts to ground knowledge in single standpoint. This has arisen as a result largely of black feminism and relativizes women's experience with other forms of oppression (Hill Collins, 1986). Thus gender is seen as only one identity and must be placed alongside race and other identities. In sum, postmodern standpoint concerns the existence of multiple and overlapping forms of experience.

In whatever form its occurs, standpoint epistemology seeks to give voice to the numerous forms of experience that have been excluded from social science in the dominant approaches. Other versions of standpoint epistemology include post-colonialism, marginalization theory, critical race theory. It has been very strongly influenced by postmodernism and deconstruction but also by multiculturalism.

While this emphasis on the situated nature of knowledge has the tendency to over-rely on experience as a criterion of scientific knowledge and thus compromise objectivity, most proponents defend the compatibility of standpoint with objectivity. It is helpful to distinguish three kinds of objectivity: 'strong' objectivity (as in positivism), a 'limited/weak' objectivity (as in sociological hermeneutics) and a socially situated objectivity. The latter, while being situated, is nonetheless an objectivity. According to Donna Haraway, a situated objectivity is self-consciously based on what she calls a 'partial perspective', that is one that rejects the illusion of a totalizing objective perspective in favour of a view that aims to capture the reality of human experience as lived. The science question in feminism, she argues, is about 'objectivity as positioned rationality' (Haraway 1988). Sandra Harding claims that in fact the kind of objectivity that standpoint epistemology achieves is precisely a 'strong' one simply because it makes available for critical scrutiny all the evidence marshalled for or against a scientific hypothesis as well as reflexively questioning the research process and the nature of evidence: 'we can think of strong objectivity as extending the notion of scientific research to include systematic examination of such powerful background beliefs. It must do so in order to be competent at maximizing objectivity' (Harding 1991: 149). This entails a commitment to acknowledge the historical character of beliefs. The notion of strong objectivity indicated in this is simply the aim to include as much as possible in making a claim to scientific objectivity. In Harding's terms, strong objectivity requires an equally strong reflexivity. Her general position can be summed up thus: 'Standpoint theory opens the way to stronger standards of both objectivity and reflexivity. These standards require that research projects use their historical location as a resource for obtaining greater objectivity' (Harding 1991: 149).

Nevertheless, there is a clear appeal to experience in feminist standpoint epistemology as a valid form of knowledge. In this a tension is set up between method and experience, with truth being located more in the latter than in the former. Method, reflexively employed, is thus only a guide to experience and is not the sole source of reliable knowledge.

Reflexivity and Social Transformation

The concern with linking reflexivity and social transformation can also be related to social movement theory. The principal representatives of this are Alain Touraine (1977, 1981, 1988, 1995) and Alberto Melucci (1989, 1996). In their work we find the vision of the role of social science as a critical intervention in society. Touraine's calls his approach 'interventionism'. Interventionism, as with Bourdieu's 'logic of practice', Unger's 'reconstructivism' (see below) and, as we have seen, feminist epistemology, is a reflexive approach. The central idea in Touraine's methodology is the concept of 'historicity', which means 'self-production' of society by social agency. Touraine is primarily a theorist of social change, and is in particular concerned with the problem of relating agency to structure. In his framework, agency has priority as a determinant of change, but the direction of social change is open in that it cannot be determined by agency itself. It is in battles to bring about social change that historicity is constituted. In order for change to be possible social actors must act upon the cultural model of society in order to generate conceptions of alternatives which are then actualized in structural change. As a theorist of new social movements, Touraine criticizes the dominant traditions in social science for failing to recognize the 'return of the actor'. Against post-structuralism and deconstructive approaches, Touraine opposes the 'death of the subject' with a theory of new forms of agency. Post-structuralism had been an intellectualism of the 1970s when the student movement and the May 1968 project appeared to have been exhausted of radical potential. But with the rise of the new social movements – the Green Movement, the Peace Movement, and Solidarity all of which had particular impact on Touraine – it looked as though the political landscape was changing for the better. For Touraine in his major works *The Self Production of Society* (1977) and *The Return of the Actor* (1988) social movements have a particularly important role in the genesis of social change even though the actual direction of social change may not be under their conscious control. The implications of the return of the actor amount to radical constructivism. In *The Voice and the Eye* Touraine (1981) outlines his interventionist approach. Interventionism necessitates the active involvement of social science in the construction of social action.

In this context mention can be made of Roberto Mangabeira Unger's *Politics: A Work in Constructive Social Theory* (1987) which is an important contribution to a radical social science in which reflexivity and human experience are connected. In volume 1, *Social Theory: Its Situation and its Task,* Unger outlines his conception of social science as a struggle to 'reinvent society'. His 'constructivist' position includes both an explanatory approach to society and a program for social action (1987: 3). Attacking the utopian ideas of the radical project of modernity associated with the Enlightenment for their false promises of emancipation, Unger argues for the need to make explicit the institutional and imaginative structure of society in order to open up the possibility for social reconstruction. Social scientific explanation and reconstruction go hand in hand. Construction is reconstruction because 'as intellectual traditions dissolve, they also provide the materials and the methods for their own dissolution' (1987: 8). He argues that 'the disintegrating tradition have forged many of the instruments for their transformation' (1987: 143). In order to release the 'radical project' from false necessity, the task of reconstruction requires self-critique, above all the self-criticism of social theory and the ideologies upon which it had previously rested. The most important legacy of modern social theory in Unger's estimation is the idea of 'society as artifact' and which can be contrasted to the notion of society and history having a 'script'. The 'constructivist task' must be disconnected from the utopian and millenarian claims that have accompanied it in the past.

For Unger there are three starting points for a reinterpretation of social theory: 'the idea of transformative vocation, the reinterpretation of the radical cause, and the discontent with social democracy' (1987: 15). In his view there is something better to be hoped for than social democracy, and social theory must recover the radical project in a new transformative politics which will draw on existing social discontent. Unger also defends his approach as realist in the sense that a normative social theory with an emancipator-reconstructive task must also embrace an explanatory dimension. In this he is not distant from Bourdieu. The problem for Unger is that social theory has been trapped either by a defence of the existing order or by utopian faith in a revolutionary rupture. Neither is satisfactory: 'The social theory we need must vindicate a modernist – that is to say, a nonnaturalist – view of community and objectivity, and it must do so by connecting the imagination of the ideal with the insight into transformation' (1987: 47). Objectivity in social science is not achieved by holding to the existing social structures, but by rendering those structures 'insubstantial' or transparent. Unger defends his constructivism on realist grounds, claiming that his approach is not one of unbridled agency overcoming structure. The undermining of structure through rendering it reflexive, will allow the construction of a new kind of community: 'With the rejection of the naturalistic premise, the content of the idea of community changes in ways foreshadowed by the shift in the idea of objectivity' (1987: 46).

Reflexivity is also central to Ulrich Beck's conception of social science. His influential book, *Risk Society* ([1986] 1992), heightened the wider societal context for reflexivity in science. According to Beck, a distinction can be made between traditional and reflexive modernization. In the first, 'the sciences are confronted with their own products, defects, and secondary problems', while in the second the sciences are confronted with 'complete scientization, which also extends scientific to the inherent foundations and external consequences of science itself' (1992: 155). It is Beck's central thesis that today in late modernity the authority of science is under-going a major challenge to its legitimacy. As a result of the rise of 'risk' – which in our late modern scientific-technological society derives not from nature but from science and technology itself which is unable to master its side effects – which is increasingly penetrating into many spheres of life, scientism (science as its own self-legitimation) collapses. New critical publics arise which challenge the authority of science and its claim to truth. 'Until the sixties', Beck argues, 'science could count on an uncontroversial public that believed in science, but today its efforts and progress are followed with mistrust. People suspect the unsaid, add in the side effects and suspect the worst' (1992: 169).

The expansion of science today under the conditions of the risk society, Beck argues, requires a critique of science by the engagement of publics outside science. This is what Beck calls 'reflexive scientization', the self-critique of science and a scientized public. Defending the Enlightenment project of modernity as unfinished, Beck argues that nonetheless science must break from the old model which divorces scientific rationality from public scrutiny: 'The sciences can no longer remain in their traditional Enlightenment position of taboo breakers; they must also adopt the contrary role of taboo constructors. Accordingly the social function of the sciences wavers between opening and closing opportunities for action, and these contradictory outside expectations stir up conflicts and divisions within the profession' (Beck, 1992: 157). With reflexive modernization the public consciousness of risk leads to protests against science. In this particular sense, then, 'potentially the risk society is a self-critical society' (Beck, 1992: 176). The result of this scientization of public consciousness is that: 'New public-oriented scientific experts emerge, the dubious aspects of the foundation of scientific argumentation are exposed with counter-scientific thoroughness, and many sciences are subjected through their applied practices to a "politization test" of a previously unknown extent' (Beck, 1992: 161).

The constructivist implications of Beck's argument are that with the crisis in the legitimacy of scientific rationality a new scientific consciousness, sensitized to public concerns, will arise: 'Science, having lost reality, faces the threat that others will dictate to it what truth is supposed to be' (Beck, 1992: 167). The question, in other words, is whether the 'organized irresponsibility' of science can be subjected to responsibility. Knowledge is not neutral or objective; it is a social construction. Indeed, risk, too, is a construction in the sense that social actors construct problems around issues of risk. Thus Beck (1995: 55) argues: 'The ecological movement is not an environmental movement but a social, inward movement which utilizes "nature" as a parameter for certain questions'. He (1992: 55) admits: 'It is not clear whether it is the risks that have intensified, or our view of them'. As a constructivist, Beck appears to opt for the latter: our perception of risk has increased, a view that is concerned in much of new social movement research. Constructions of danger do not always require an objective reference point. (In a more recent essay, Beck (1996) has attempted to resolve this paradox.)

In the broader context of philosophical debates on methodology, one of the implications of Beck's arguments is that the identity of social science can no longer be defined in terms of post-positivism. Beck's attack on science is ultimately aimed at the natural sciences which he argues cannot be explained in terms of a coherent positivism. The social organization of science contradicts the basic premises of positivism: scientism, neutrality, objectivity. Beck has demonstrated that scientific knowledge and nature are constructions, and, moreover, to the extent that the critique of science borrows from science its scientistic discourse, this too will be a construction. In place of objectivism, the new discourse, binding science and society, is one of societal responsibility, which Beck hopes will be the foundation of a new modernity.

As a result of public challenges to science, 'the central question becomes, not only *what* is investigated, but *how* it is investigated' (1992: 175). In Beck's view the social sciences have a role to play in the construction of an alternative scientific rationality. The guiding question is: 'how can social science and social experience be related to each other in such a way that the spectrum of unseen secondary consequences is reduced' (Beck, 1992: 180–1). The mediation of science and experience is central to the constructivist understanding of science. For Beck this task of social science extends beyond social science to the natural sciences themselves. Having established the case of the existence of 'latent reflexivity' in public consciousness, the challenge is to transfer this into scientific consciousness (Beck, 1992: 181). It would appear that this is the special role of social science.

Reflexivity, Practices and Objectivity

One of the main challenges for the social sciences for Pierre Bourdieu was the task of preserving a space for critique (Bourdieu, 1990, 1992, 1995, 1996, 2004). Science is a product of the social world while at the same time being autonomous from it. Social science must retain a critical distance from its object in order precisely to be able to offer critical and objective knowledge. The object of knowledge must be theoretically constructed by science. But this requires expressing what he calls 'radical doubt' or a reflexive relation to the scientific process by which the social scientist recognizes the context-bounded nature of science. Reflexivity for Bourdieu is considerably more tied to the autonomy of science than in feminist epistemology, where there is a stronger acceptance of the standpoint of the social actor. Reflexivity is a way of viewing the social world in a way that allows objectivity to be possible while aware of its limits.

Bourdieu's approach has both an objective and a subjective dimension. The former refers to the structural order, for in his framework society is an objective reality independently of its perception by social actors and social scientists. In this he has retained a strong Marxist sense of the objectivity of structure. Bourdieu, however, goes far beyond simplistic structural determinism in arguing for a subjectivist or constructivist account of how first-order concepts, that is those of social actors, constitute social reality in the production of meaning. In this way, he resists the dangers of objectivist structuralism and subjectivist hermeneutics. Objectivism refers to the social and structural condition of belief systems, or subjectivism. It is of course Bourdieu's contention that the constructions of social actors vary depending on their position in the objective structures of society. For this reason, he gives priority to the structuralist or objective dimension.

By means of the concept 'reflexivity', Bourdieu argues social science cannot escape its own self-reference. What this means is that social science is an intellectual practice embedded in a cultural context which is always greater than what the individual scientist can consciously reflect upon. Bourdieu writes about the collective unconsciousness underlying the social organization of social science and which constitutes what could be called its paradigms. Like social actors, the social scientist has a social location, or 'habitus', which conditions knowledge. The aim of reflexivity is to make the social field of social scientific knowledge explicit in its social organization and in its cognitive structures: 'Reflexive analysis must consider successively position in the social space, position in the field and position in the scholastic universe' (Bourdieu, 2004: 94). Science cannot escape its own historicity, but it can make its situatedness reflective in order to distinguish between the realms of freedom and necessity. It is in this way that social science is committed to an ethical role. As a political-reflective practice, his social science, which he calls the 'theory of practice' (Bourdieu, 1990), is also transformative in that it is ultimately aimed at the creation of a new subjectivity in its confrontation with objectified social structures. It is in this specific sense that his approach can be called constructivist in that the aim of social science is to enhance the power of social agency over social structures. Bourdieu's reflexive constructivism thus involves the freeing of agency from oppressive social structures by raising to the level of reflexivity the degree to which existing forms of cultural production are limited by social structures. On a more practical level, Bourdieu sees as the task of social science the preservation of the autonomy of intellectual critique. For him the social scientist is first and foremost an intellectual and one of the most important tasks today is the need to create social spaces for intellectual activity. The social scientist as a member of an intellectual community is a constructivist for the social production of knowledge is also the construction of a rationally organized society.

The Rational Actor: Rational Choice as Explanation

The reflexive turn in the philosophy of social science can be contrasted with rational choice which can also be viewed as an approach that is strongly based on the social actor. In this case the emphasis is not on the social actor as reflexive but as rational and corresponding to this is a view of social science as an explanation of rationality. Although not a philosophy of social science, rational choice has become influential in recent years, especially in economics and political science, but is also important in public policy and to a lesser extent in sociology. The classic accounts of rational choice include Mancur Olson's *The Logic of Collective Action* (1965), Homans's 'Social Behavior as Exchange' (1958); Peter Blau's *Exchange and Power in Social Life* (1964) and T. C. Schelling's *Strategy of Conflict* (1960). Later works are include Axelrod's *The Emergence of Cooperation* (1984) and Coleman's *The Foundations of Social Theory* (1990). Rational choice is based on the assumption that the social actor, generally held to be an individual, seeks to optimize rationally gains within the limits of the objective situation in which the actor exists. In this respect there also parallels with some of the other positions discussed in this chapter in so far as rational choice is based on a situated concept of the social actor. However, rational choice assumes self-interest and optimality as the key feature of social action.

One of the attractions of rational choice theory is its undoubted capacity to offer an explanatory account of social relations. The explanatory models in rational choice differ from positivistic ones in that they are regressive, beginning with outcomes at the macro level which is explained by a series of actions that can be traced back to the actions of individuals. The assumption is that macro-level outcomes (social structures) can be explained by micro-level actions (the choices people make). Unlike functionalist accounts, the explanation of social action is not in terms of a functional outcome but rather in terms of a model of intentionality. Intentionality is thus the basic unit of analysis. For rational choice the simplest possible model of explanation is desirable.

Rational choice is mostly concerned with explaining social behaviour in the context of non-cooperative situations, that is in situations where the outcome of an action is never entirely determined by the individual who must take into account the actions of others. Non-cooperative situations arise when social actors are co-operative only to achieve their own interests. Rational choice theories are also becoming more relevant in the context of contingency, since what is central to these approaches is the availability of information relating to the choices of other actors, as in the so-called 'Prisoner's Dilemma', which demonstrates the paradox that the collective outcome of an individual preference may be detrimental for everyone and that therefore rationality leads to irrational outcomes (see Baert, 1998: 153–74; Abel, 2000). This scenario can arise whenever people try to design a public good. Rational choice analysis applied to such situations would try to identity ways in which social institutions can be designed to eliminate the Prisoner's Dilemma.

Rational choice approaches have been criticized for their methodological individualism, although there is no reason in principle for restricting rational choice explanation to the individual. Rational choice approaches have also been heavily criticized for their non-sociological view of the social actor, who is generally seen as making rational and culturally neutral choices in artificial situations. Moreover, it assumes social arrangements can be explained by the choices people make, whereas in reality people make decisions on non-rational grounds.

In sum, while being oriented toward explanation, in the view of the critics, rational choice theorists over-stress intentionality and attribute rationality where it might in fact be absent. This might lead to relativism, as in the rationality debates concerning the belief systems of different cultures (see Wilson, 1970) but it could also be interpreted in different terms. Two examples will suffice to illustrate the contested nature of rationality, Davidson and Habermas. The analytical philosopher Donald Davidson ([1974], 1984) has proposed a revision of the concept of rationality that takes into account what could be called a social conception of rationality whereby rationality is seen in others, including in those who may be in many respects very different, in terms of criteria very similar to one's own. In a similar way, Habermas has argued for a notion of rationality as discursive agreement rather than methodological individualism (see Chapter 5).

Conclusion: Reflexivity versus Explanation

The reflexive turn in the philosophy of social science has brought a very new perspective to bear on social science. The turn to social context and experience as the object of study for social science requires the social scientist to address the question of knowledge from the perspective of social positioning in which knowledge, thinking and acting are related. As is particularly highlighted by feminist standpoint epistemology, knowledge is not just socially contextualized but is also a transformative process arising out of the reflexive investigation into people's social positioning. Where sociological hermeneutics since Max Weber banished evaluation from the research process, the cognitive evaluations associated with various standpoints or positioning is the basis of social scientific knowledge.

The adoption of a reflexive approach, it has been argued, preserves a claim to objectivity; indeed, making possible an enhanced objectivity. According to Tim May, 'the explanatory power of social science is obtained methodologically from the relations between an understanding of social actions, including the points of view and attributes of those involved and how they are seen by others, in relation to the explanation of conditions under which those actions take place' (May, 2000: 169). The purpose of social science is not then experience as such but a critical awareness of the social context of an actor's position in society. Viewed in this way, explanation is not compromised by common-sense understandings of social reality.

7

Constructivism and Realism

Introduction: The Constructivist–Realist Controversy

A central concern of much of recent philosophies of social science is the reopening of the question of the social context of knowledge: the indeterminacy of scientific knowledge can be related to its social context in the emergence of new links between democracy and knowledge. Feminist epistemology, discussed in the previous chapter, challenges many of the presuppositions of social science as a pure cognitive system, as does the sociology of interventionism of Touraine. These approaches point to a deepening of the idea of a critical hermeneutics beyond Habermas and Apel's reconstructive approach, which failed to see the links between natural and social science, a relationship which now lies at the centre of recent philosophies of science. The conceptualization of social science that is now emerging is one that is pointing in the direction of new links between the natural and social sciences. In this context of central importance are constructivism and complexity (the latter will be considered in the next chapter).

Among the issues that constructivism raises is the question of the extent to which social science offers knowledge of socially constructed realities. In what ways can social science construct public discourse? To what extent is science as a cognitive system part of the social production of knowledge? Can the institutional structure of science be radicalized by democracy? It is on these issues that constructivism and realism diverge, though not to an irreconcilable extent.

Constructivists maintain that social reality is not something outside the discourse of science but is partly constituted by science.

In constructivism, the subject is an active agent as opposed to the passive conception of subjectivity in the value-free social science of positivism and hermeneutics. While the hermeneutical approach does involve a degree of constructivism in the sense that hermeneutical knowledge enhances self-understanding, the constructive moment has not been central to this tradition. In radical constructivism social scientific knowledge is neither a representation of society nor a reproduction of it. The knowledge social science provides is a mediated knowledge; it is a mediation of science and reality. Constructivism does not hold to the idealist thesis of epistemological idealism that reality is creation of the mind, but that reality can only be known by our cognitive structures. Such a position does not deny the existence of external reality itself, but simply holds that the empirical world of reality is known through the structures of science. In this way social science, like all of science, is a construct designed to produce knowledge of something other than itself but is forever confined to the limits of its own methodology. Constructivism therefore entails a degree of 'reflexivity'.

The critical realist school, on the other hand, although not opposed to reflexivity, argues for a stronger sense of objectivism in the social scientific method. It is less concerned with the actual construction of objective reality than is constructivism for which all knowledge is necessarily mediated by the discourse of science. Like Habermas, Bhaskar's aim is to go beyond both positivism and hermeneutics while retaining a commitment to critique. However, unlike Habermas, he does not see communication as playing a central role in the production of social scientific knowledge. Opposed to naive naturalism, Bhaskar defends a qualified naturalism, which he calls 'critical realism', which is aimed at getting at the truth of things. The primary difference between critical realism and constructivism lies in the former's concern with discovering generative mechanisms within an objectively existing social reality. Both Habermas and Bhaskar share a concern with relating knowledge to social change.

In this chapter I shall outline the constructivist and critical realist positions. The direction of the argument is to show that a reconciliation of radical constructivism and critical realism is possible, but in a way that will entail a movement beyond these positions.

The Revival of Constructivism

While constructivism has it origins in the various kinds of philosophical idealism (the positions associated with Hume, Berkeley and Kant, who argued in different ways that knowledge is shaped by human cognitive structures) the great exponents of modern constructivism in social science were Max Weber and Karl Mannheim. The idealist schools confined their constructivism to epistemological individualism, neglecting the social dimension in the construction of knowledge. Unlike Durkheim, who was writing in the French positivist tradition of Comte and the rationalizing culture of the Enlightenment, Weber writing in the tradition of German neo-Kantian idealism questioned the possibility of a strong objectivity in social science which constructs through ideal types social reality. Durkheim's anthropological works reveal him to be an early proponent of the sociology of knowledge. However, his writings on the social construction of belief systems in primitive societies were not extended to modern Western societies and their conceptions of scientific knowledge.

Within the classical tradition of sociology it was the achievement of Karl Mannheim, the founder of the 'sociology of knowledge', to establish constructivism as one of the key methodological issues in social science. One of the most important statements of this is his essay 'Competition as a Cultural Phenomenon' ([1928], 1993). Mannheim's importance in the philosophy of social science consists of his attempt to relate knowledge to its social producers. He argued that knowledge was always produced from a specific social and historical standpoint, reflecting the interests and culture of the groups in question. Truth is ultimately a product of its social location. Unlike his Marxist contemporaries, such as Georg Lukacs, Mannheim did not confine constructivism merely to culture in general or ideology, but angered Marxists by relating constructivism to political beliefs as well, thus undermining the Marxist faith in the objective status of the Marxist claim to valid knowledge.

Mannheim was particularly interested in ideology as a form of knowledge which expresses the thought of a dominant group. Ideology was a contrast to utopia which reflected the aspiration of those struggling to bring about change. The intellectual problem for Mannheim was to transcend ideology and utopia. It was his conviction that only specific kinds of intellectuals (the 'free-floating intellectuals') could achieve genuinely historical knowledge and in whose hands sociology rested in order to grasp the *Zeitgeist* of the age. An approximation to objectivity could be reached by social science in its self-diagnosis of the age. However, Mannheim fell victim to positivism in that he believed the natural sciences and mathematics lay outside the social construction of knowledge. Mannheim's sociology of knowledge was reflected in the American tradition of symbolic interactionism, which is best associated with G. H. Mead and the sociology of knowledge. In general, the proponents of the 'sociology of knowledge' tend to restrict the theory of the social production of knowledge to ideological knowledge, which can be contrasted to scientific knowledge.

Since Mannheim, constructivism tended to have been obscured by the positivist debate and the rival philosophies of hermeneutics and Marxism. With the decline of these challenges constructivism has been rediscovered (Stehr and Meja, 1984). Constructivism has been the social scientific methodology of the 1980s, but has resonances in a wide range of other and related epistomologies (Knorr Cetina, 1993; Sismondo, 1993; Gergen, 2001; Gergen and Gergen, 2003). It is increasingly being more and more recognized that our knowledge of social reality is a construction of social science in the sense that social scientific knowledge is a reflexive knowledge which constitutes its object. Clearly, the object, social reality, exists independently of what social scientists do, but there is a sense in which social science itself plays an active role in the shaping of knowledge. Habermas and Apel's theory of the link between knowledge and interests also presupposed certain constructiveness on the part of science. Constructivism has a strong political resonance in the notion of the governance of science (Fuller, 2000b).

Three Kinds of Constructivism

Three kinds of constructivism can be identified: social constructionism, scientific constructivism, and radical constructivism.

As previously mentioned, one of the older assumptions of post-empiricist epistemology is that knowledge is not confined to the world of science but is also to be found in the everyday world where social actors creatively construct their world using cognitive structures. In this view, the social world is socially constructed. A famous example of this sense of constructivism is the book *The Social Construction of Reality* (1966) by Peter Berger and Thomas Luckmann. 'Constructionism', as opposed to the stronger notion of constructivism, is the 'weak' argument that social science is principally concerned with interpreting the process by which social reality is constructed by social actors. Social constructionism can also refer to the recognition that social factors enter into science and that science must be seen as historically constituted (as in Kuhn and Foucault). A stronger sense of constructivism can be associated with what may be called Social Constructivism, sometimes called 'scientific constructivism'. The use of the term 'constructivism' as opposed to 'constructionism' tends to suggest this, although the terms are frequently used interchangeably. This is the stronger thesis which advances the controversial claim that science is constructed by social actors. Increasingly, this is generally what is meant by constructivism, a term that has become associated with a wide variety of positions (it had its origins in mathematics). Beginning with the so-called 'strong programme' of the Edinburgh School and the now famous book by David Bloor, *Knowledge and Social Imagery* ([1976], 1991), the idea emerged that science is not merely influenced by social factors, as the older sociology of knowledge and sociology of science claimed, but its actual content, as opposed to its external form, may in fact be socially constructed.

This 'strong' thesis is often associated with the new Sociology of Science and a new interdisciplinary sub-field, Science and Technology Studies. Examples of this approach are to be found in Karin Knorr Cetina's *The Manufacture of Knowledge: An Essay of the Constructivist and Contextual Nature of Science* (1981). Knorr Cetina (1981, 1984) argues 'facticity' is a 'fabrication' and is not therefore objective for knowledge can only be understood in terms of the social processes of production. Science, she argues (1984: 227), is more constructive than descriptive: the 'products of science are contextually specific constructions which bear the mark of their situational contingency and interest structure of the process by which they are generated, and cannot be adequately understood without an analysis of their construction'.

Other proponents of constructivism in science are Woolgar and Latour (Latour and Woolgar, 1986; Latour, 1987; Woolgar, 1988a, 1988b) who take a more extreme position on scientific knowledge as a socially produced system of knowledge. In their view the cognitive content of science cannot be separated from its social context. This position has come to form the core idea of Science and Technology Studies (STS) for which the objects of scientific research are constructed by the conventions of science. These debates, such as those associated with the Edinburgh School of the Sociology of Scientific Knowledge (SSK) are mostly confined to natural science. SSK and the so-called 'strong programme' entails the view that science as a cognitive system can be explained only by its social situation. This school of thought has been very successful in opening up new debates on the social construction of science in many disciplines (Simons, 1990; Sismondo, 1993; Gergen, 1994). Steve Fuller (1993, 1994) has explored the wider relevance of this approach for the social sciences. He emphasizes the centrality of the thesis of reflexivity in the construction of knowledge. A system is reflexive if it applies something it has learned about its environment to its own internal working (Fuller, 1993: 341).

Radical constructivism term was introduced in the 1970s by Ernst von Glaserfeld, but the roots of the tradition lie in cybernetics, particularly in the work of Heinz von Foerster on self-organizing and self-observing systems, as well as in developments associated with Jean Piaget's psychology. The key idea is reality can be viewed as a system which is structured as an information-processing entity. Reality is thus essentially an endless process of constructing information in order for a system to distinguish itself from its environment. This kind of constructivism is termed 'radical' because it sees reality as a set of self-reproducing mechanisms and processes. Within social science, a major example is Niklas Luhmann, who was influenced by cognitive biology and cybernetics and developed a systems theory.

From the perspective of systems theory, Niklas Luhmann developed an alternative concept of constructivism which dispensed with notions of structure and agency. This is based on the view that society is composed of a set of quasi-independently existing subsystems, which reproduce themselves independently of social agency. Science is one such functionally differentiated system. The central theoretical idea is 'autopoetic constructivism'. Autopoiesis means 'self-perpetuating system' (from 'auto' meaning self and 'poiesis' creation).

Before remarking further on this, it must be mentioned that autopoetic constructivism owes its origin to developments in cybernetics (for example, Von Foerster, who is generally credited with being the originator of autopoiesis as self-organization) and biology (for example, Manturana and Varela) and is particularly influential in psychology today (Schmidt, 1987, 1992; Nüse et al., 1991). Cybernetics is the science of self-regulating systems of information. These cybernetic and biological models had a certain impact on Luhmann's philosophy of science, which has been influential in social science. An earlier and important proponent of constructivism was the psychologist and biologist Jean Piaget, who advocated a Kantian epistemological structuralism which stressed the constructivist activity of the mind. Piaget sometimes referred to his approach as 'dialectical constructionism' (Boden, 1979: 15 and 91). He argued that the mind possesses transformative capacities which derive from self-regulating structures. In general the concept of autopoiesis in social science is a variant of the idea of self-organizing and operationally closed systems in natural science (Mayntz, 1992).

Luhmann (1984a, 1984b, 1984c, 1986, 1988, 1990a, 1990b, 1995, 1996) differs from many radical constructivists in that he demands a sharp distinction between science and non-science and, moreover, stands for uncompromising relativism in social science: meaning in science can only come from the cognitive systems of science and not from its institutional context. For him scientific knowledge is produced only within the sub-system of science, which is a hermetic system having no connection to things that are not science. Politically, Luhmann's position is that scientists should confine themselves to science, leaving the social implications of science for other people to sort out, for the discourse of societal responsibility does not belong to the field of science. In short, Luhmann defends the sharp separation of the expert from the intellectual. Science for Luhmann is a closed system and one which is self-perpetuating, that is, it is self-generating or autopoietic. 'Knowledge', he writes 'is and remains bound to self-reference at the levels of individual events, of processes, and of systems' (Luhmann, 1984a: 123).

Luhmann's autopoietic constructivism is based on a theory of communication. His understanding of communication is very different from Habermas's theory of communicative action, for it surrenders agency and the concept of a knowing subject in favour of an autopoietic system. Scientific communication for Luhmann is not based on the primacy of the individual scientist but on science itself. The semiotic dimension to Luhmann's autopoietic model of scientific communication is a 'decentred' one. Science, as with all other discourses in modernity, has suffered the fate of fall of the subject and the collapse of 'centres'. Luhmann rejects Habermas's attempt to link communication to ethics, claiming that the autopoietic theory of communication does not need to have recourse to an acting subject: 'On the contrary, it takes communication as a recursively closed, autopoietic system, and actually as a structurally determined system that may be specified only by its own structures and not by states of consciousness' (1996: 263–4).

Beyond Constructivism: Actor Network Theory, Complexity Theory and Cognitive Social Science

Contructivism can be related to Actor Network Theory (ANT), which argues that there is no essential difference between nature and society, proposing a relational conception of the social world. The major statement of this is Bruno Latour's *We Have Never Been Modern* (1993). Latour's work with Woolgar, referred to above, suggests a strong constructivism. However, ANT is different: science is not only a social creation, but scientists construct nature and the only reality that exists are networks, seamless webs of interactions. Latour has been seen as a radical anti-scientist, denying the objectivity of the scientific enterprise. Moreover, what is particularly characteristic of his approach is that Latour sees society as a network of things and social actors. Society is not merely social but is also made up of things, including nature. For this reason, Latour prefers to see society made up of what he calls 'actants', that is any thing or actor that plays a role in constructing reality. One of the consequences of ANT for the philosophy of the social sciences is that it denies the centrality of causal analysis, for in place of cause-effect relations is a new emphasis of seamless networks in which social agency is not central.

In place of causal relations is instead the notion of translation. Latour is interested in the way reality is constructed out of constructivist processes by translation. Scientists, for example, translate nature into scientific categories which then become the resulting reality. Hybridization is another example of translation at work in the construction of reality.

Constructivism is characterized by an emphasis on how social interests and, above all, social context enters into the world of science. Actor Network Theory, which can be situated within the broad spectrum of constructivism, is an example of a move within constructivist philosophy of social science beyond it to a concern with the creative process of translation.

Complexity theory is another example of a move within a broad constructivist camp towards a position that, while not being a philosophy of social science, suggests a new approach to knowledge. Complexity theory, which is most closely allied with Luhmann's autopoietic constructivism, concerns in first place issues that are specific to neither the social or the natural science but cut across both, such as non-linearity, contingency and self-organization.

With its origins in biology, complexity theory has implications for the social sciences in many ways (Byrne, 1998; Medd, 2002). This is more than a view of the social world as complex. Firstly, complexity theory is predicated on the assumption that the natural sciences deal with a fixed conception of reality is untenable and reveals an entirely incorrect understanding of the natural sciences for which nature is now seen in terms closer to the social world. Secondly, complexity theory draws attention to the centrality of a conception of social reality in terms of relationships, that is with the connections between things. It is often the case that the connections between things are more significant that the things themselves. An example of this is hybrid phenomena, as in the ATN. Complexity theory thus concerns a relationist view of social reality and is particularly relevant to an understanding of globalization, which is increasingly seen in terms of a model of networks (Urry, 2003). Thirdly, complexity theory has direct implications for epistemology with its emphasis on the process of knowing, rather than on a knowing subject or an objective reality that exist outside the cognitive process.

In this latter sense complexity can be seen in the context of postmodernist thought in its critique of a foundational subject. Where postmodernism emphasizes multiplicity, complexity theory is concerned with the incompleteness of knowledge which is always from a limited perspective. In this respect what is important is less deconstruction than self-reference or a reflexivity that is concerned with a model of knowledge that is based not on knowing something external but on the very processes and mechanism of the cognitive operation itself.

Piet Strydom has characterized the various positions within constructivism, in particular Luhmann's autopoietic constructivism, and related developments such as 'connectionism' in terms of a cognitivism (Strydom, 2000, 2002, 2005). Cognitive social science intensifies constructivism around the ways in which social realities emerge out of cognitive frameworks. In this framework elements of different kinds are combined in such a way that an emergent reality – whether problems, issues, facts – results. The emphasis here shifts towards the dynamic construction of the social world, which remains radically indeterminate. This is a view of the social reality as made of up different and competing cognitive frameworks – discourses, normative ad symbolic structures, frames and master frames, repertoires, modes of legitimation and cultural models – which create the social world in situations of contestation.

In this context of importance is van den Daele's (1992: 531, 552) thesis of a shift in contemporary social science from an 'objectivist to a constructivist perspective'. In the language of constructivism, argues van den Daele, 'every reality is an observed reality'. He points to the radical possibility of new norms being introduced through public debate, professional discourse, and political regulation. This position is reflected also in Eder's (1996) recent work on the social construction of nature and the post-corporate order and is also present in Fuller's (1993, 2000) theory of knowledge policy.

The upshot to this is a view of social science as an intellectual framework by which the social world can be transformed by the very processes that make up the social world.

Critical Realism

The previous section looked at varieties of approaches which can be characterized as constructivist. The principal characteristic of constructivism is its view that knowledge, both everyday and scientific knowledge, is a construction shaped by its context. I have shown that this view varies from emancipatory schools to the value-free school of systems theory and that within these diverse schools there is an ambivalence as to the status of reality. Except for extreme constructivism, constructivists do not deny the existence of social reality as an objective entity. The stress, in general, is on how social actors construct reality, with implications that this has for the methodological self-understanding of social science largely unexplored. In this section I shall bring the debate one step further by introducing critical realism. As indicated earlier, there a case for seeing realism as the main alternative to constructivism.

Realists, unlike constructivists, emphasize that realities underlying knowledge do exist. As the term suggests, realists hold that an external reality which is independent of human consciousness exists and can nevertheless be known. Realists do not make the naive assumption that reality is easily observable, but rather claim reality as morphologically 'emergent'. Therefore there can be no simple recourse to observable causes, as in the positivistic approach to causation where regular occurrences must be explained in terms of observable cause and effect.

The new realism in social science today is an anti-positivist and post-empiricism which wants to hold onto 'the possibility of naturalism', to use Bhaskar's phrase (Bhaskar, 1979). Critical Realism can be contrasted to empirical or positivist realism, which reduces the social world to observable objects or facts. For critical realism there is a basic distinction to be drawn between our knowledge of the world and the reality of the social world. Realism too stands for the separation of the sciences both in terms of their subject matter and method. It is therefore a comprehensive anti-positivism, so much so that realists disagree with Habermas's characterization of positivism as the method of natural science. For realists, positivism is an anachronism and therefore the case for an anti-positivist philosophy of social science cannot be made on the basis of an attack on natural science. As a philosophy of social science, realism attempts to integrate three methodologies. First, it defends the possibility of causal explanation. This is the most distinctive characteristic of realism. Second, it accepts the hermeneutic notion of social reality as being communicatively constructed, without drawing constructivist conclusions. The problem with the hermeneutical approach is that it does not address causal mechanisms and accepts the construction of social actors. Third, most varieties of realism, though not necessarily all, involve a critical dimension. Post-positivist realism is therefore called 'critical realism'.

Roy Bhaskar is generally regarded as one of the leading representatives of realism. Other representatives of realism are Harré (1986), Outhwaite (1987), Archer (1995), Sayer (1984, 2000), Keat and Urry (1975). According to Bhaskar, there are three levels of reality, the real, the actual and the empirical. These levels constitute the realist ontology. The real is whatever exists, regardless of whether social actors are consciousness of it. The real can be a natural reality or a socially created one. An important feature of the real is that it is composed of structures and causal powers. Whereas the real is largely the objective world, the actual is the reality that happens when the real is activated. Thus, the objective reality of power becomes actual only when it is activated. The empirical concerns the realm of human experience, that is the way in which either the real or the empirical is subjectively experienced.

Realist ontology is a morphological reality. One of the central ideas of Bhaskar's approach is that social reality is composed of what he calls 'generative mechanisms' and that these mechanisms generate 'events'. It is a non-atomistic view of society as being causally structured. Bhaskar insists that generative mechanisms, which are causal laws, are independent of the events to which they give rise. It is important to stress that causal laws for realists are not universal deterministic laws as in positivism, but are contingent and emergent. Moreover, both causal mechanisms and the events they give rise to are not necessarily reflected in experience. For this reason, traditional forms of positivism and empiricism are untenable since experience does not provide us with knowledge of generative mechanisms. In Bhaskar's theory there is a difference between the transitive and intransitive objects of science. The former refers to the concepts used by science and the latter refers to the real world. The task of science is to penetrate to the generative mechanisms operating in the real world.

A concern with explanation is thus central to critical realism, which argues for an anti-positivistic conception of causation, that is a model of explanation that explains how something is brought about. Such a logic of explanation would differ from the positivistic conception of explanation in terms of establishing a relationship between cause and effect. There are different levels of causation that go beyond reductive cause-effect models of explanation, as in the view that for every observable effect there is an observable cause. Critical realists instead investigate the mechanisms by which effects operate, the powers and properties that they produce and the intricate inter-linkages between the different levels of structures which all make causation very complex and thus, irreducible to single factors.

Science has this power to provide knowledge of reality as it really exists. Social scientific knowledge is ultimately explanatory knowledge, something which it shares with natural science. In this respect realists adhere to the unity of science while rejecting positivism. Bhakar's version of realism in fact is not unlike Habermas's in that he believes science to have an emancipatory function. However, what marks realists off from constructivists is that the latter lay less stress on an objectivity outside the discourses in which it is articulated. In other words, science is about something other than science.

In Bhaskar's theory of science, phenomena are identified which are then investigated and explanations are proposed and empirically tested. His model of scientific progress is one of science digging deeper and deeper into the depth structures of social reality identifying generative mechanisms. Andrew Collier (1994: 50), in a study on Bhaskar, contrasts this metaphor of science digging forever deeper into the ontological depths of reality to the empiricist metaphor of science collecting bits of knowledge, while relativists use the metaphor of 'gestalt switches', or 'coming to see the world differently'. Bhaskar defends the possibility of science as a form of valid knowledge without embracing scientism, for scientific knowledge is never entirely context-free and is always falsifiable. He is also fighting reductionists (who assert that lower levels of reality have more causal power) and dualists (who assert the independence of the different levels of reality from each other). A more recent work on these questions is Archer's (1995) morphogenetic approach which stresses the importance of social change in terms of a transformative model of structure and agency.

One of the most important and far-reaching concepts in critical realism is the notion of emergence, a concept that has resonances in cognitive social science. Emergence refers to a condition of contingency by which social reality emerges out of the interaction of different processes. A given social entity is always more than its parts. The problem with positivistic approaches is that they ignore the emergent nature of the social world. This concept is similar to the Hegelian-Marxist notion of dialectics, whereby the social world is created by a self-transformative logic of conflict entailing subjective and objective processes. For Critical Realism the social world is inherently transformative and social science must reflect the emancipatory possibilities contained within it and which lie beyond the realm of necessity.

Conclusion: Integrating Constructivism and Realism

One of the challenges for the philosophy of social science today is to integrate realism and constructivism into a new critical theory of science. In this concluding section, I shall attempt to sketch the main issues that are at stake.

With respect to constructivism there is widespread unclarity as to whether reality is something constructed or whether there is an underlying reality which is constructed by social actors. This is of course primarily a theoretical issue for social theory, but it does have implications for the philosophy of science in that it raises a question about the function of science in relation to knowledge of it. If all knowledge is constructed can there be universally valid social scientific knowledge?

Constructivism has become a widely accepted methodological practice in the social sciences, and has been particularly useful in the study of 'social problems'. Studies on environmental discourse frequently adopt constructivist approaches (see Hannigan 1995 or Eder 1996). In the sociology of science constructivists such as Latour and Woolgar (1986) have argued for a view of science which denies its objectivity. Their theory of science dissolves all knowledge, including that of science into a semiotic idealism. According to Barnes (1995: 106–11) this ambivalence as to the status of reality in constructivism is also present in Beck. In Barnes's view Beck must decide whether the risks are real or whether they are constructions. Barnes accuses Beck of advocating an idealist version of constructivism. Beck's constructivism is thus caught in the bind that to admit that the risks are real would be to admit the validity of scientific knowledge, which is precisely what is being challenged. Clearly constructivists such as those discussed in the previous section – in particular Bourdieu, Unger, Touraine and Beck, who self-consciously adopt constructivist methodologies, but also feminists, Habermas – accept a realist ontology of the social. Given the Marxist pedigree of many of these theorists, few would deny the objectivity of structures of domination. Only extreme constructivists, such as Woolgar and Latour, or deconstructionists, for whom the image is more real than reality, would deny the existence of underlying structures.

On the other side, the realists, while advocating the objectivity of the social and the possibility that science can provide knowledge of things other than science, do not deny a dimension of constructivism in knowledge. One of Bhaskar's themes is the social production of knowledge by means of knowledge. Knowledge, not even scientific knowledge, exists in a closed system. Bhaskar even goes so far as to acknowledge his depth to Bourdieu and Giddens for his transformational model of society and the idea of the 'duality of structure', the notion that social action and structure are mutually implicated. All of social action is transformational and it is the aim of science to express this. However, given his commitment to realism, Bhaskar is more concerned with the possibility of providing depth explanations, a position that results in an infinite regress of explanations (Byrant, 1995: 86).

What is apparent from Actor Network Theory and the various kinds of constructivism discussed above is a concern with the way in which reality is constructed as a creative process in which elements of some sort get put together in a combination such that an emergent reality – whether problems, issues, facts – results. For this reason, many of its proponents situate themselves within a broader realism, where what is real is precisely the capacity to construct social and natural worlds. However, the difference from realism and from the earlier social constructionism is a more reflexive stance. Different forms of constructivism or constructionism are defined by their particular choice of conceiving of the process, the agents, the elements, and the make-up of the various combinations of elements and hence their emergent constructs. An example of this is Knorr Cetina's constructivism, which focused on the internal practices of the scientific enterprise in which transactions, competition, conflicts and negotiations between scientists lead to emergent outcomes such as conceptual orders, theories, diagrams, laboratory phenomena, facts and knowledge.

Ian Hacking (1999) has written an extensive critical analysis of constructivism, arguing with Hillary Putnam, that the very term is confused. Reality is not a single thing but is constantly renegotiated and is differentiated. This is something critical realists generally agree with. Thus, child abuse is real but the idea of child abuse is constructed. Constructivism draws attention to the role of social context in science, but does not answer some of the major questions that science is concerned with. Instead, he argues for an interactive conception of social reality and social action; the real with the idea of it. The real versus construction tension in his view is a minor issue concerning the creation of social classifications. Where social constructivism makes sense, it is mostly a truism, as in the statement that everything that exists is a social construction or that if something is socially constructed then it exists. As Bourdieu has written: 'Science is a construction which brings out a discovery irreducible to the construction and to the social conditions that made it possible.' (Bourdieu, 2004: 77).

The principal conclusion I wish to draw in this chapter is that the constructivist–realist divide is in fact a false dichotomy and that the two sides can in fact be interpreted in a reconcilable fashion. Constructivists and realists are both united in the rejection of correspondence theories of truth. Realists such as Bhaskar acknowledge the importance of hermeneutic issues: science cannot opt out of the double hermeneutic. And, as Outhwaite (1987: 91) adds, both sides are united in their support for an emancipatory critique. Bhaskar then is not too far removed from critical theory in believing that critical realism involves an explanatory critique of the generative mechanism of false consciousness. It is difficult, then, to find real points of difference in philosophies that are coming from quite different intellectual differences. It would then in fact appear that the real differences lie within constructivism than between constructivism and realism. I hope to have indicated that the divisions within constructivism are much more consequential than those realism pose. Constructivists are divided between those who adhere to the possibility of an emancipatory critique and those who in adopting the autopoietic approach defend the value-freedom of science as a closed system. If we add to this the deconstructionist approaches (which clearly also adopt a constructivist position on knowledge which can only be deconstructed), constructivists who want to retain the possibility of critique are best allied with critical realists.

Beck (1996: 7) has attempted to reconcile the theoretical problems arising from the realist–constructivist debate, arguing that realism and constructivism are not mutually exclusive. In his view they can be exclusive only if they are conceived naively. Naive constructivism fails to see that behind the constructions of social actors there are objective realities and naive realism neglects the extent to which social actors and science constructs reality. Taking the ecological discourse as an example, he argues:

> realism conceives the world ecological problematic as 'closed', whereas constructivism maintains it openness in principle. For the one, it is the dangers (the doomsday scenarios) of the world risk society that are the central focus; for the other, it is the chances, the contexts in which actors operate. For the one, global dangers must first of all give rise to international institutions and treaties. For the other, talk of global environmental dangers already assumes supranational discourse coalitions engaging in successful action.' (Beck, 1996: 6–7).

He defends a 'reflexive realism' in opposition to 'naive constructivism' in order to arrive at a notion of 'constructivist realism'.

Reflexive realism 'investigates how self-evidence is produced, how questions are curtailed, how alternative interpretations are shut up in black boxes and so on'; in other words, it examines how reality is constructed by social actors who define what is to count as knowledge. Reflexive realism can therefore be understood as constructivist realism in which reality, the sign system and the interpreter together interact. In other words, if knowledge has a constructivist dimension this openness can be radicalized by the growing reflexivity of social actors in the extension of discursive democracy into the cognitive framework of science. This ties in with the conclusions of the Gulbenkian Commission Report (1996: 93):

> In short the fact that knowledge is socially constructed also means that more valid Knowledge is socially possible. The recovery of the social bases of knowledge is not at all in contradiction to the concept of objectivity. On the contrary, we argue that the restructuring of the social sciences of which we have been speaking can amplify this possibility by taking into account the criticisms of past practice that have been made and by building structures that are more truly pluralist and universal.

The wider implications of this with respect to the relationship between knowledge and democratization will be discussed in the final chapter.

In the previous chapter I argued that postmodernist forms of deconstruction are unable to answer the question of how are we to conceive of solidarity and emancipation, concerns which are central to feminism and new social movements. Moreover, society cannot be viewed simply as a text and open to multiple readings without facing the question of alternative social relations. This is the central task of a critical social science: the recovery of the public role of science. In the following chapter I shall take up some of these issues which are implicated in the turn to reflexivity in the social sciences, such as the role of social science in the public identification and definition of collective problems, the contribution made by social science to public debate and democratization, the relation of social scientific knowledge to other kinds of knowledge contributing to public discourse, the impact of the ordinary everyday perception and articulation of problems on social science, and the relation between social scientific problem definition and media agenda setting.

8

Social Science and Public Discourse

Introduction: Social Science and Modernity

A pervasive tendency in the social sciences over the last few decades is an interest in a communicative concept of knowledge. In a whole range of recent developments, science is becoming increasingly conceived as a communicative system that interacts reflexively with society. In the extreme version this is the view that there is ultimately no difference between the forms of knowledge embodied in science and in society. While positions on the relation between science and society differ, it is becoming more and more apparent that the alternative to positivism and scientism is not a highly normative critique or a special status for scientific knowledge. That science might be a form of human communication goes against some of the fundamental assumptions of modernist science, for since the Enlightenment a belief dear to modern science is the inherent superiority of science over all other forms of knowledge. This self-legislating conception of scientific knowledge ran counter to the idea of science as communication simply because the republic of science and the life-world were incommensurable. Scientific knowledge existed for its own sake or for the community of scientists and if it had a public role it was not one that had much to do with communication. In short, science could enlighten society but could not be enlightened by the non-scientific. Today it is a different matter: science is coming increasingly to be seen as a form of social action, responsive to social context, and exhibiting a new reflexive capacity that is illustrated in new science and society links. These new links are not entirely new but have been part of social science for a long time.

The Finalization of Science

A concern with the communicative role of social science is the basis of the 'finalization' in science in Germany from 1976 to 1982 (Schäfer, 1983a). While this refers mostly to developments in natural science it has implications for social science. The finalization thesis postulates a link between theoretical knowledge and policy specifications. Ultimately it implies a normative link between science as a cognitive system and science as an institution. The finalization argument is that a point is reached when science as a mature system of knowledge has reached the limit of its cognitive expansion and that any further development requires a revision of its fundamental normative goals. In other words, the limits of scientific knowledge are reached when a particular paradigm can no longer be improved and actual research is therefore confined to improving that paradigm. The alternative is a major revision of normative goals by 'extra'-scientific forces. This reorientation can only be undertaken through a rethinking of the theoretical presuppositions of science by forces outside science. The proponents of the finalization thesis do not deny that this amounts to a policy directed science or the social steering of science, a new kind of knowledge policy; in fact, they defend the finalization thesis on precisely the argument that science today can only be finalized by a rethinking of its public utility.

The finalization position amounts to the recovery of the 'external' or social goals of science, which is no longer determined by its own internal cognitive structure. The consequence of this position is the questioning of the autonomy of science as a value-free activity. One of the leading representatives of the finalization thesis, Germot Böhme, argues that the finalization of science favours the development of critical potential of science and therefore implies a retreat from the self-regulating 'republic of science', its instrumentalization and academization (Böhme et al., 1983: 161). This involves a fundamental departure from the historic position worked out in the late seventeenth century when science was institutionalized by the absolute state as an autonomous institution having been forced to relinquish its extra-scientific dimension (see Chapter 1). The finalization argument points to the convergence of two types of discourse: theoretical discourse about objective knowledge and practical discourse about social interests (Schäfer, 1983b: 213).

Obviously the finalization thesis owes much to the Kuhnian

conception of science in its view of the limits of a paradigm of 'normal science.' The theoretical breakthrough achieved by the finalization position is that the period of breakdown of the paradigm is now seen in positive terms and points towards the finalizing of science in society. In place of the menace of relativism which pervaded Kuhn's theory science, the finalization argument defends a normative conception of progress.

The finalization argument helps to overcome an ambiguity in constructivism which is often unclear as to the question whether social agency or expert system determines the goals of science. In the next chapter by way of conclusion, I shall be arguing for a position which recognizes the democratic constructivism of science. It is in this sense that I wish to use the term, 'the radical discourse of constructivism' (Schmidt, 1987, 1992).

The finalization thesis is primarily concerned with developments in natural science, but the questions it raises concerning natural science cannot be ignored by social science. For instance, it has been suggested that ecological thinking should serve as the prototype of a normative natural science, which unlike traditional positivistic natural science, involves normative elements, such as universal social norms, in its cognitive system (Schäfer, 1983b: 214–15). The ecological question is something that cuts across the sciences, uniting natural and social sciences, and moreover touches upon questions of the democratization of knowledge. The unity of the sciences is not constituted by its methodology or subject matter, but by its location in a social context. This context provides the basic normative questions for science and cannot be derived from the cognitive system of science itself. The finalization thesis was taken up in slightly different terms by Beck and Bonss (1989), who questioned the definition of the social science in terms of either Habermas's model of enlightenment or Luhmann's autopoetic model. They proposed a more pragmatic model of social science as a normatively regulated form of knowledge.

Examples of common normative concerns in the sciences relate to new conceptions of nature and natural science. Nature opens up the possibility for a different kind of a hermeneutic link between the sciences. The authors of the Gulbenkian Commission Report (1996: 61) argue:

> Post-positivist natural science no longer sees nature as an unchanging object but one that is being continuously constructed by society. New

> developments in the natural sciences emphasize nonlinearity over linearity, complexity over simplification, the impossibility of removing the measurer from the measurement, and even, for some mathematicians, the superiority of qualitative interpretative scope over a quantitative precision that is more limited in accuracy.

Positivism ultimately collapses in the recognition that it is not only society which changes but also nature and that there might be commonalites between change in society and change in nature. The re-emergence of nature as a discourse in contemporary society with implications for science is connected to a changed conception of time. Our changing natural and social worlds are shot through with the experience of time, which it may be suggested is replacing space as the dominant cognitive and normative frame of reference today. This new ontology of time is not unrelated to the idea of societal responsibility (Strydom, 2002).

Wolfgang van den Daele (1983: 247) points to the importance of responsibility for the consequences of knowledge. His argument is that responsibility cannot rest with scientists alone, but with society which institutionalizes science. This is a position, it will be recalled from Chapter 1, which was represented by Paul Feyerabend, who stood for a participatory democracy which also applied to science. Increasingly, the question of the penetration of the social into science is becoming more and more a theme in the philosophy and sociology of science. Radder (1988) argues the 'materialization of science' in society is always a social realization for theoretical knowledge but can never be a purely internal scientific question. Biertvert and Dierkes point out (1992: 13–14) that an emerging characteristic of social science is a new semantics of self-reflexivity, which links up with a similar kind of self-diagnosis in natural science, which allows it to bring about normative innovation. This raises the question of new kinds of 'knowledge transfers' between the natural and the social sciences and which cannot be understood in terms of positivism. The consensus on this question appears to be that the post-empiricist dialogue between the sciences is fruitful, but there does not appear to be a fundamental shift in the differentiation of the sciences (Mayntz, 1992). Indeed, many of the commonalities are purely metaphorical or semantic, serving heuristic tasks. A more fundamental question is the very self-understanding of the social sciences.

Three Conceptions of the Public Role of Social Science

Peter Wagner's *Theorizing Modernity* is a good example of the attempt to make explicit some of the central assumptions of the identity of the social sciences as an interpretation of socio-historical experience. By locating the discourses of the social sciences within the structures of experience that characterize modernity, Wagner in effect introduces a high degree of reflexivity into social science. His central argument is that because social science arose out of central experiences that are constitutive of modernity it is constantly presented with certain questions that are 'inescapable' but which are 'unattainable'. This is a contrast to the dominant assumption of positivistic science that science is self-legislating and can attain all that it sets out to achieve. The implication, too, is that much of postmodernist thought has sent social science in the wrong direction. However, one of his key points is that both modernist social science and its later critiques all represent valid modes of reasoning. Modernist social science began as a self-legislating project that rejected all traditional foundations for universalistic principles and formal kinds of communication that were not tied to substantive structures or transcendental principles. But this Enlightenment spirit became challenged by two alternatives: the postmodern position that sees modernity as seeking a different kind of foundationalism identified largely with science itself and a position that rejects both modernist and postmodernist alternatives but which does not simply seek to retreat to the premodern. This second position might be a more nuanced reinterpretation of the postmodernity already within modernity, a thesis that can be associated with a broad range of positions, ranging from Bauman to Habermas and Touraine. The social sciences emerged initially as part of the concern of modernity with reflexive self-understanding but increasingly lost this capacity as they distinguished themselves from philosophy, which in turn became preoccupied with other concerns and to which social science cannot return. Instead, there are certain key *problematiques* which have survived within social science and are constitutive of social science and social theory. The contemporary task is to recover such *problematiques*.

In this view, which can be related to Castoriadis, science derives its meaning from the concern with human autonomy that is central to the radical imagination of modernity and which is always in tension with the other face of modernity, namely rationality, the assumption that the world is in principle intelligible (Castoriadis, 1984). The problem, however, is that social science has lost its way: it has lost its capacity for self-questioning by assuming that autonomy and rationality are foundations rather than modes of problematization. In Wagner's view, social science must recover the project of modernity as a critical and therefore a self-limiting philosophy in the sense of a project that is willing to reflect on the conditions of the possibility of knowledge. This all suggests a deep sense of critique as a self-limiting mode of reasoning but one that, despite its modesty, offers many possibilities for social science. Wagner argues 'that there are *problematiques* that have been and will remain constitutive for socio-political modernity. Modernity is characterized by *problematiques* that remain open, not by specific solutions to given problems' (Wagner, 2001: 8). Some of the main ones are those of the certainty of our knowledge, the viability of the polity, the continuity of the self, the accessibility of the past and the transparency of the future. What is distinctive about these questions is their persistence not just in time but in all intellectual traditions. This is because answers can never be settled for once and for all and, more importantly, the different intellectual traditions are responses to the same problems. For this reason, it is important that social science must recognize a plurality of modes of theorizing and the possibility of some degree of communication across them.

A striking idea is that the social sciences occupy an 'interpretative space' in society, and in this sense the book offers a contribution to my theme of science as communication. The social sciences are part of the discursive self-understanding of social life and therefore entail an openness to the social that has always been denied in modernist social science. Since the 1990s this has all changed and social science has become more and more part of its object, as developments in postmodernism, constructivism, standpoint epistemology all illustrate. The result is that the door has been open to all kinds of relativism and to erasing the boundary between science and the social. One of the many merits of this position is that such radical contingency must be resisted in favour of a cognitive and epistmological imaginary within social science. In a move that is not too distant from Rorty's postmodern pragmatism or the sociological pragmatism of Boltanski and Thévenot, Wagner preserves a cognitive space for social science as a practice that is part of its object and yet with a rationale of its own (Boltanski and Thévenot, 1991). This space of social science is in those moments of crisis when social life becomes problematized. Much of the history of the social sciences and of social philosophy can be read as knowledge claims being made in problematic situations and with the practical aim to solve those problems.

This position in fact goes beyond pragmatism, which is limited in that it is confined to the unproblematical, whereas the position Wagner argues for is one in which epistemological claims are made in the process of solving problems. It is this respect that a communicative concept of knowledge becomes evident. Pragmatism '[u]underestimates the significance of the argumentative means to settle disputes in situations in which the interpretations of the "problem" as well as the proposals to deal with it are diverse and contradictory' (Wagner, 2001: 31).

Bent Flyvbjerg's *Making Social Matter* gives a strong argument for the public relevance of social science today (Flyvbjerg, 2000). He takes his cue from Aristotle, who he reinterprets via Foucault. The objective is to reposition the social sciences in terms of a theory of values and power. Aristotle's notion of *phronesis* (practical value knowledge) stands for a conception of knowledge that is different from *episteme* (scientific knowledge) and from *techne* (technical or instrumental knowledge), he argues. It represents a form of knowledge that is particularly pertinent to the social sciences in that it addresses the role of action in human knowledge. This is a strong argument for the distinctiveness of the social sciences. Despite the critique of positivism, the social sciences have been dominated in practice by the epistemological methods of the natural sciences. But the real strength of the social sciences is not in predictive or explanatory theory but in reflexive understanding, which is the weakness of the natural sciences.

The central questions are those of what is knowledge, what are the conditions of the possibility of knowledge? However, his questioning is more direct and more Aristotelian than Kantian, but contains the same pragmatism: 'how do people acquire knowledge and skills?' His point of departure is the essentially phenomenological role of context, judgement and practical knowledge in human learning. Rejecting the dominant paradigms inherited from the natural sciences, Flyvbjerg argues for the appropriateness of this model of learning for the social sciences, which must recover their hermeneutic capacities. Before commenting further on this it must be noted that this book rejects any common ground between the natural and the social sciences. This is surprising as recent tendencies suggest the emergence of a post-positivistic natural science. Admitting that the epistemological basis of the natural sciences has become more complex, any convergence is rejected by Flyvbjerg as the arguments for such convergence are weak. The reality is that the social sciences are too different, they do not have the same tendency towards paradigm formation, progress and above all their object is interactive. The distinctive feature of the social sciences is precisely that their objects 'talk back', necessitating what Giddens, following Garfinkel, has called a 'double hermeneutic': social science as a second-order interpretation. This is the tradition Flyvbjerg represents and which he associates with Aristotle: 'Today the Aristotelian question of balancing instrumental rationality with value-rationality is forcing its way back to the foreground. Problems with both biosphere and sociosphere indicate that social and political development based on instrumental rationality alone is not sustainable' (Flyvbjerg, 2000: 53).

It is of course only in a very loose sense that this is an Aristotelian approach, but a contemporary reading of Aristotle does offer a challenge to the modernist preoccupation with *episteme* and *techne* as dominant forms of instrumental rationality. This reading is one that emphasizes the ethical dimension in phrenetic social science as a deliberation about values as embodied in social action and human experience. In so far as it is oriented towards action, it suggests a certain pragmatism. But where Flyvbjerg differs from other hermeneutic approaches is in the central position he gives to power. In a reading of Habermas and Foucault, he introduces the idea of power as constitutive of social science, and in this discussion he adopts a more Foucauldian approach. The value of Foucault's approach is that it emphasizes the pervasiveness of power in social relations. Public discourse as in Habermas's terms must be reconceived in terms of power. An important point in comparing Foucault to Derrida: the former's genealogical approach is essentially an argument for contextualizing social science, while the latter's deconstructivism is essentially a 'textualization': 'The context of practices disciplines interpretation' (p. 115). In short, Foucault's contextualization does not amount to the relativism that has been characteristic of the poststructural movement and which has become a central feature of postmodern thought.

Adapting Foucault's notion of power to the Aristotelian phronesis, a conception of social science emerges that is very strongly based on qualitative case study research. While quantitative research has its role in social science, the real achievement of the social sciences is not breadth but depth of analysis. Flyvbjerg argues that Foucault offers a basis for this kind of social science for in his work we find the Aristotelian phrenetic concern with 'particular circumstances'. This produces a new set of questions for social science, such as: What are the most immediate and the most local forms of power? How are the different kinds of power linked together and what kind of rationalities have they created? How can power be challenged? Social science has a future, according to Flyvbjerg, only if it does three things. It must firstly cease to imitate the natural sciences. It will never have the same predictive and explanatory power as the natural sciences. A second challenge is that it must focus on issues of values and power in real-life contexts. Thirdly, it must have a public role rather than being a sterile academic pursuit. In all of these senses, this is a conception of social science that places communication at the centre of scientific knowledge. By this is not meant the communication of an established body of knowledge, but a more dynamic set of practices.

This conception of social science has much going for it. It is mostly a defence of what is already the practice in social science and as such it avoids an overly normative critique of research. It also avoids unnecessary issues of relativism, since today we have to accept at some level a self-limiting universalism. In Flyvbjerg's case there is no suggestion that the actual practice of social research is driven by theory; although this move beyond the concerns of modern social theory does come at a cost since social science is reduced to a very specific set of problems that are amenable to case study research. However, the question is not this important question of theory and research but whether Flyvbjerg has defined too tightly the identity of the social sciences as in opposition to the natural sciences and as a result underestimates the penetration of communication into all the sciences. He clearly thinks the natural sciences are too closed and that their impact on the social science has been at best very damaging. I think it has been established that the latter has indeed been the case but this does not mean that the natural sciences are in fact closed in positivistic discourses; that is, non positivistic communication between the natural and social sciences is now possible. But this is perhaps to go beyond the scope of this book, whose aim is limited to the territory and method of the social sciences. In sum, Flyvberg's book provides the social sciences with what they need: a defence of their autonomy against positivism and a defence that can be made in terms of the actual practice of social science as having a public role.

The idea of a public science is also present in Helga Nowotny, Peter Scott and Michael Gibbons's *Knowledge and the Public in an Age of Uncertainty*. While their concerns are not confined to social science, but with the institution of science more generally, their interpretation of the current status and function of science in the 'knowledge society' is highly relevant to the issues considered above. The point of departure here is neither primarily epistemological nor methodological, but an institutional analysis of knowledge cultures.

This book is a development of, and response to the debate around, their earlier *New Production of Knowledge* which announced the arrival of a new Mode 2 knowledge that is shaped in the context of application and which is more reflexive than Mode 1, which is disciplinary bound and basic rather than applied (Gibbons et al. 1984). The present book is more concerned with the social implications of the production of knowledge than the earlier book which was conceived more empirically and led many critics to the view that it was endorsing the turn to applied science. The authors argue that the division between science and society is breaking down in the emergence of a contextualized science. Communication is now two-way: from society to science as well as from science to society. A key idea is that science like much of culture is 'transgressive', in that there is more and more de- differentiation in relations between the state and the market, science and other forms of knowledge, science and politics for example: 'the great conceptual, and organizational, categories of the modern world – state, market, culture, science – have become highly permeable, even transgressive'. It is not only in the social sciences that society can answer back to science, as Flyvbjerg assumes. All of science is more responsive to the social than ever before: 'The context speaks back', the authors argue. The relation between science and society is not causal and linear but reflexive and interactive. Both society and science are having to live in a world of ever greater uncertainty.

The penetration of uncertainty into the heart of science does not mean a total loss in the autonomy of science or the reduction of science to applied pursuits in which it is driven by instrumental dictates, such as those of the market. New spaces are emerging in which science is conducted, such as transdisciplinarity, as opposed to the weaker models of interdisciplinarity. However, these spaces are not literally spatial but reflexive in the sense of a discourse that is becoming constitutive of the object it portrays (Nowotny et al., 2001: 109). Many examples of this contextualization of science in society are given, suggesting a weak constructivist position. The intention is not to reduce reflexivity to an instrumentalization of science. Contextualization can be 'weak' or 'strong'; it is 'socially robust' in that it is shaped by ever more social actors. This means that science is more contested today as a result of the increasingly presence of multiple actors in the domains of science. However, it does not mean a crisis for science, for there is no reason the emergence of a more socially robust science is less reliable. For the authors of this book the conclusion is that the epistemological core of science is empty: 'Our contention, contentiously, is that the epistemological core is empty – or, alternatively and perhaps more accurately, crowded and heterogeneous. That irreducible core of cognitive values and social practices, which once enabled good science to be distinguished from bad science (if not – quite – truth from untruth), has been dispersed, or distributed, across more, and more heterogeneous, knowledge environments' (Nowotny et al., 2001: 179).

But this in fact leads paradoxically to an increase in the power of science: on the one side, there is a general loss in the ability of science to define reality and on the other side a growing ability of science to intervene in the world (Nowotny et al., 2001: 184–5). The crucial task for science as it becomes more and more a part of the agora – the public realm – is to become more communicative and interconnected with society: 'Our conception of science has to find room for the wide range of people who engage in material scientific activities and are linked in concrete ways to other social spaces in the agora that go far beyond the laboratory' (Nowotny et al., 2001: 197).

As a result of changes within science and within society more generally, a communicative kind of science is more possible. There has always been what the authors of this book call a 'co-evolution' of science and society. Today, these forms of evolution have become more intertwined, necessitating a new way of thinking about science as a form of communication.

The three positions discussed here share a view of science as open to new questions. For Peter Wagner's book this was conceived in terms of certain epistemological questions that provide the basic cognitive structures of modern social science; for Flyvbjerg the methodological practice of social science can be seen as a deeper form of social reflexivity; and for Nowotny, Scott and Gibbons all of science is becoming more and more contextualized, and as it does, it becomes more communicative. The emerging picture of knowledge that emerges from their work is one of the incompleteness of science in an ever more public context. A sense is conveyed that one of the strengths of science is its capacity for reflexive engagement with its object and that the new climate of uncertainty is not a threat to science. All positions affirm the resilience of social science, which is variously seen as methodologically, epistemologically and institutionally adaptable to changing circumstances without losing its reliability. In this respect the debate on method can move beyond the postmodernist and constructivist critiques with their announcements of the end of science. The move from a self-referential, modernist and universalistic conception of science to a more contextualized one in which relativism and uncertainty become more pronounced offers the possibility of a communicative science. However, this will require greater agency on the part of social science than is currently the case to take advantage of the opportunities of what is not only a knowledge society but is also a global society. The biggest problem is that the three dimensions of epistemology, empirical method, and social relevance do not amount to a common framework for social science. Consequently its communicative capacity is limited and social science can easily be either marginalized or instrumentalized. What is often forgotten too is that social science is also a mode of reflection that is primarily expressed as a form of writing. In the cases of disciplines such as sociology and anthropology this is particularly the case. Sociologists produce written texts and it is probably in this that they are closest to the human sciences. Written discourse plays a lesser role in the experimental sciences. When one considers the most influential works in sociology, it can be seen that they all share a capacity to offer far-reaching interpretations of the age. But it is the nature of these interpretations that their message cannot easily be finalized, as has been argued by Peter Wagner. The defence of social science as a publicly relevant activity must not lose sight of the openness of its particular kind of communication.

Conclusion: Social Science as Discursive Practice

The historical overview of the philosophical debates on social science presented in this book has been undertaken from the contemporary situation of social science at the end of the twentieth century. This presupposes a particular understanding of the present situation of social science. For over one hundred years the positivist dispute has shaped the self-understanding of social science. The argument I have proposed in this book is that when we look at contemporary debates on science there is very little left of that controversy: nature and society no longer seem to be the opposites they were previously believed to be. Since the 1970s the philosophy of social science has moved onto new issues beyond those of the neo-Kantian heritage of explanation and understanding. My overview points to new areas of contention, of which one is between realism and constructivism. This debate does not coincide with positivist explanation and hermeneutic-interpretative understanding since the proponents of realism do not hold to a positivistic conception of science, whether social or natural; and the proponents of constructivism do not confine themselves to the purely hermeneutic.

One of the implications of recent debates in the philosophy of science is that natural science no longer corresponds to the model of positivistic knowledge. Thus, radical constructivism, finalization research and the idea of a policy-oriented science point to a new conception of the link in the relationship between knowledge and society, or science as a cognitive system as an institutional system. Reality is no longer seen as an object but is itself constituted by scientific discourse, which also can no longer be seen to be independent of society. While the social sciences have continued to retain their autonomy from the natural science, there are indications of common concerns. The most significant of these relate to the rise of a self-reflective kind of knowledge involving new links in the relationship between the cognitive and the institutional structures of science. It has been suggested that a new commonality between the natural and the social sciences lies in the area of nature, for nature as a social construction has become a new theme in a social science responsive to changing social and natural worlds. The fact that nature for late modern society has exceeded its carrying capacity–a situation that has given rise to new questions about the democratization of science and technology – points to the broader issue of the public role of all of knowledge. The way we conceive of this undoubtedly will be one of the central questions in the future. It may be suggested that the way forward for science will be whether it can align itself with democratic change in society. As Steve Fuller (1993: 281) argues, the crucial question is whether science is compatible with democracy. We are not only living in a world dominated by science but also one shaped by democracy. Science and democracy are the two great value systems of modernity, but have not yet been brought together. From a theoretical point of view this raises the possibility of discussing the social production of knowledge from a constructivist standpoint (Fuller, 1993: 254). Can constructivism be conceived democratically? This is one of the central issues in new debates on knowledge.

The varieties of constructivism and realism I have emphasized are united in their adherence to a critical social science. While the two sides reveal many differences, they also have much in common, suggesting that the future direction in the philosophy of social science may point towards reconciliation. Such a reconciliation may not be unlike that undertaken by Max Weber, who sought to overcome the neo-Kantian dualism of the sciences, or Habermas's and Apel's attempt in the 1960s and 1970s to reconcile explanation, understanding and critique in a reconstructive critical hermeneutics. If such a synthesis is possible between realism and constructivism in the future the conception of social science that will emerge will therefore be more an expression of the divisive heritage of post-empiricism. In other words, there is little to be gained by defining social science in opposition to natural science when in fact the most serious problems derive from the practice of social science itself.

These problems relate to the question of the connection between knowledge and its public role. Since the late 1980s, a central question in this context has revolved around the notion of policy-oriented social science. Many social scientists have become conscious of the failure of the social sciences to deliver the promises of founders whose vision of social science was the amelioration of social evils and the rational reconstruction of society (Beck and Bonss, 1989; Wagner et al., 1991; Biervert and Dierkes, 1992). While the idea of 'policy science', in the sense of a commitment to the improvement of public policy, goes back to the late 1940s and was always an essential dimension to the evolution of social science as a profession, the question of the public role of social science has become a more recent and pressing question. However, the terms of the debate are very different today for it is no longer a question of the institutionalization of social science as a professional activity but is a matter of the public role of knowledge. Debates around the 'implementation' of scientific research raise questions that penetrate to the heart of science and its relevance for society.

As indicated in the previous chapter, I believe contemporary developments in the philosophy and sociology of social science point less to a confrontation between realism and constructivism – though this is quite clearly where the debate lies at the moment – than one within constructivism. The principal issue at stake in the internal division of constructivism relates to the question of agency with respect to self-reflexivity. Constructivists are divided on whether self-reflexivity refers to agency or autopoetic systems. The synthesis between realism and constructivism I am arguing for, will require an internal critique of constructivism since this is also a too diffuse and indeed a confused category. Above all, what is needed is a clear sense of what I have been calling radical or critical constructivism as opposed to the autopoetic notion of constructivism or even deconstructionism. This is so because a close reading of constructivism reveals that those who advocate a critical constructivism are closer to critical realism than to postmodernist deconstructionism and systems theory. Realism, on the other hand, will have to undergo a reappraisal of its commitment to critique, which occupies an unclear status in realist philosophies.

At the moment post-empiricist social science is too internally divided for any one philosophical position to claim paradigmatic dominance. This is all the more reason why a synthesis is required in order to bring social science out of its present malaise.

What needs to be fundamentally rethought is the concept of reflexivity. This is the key to rescuing constructivism from its present situation. Reflexivity points to the ability of science to transcend itself. Theorists have understood this in different but closely related ways. Giddens emphasizes the ability of science as an institution to reflect upon itself. In his model scientific reflexivity is primarily carried out by expert-systems (though some of his recent work (1996: 69) which emphasizes the idea of the 'knowledgeable human agent' and the need for a recovery of 'practical consciousness' suggests a different reading). Beck demands a more open form of reflexivity which is carried out by opposition publics. In contrast to both Beck and Giddens, Wynne (1996) argues for a greater mediation of experts and lay cultures. This position is also represented by Fuller (1993) who defends the democratization of knowledge as an empowering of the public. Nico Stehr (1994: 95) develops Giddens thesis of the fundamental 'knowledgability' of social actors and advances the theory of the 'knowledge society' in which the capacity for society to act upon itself and bring about normative innovation is increasing.

While Giddens and Beck have mostly written about reflexivity in relation to natural science, Bourdieu emphasizes a more transformative kind of reflexivity which points to the core of social science. His concept of reflexivity emphasizes the public commitment of social science. This concern with the political-ethical foundation of science is also central to Habermas and Apel's theory of communication. The central and concluding thesis of this book is that the most important challenge for the philosophy and sociology of social science is to radicalize the thesis of scientific reflexivity around a theory of the social communication of science: it is neither a question of self-reflexivity by expert systems nor one of oppositional cultures, but of the mediation of science and society around public discourse. To conceive of social science in this way is to locate social scientific knowledge as a part of a wider discourse of discursive democratization (Habermas, 1996a).

I wish to suggest that social science in breaking from positivism generated new kinds of problems, of which the most consequential has been the failure of social science to mediate with society. None of the post-empiricist philosophies of social science have radicalized the idea of self-reflectivity which they have presupposed. In short, the problem of social science today is the problem of the relationship of science to society. It is a question of the public role of social science. How are we to conceive of this relationship? Extreme constructivists, and some postmodernists, deny the possibility of science having an emancipatory function. Social science is confined to the practice of deconstructing social constructions without offering an alternative. In jettisoning an ethical foundation, deconstructionism generated a new kind of relativism which leaves the problem of indeterminacy too open. The proponents of systems theory, such as Luhmann, advocate an autopoietic conception of science encased in its own self-generating discourse: scientific communication can never mediate itself with public discourse since these operate within different systems which never come together. For Luhmann science is a closed system.

In order to bring the debate one step further I wish to propose the concept of social science as a 'discursive practice' to characterize the contemporary situation. This concept is intended to express the communicative presuppositions of science as a social institution, or as Richard Harvey Brown (1989) says, 'social science as a civic discourse'. The idea of social science as a discursive practice is addressed to the question of the mediation of scientific discourse with social discourses. To envisage social science as 'discursive practice' it must be recognized that the social situation of science today is one in which science has on all fronts lost its claim to uniqueness. The implications of Beck's critique of science apply not only to the technical and natural sciences, but also to the social sciences. Social science cannot hide behind a protective veil of methodology and theoretical discourse any more than the natural sciences can resist the public critique of scientism and demands for accountabilty.

Such a perspective allows us to defend the prospect of social science as a professionalized discourse without being the closed autopoietic system as in Luhmann. The question of the public role of social science as a communicatively permeated discourse refers less to the question of whether the social scientist is an intellectual in so far as this is a relationship which excludes everyday life and the concerns of critical publics. In this context, the theory-research problem is also pertinent to the extent to which the problem of social science today is one of both the practical relevance of both theory and research. The tendency in recent years has been for a divorce between theory and research to the extent to which theory itself is becoming a new professional discourse as irrelevant to social communication as traditional positivistic empirical research. One of the challenges for the future will be the incorporation of theory into empirical social research.

The discursive turn in science being advocated here is a response to the rise of a new social trend in which society has become 'scientized' and science 'socialized'. What this means is that society has come to challenge science's monopoly of scientific rationality and as a result science is becoming socialized. As Beck has argued, the tendency towards the scientization of society has been apparent for some time in the case of the natural sciences which cannot be seen as closed systems. However, Beck emphasizes the oppositional nature of social reactions to science neglecting the fact that science itself is being shaped by society. The model I am proposing, then, is one that stresses far more the discursive component in the science-society nexus. In the social sciences something similar can be observed, though with the difference that social science unlike, for instance biotechnological science, does not present a threat to society in the same way. Yet, the question cannot be avoided of why does society need social science. What is the relationship between science and society?

A discursively mediated relationship between social science and society takes place in the public identification and definition of collective problems. This is the crucial dimension to social science as a discursive practice. Social science is shaped in the definition of problems. To that extent it itself is constructed in the process of problem identification. The question of the normative foundations of social science cannot be answered merely by reference to science as an expert culture. The professionalized culture of social science does not itself construct social problems from its own discourse but does so in response to public and media agenda-setting. Problem construction is a dynamic process involving many social actors who define, negotiate and thereby construct problems. In this way social reality enters social scientific discourse as a constructed reality and one which is the product of contentious action. Habermas (1996b: 5) has commented:

> Today in contrast to the 1970s, we find that in politics the euphoria over planning has ceased, together with the belief in science. This change in climate has had some benefits, as is evident in the sensitization concerning the dangers of nuclear and gene technology. Concerns with the consequences of technology have emerged in diverse fields. Here, a kind of counter-expertise came to be established which recognizes that there is no one Science which itself is neutral; scientific activity is anything but monolithic – it fragments into a number of competing viewpoints that are shot through with values.

The problem with Marxism, Habermas argues, was that it was too much focused on crisis theories, 'with the consequence that there are today no constructive models' (1996a: 7). In my estimation, the discourse theory of Habermas and Apel provides an important basis for a new constructivist conceptualization of social science around communication and democracy.

These considerations suggest that social science as a discursive practice does not speak in the name of emancipation as such. This is because the nature of discourse is 'indeterminacy', the theme of

James Bohman's (1991) important study: Social science can not itself provide answers to social problems. Social science must accept the burden of the loss of certainty in our post-ideological age. Indeterminacy is the epistemological condition of science in an age of uncertainty. With the collapse and disintegration of the great ideologies of modernity, there has been a loss in the sense of certainty that has characterized the period of time that has been influenced by the Enlightenment. Habermas refers to this as a new 'obscurity' (1989b: 54) which results from the loss of faith in the ideal of a society organized around social labour: 'The New Obscurity is part of a situation in which a welfare state program that continues to be nourished by a utopia of social labor is losing its power to project future possibilities for a collectively better and less endangered way of life'. The uncertainty that has characterized Western societies for the last decade has now penetrated into the heart of modern social science. Indeterminacy and reflexivity are therefore closely bound up with each other: the uncertainty in the political-utopian direction of society encourages reflexivity in cultural production. Social science shares this sense of uncertainty, which is why the concept of indeterminacy cannot be confined merely to the reflexivity of science. Such concerns have been central to postmodernism, but as I have argued postmodernism failed to express the democratic possibilities that the advent of the 'knowledge society' has brought about. However, by shifting the terms of debate beyond postmodernism to new debates on radical constructivism we can see how the indeterminacy of our knowledge society offers new possibilities for science and democracy. As Alberto Melucci (1996: 224) wrote: 'The intellectual has no new truths to bring into the world; these are all deeply embedded in people's own experiences and ways of defining their own worlds. The social scientist among them can only aid the actors in releasing the suppressed contents constituting their self-understanding'.

The emancipatory function of social science is confined to its mediatory role in clarifying the direction of social change. This, then, places the idea of social time at the centre of the philosophy of social science, for time itself is a socially constructed variable. The idea of indeterminacy highlights the contemporary experience of a new time consciousness taking shape around reflexivity and social transformation. One of the great failures of the classical approaches is that they failed to grasp the transformative power of agency. The positivist tradition confined its analysis to the atomistic units of society' and in its French classical phase social change was subordinated to a historicist model; the hermeneutic tradition did not look beyond the creation of meaning to provide an analysis of social structures; and Marxism attributed to agency a privileged role in history. The problem of Marxism from the perspective of a conception of social science as discursive practice is that its cognitive system derives from a non-communicative understanding of knowledge.

It may be the case that a new unity of science is emerging with nature as a mediating focus. The ecological debate (Lash et al., 1996) reveals the link between time and nature. As Barbara Adam (1996) argues, we need to have an ethical engagement with the future, a theme which is reflected in much of contemporary ecological debate. This reflexive turn in modern consciousness must be extended to the social sciences in order that they will respond to the changed ecological environment.

Reflexivity in social science is part of a wider social discourse whose contemporary manifestation is the idea of societal responsibility. The *leitmotif* of responsibility challenges both the conservative positivistic view that science is value free and the radical view that science holds the key to political practice. John O'Neill (1995: 185) writes about the politics of mutual knowledge. In his view 'we may formulate the problem of the relationship between science and democracy as a communicative task to be addressed to the mobilization of members' commitment to the goals and institutionalized allocations of scientific and technical resources employed to translate social goals into daily conveniences, rewards, and deterrents'. O'Neill argues that democratic legitimation is formed in the constitution of a communication community in which scientists and politicians are open to responses from the public. Science thus has a crucial role to play in the articulation of social goals. He disagrees with Giddens, claiming that common-sense knowledge and values do not depend upon scientific reconstruction for the exercise of critical reflection (1995: 189). 'In short', he argues, 'the social world is not, as constructivist analysts wish to make out, an intrinsic puzzle that requires scientific mediation and reconstruction in order to make rational sense' (1995: 162).

Post-empiricist social science cannot assume that the problems with the older models can be overcome in the forging of new links between theory and practice. The change in the context and conditions of the application of social scientific knowledge during the past few decades has fractured the assumption of a link between theory and practice. It is precisely the severance of this connection that has plunged social science into the deep waters of communication and discourse, or, more generally, mediation.

Bibliography

Abell, P. (2000) Sociological theory and rational choice theory, in B. S. Turner (ed.) *The Blackwell Companion to Social Theory*, 2nd edn. Oxford: Blackwell.

Aboulafia, M., Bookman, M., and Kemp, C., (eds) (2001) *Habermas and Pragmatism*. London: Routledge.

Adam, B. (1996) Re-vision: the centrality of time for an ecological social science perspective, in S. Lash, et al. (eds) *Risk, Environment and Modernity: Towards a New Ecology*. London: Sage.

Adorno, T. W. et al. (1976) *The Positivist Dispute in German Sociology*. London: Heinemann.

Alexander, J. (1982) *Theoretical Logic in Sociology*, vol. 1. *Positivism, Presuppositions, and Current Controversies*. Berkeley: University of California Press.

Alexander, J. (1996) The centrality of the classics, in S. Turner, (ed.) *Social Theory and Sociology: The Classics and Beyond*. Oxford: Blackwell.

Apel, K.-O. (1978a) *Diskurs und Verantwortung*. Frankfurt: Suhrkamp.

Apel, K.-O. (1978b) The conflicts of our time and the problem of political ethics', in F. Dallmayr, (ed.) *From Contract to Community: Political Theory at the Cross Roads*. New York: Dekker.

Apel, K.-O. (1979a) The common presuppositions of hermeneutics and ethics: types of rationality beyond science and technology, *Research in Phenomenology*, 9: 35–53.

Apel, K.-O. (1979b) Types of social science in light of human cognitive interests, in S. Brown (ed.) *Philosophical Disputes in the Social Sciences*. Brighton: Harvester Press.

Apel, K.-O. (1980) *The Transformation of Philosophy*. London: Routledge.

Apel, K.-O. (1984a) *Understanding and Explanation: A Transcendental-Pragmatic Perspective*. Cambridge, Mass: MIT Press.

Apel, K.-O. (1984b) The situation of humanity as an ethical problem, in *Praxis International*, 4, (3): 250–65.

Apel, K.-O. (1997) Auflösung der Diskursethik?, in *Auseinandersetzungen: In Verteidigung des transzendentalpragmatichen Ansatzes*. Frankfurt: Suhrkamp.

Archer, M. (1995) *Realist Social Theory: The Morphogenetic Approach*. Cambridge: Cambridge University Press.
Aronwitz, S. (1988) Foreword to Alain Touraine's *Return of the Actor*. Minneapolis: University of Minnesota Press.
Ashmore, M. (1989) *The Reflexive Thesis: Writing the Sociology of Scientific Knowledge*. Chicago: Chicago University Press.
Axelrod, R. (1984) *The Evolution of Cooperation*. New York: Basic Books.
Baehr, P. and O'Brien, M. (1994) Founders, classics and the concept of a cannon, *Current Sociology*: 42 (1) 1–148.
Baert, P. (1998) *Social Theory in the Twentieth Century*. Cambridge: Polity Press.
Baert, P. (2004) Pragmatism as a philosophy of the social sciences, *European Journal of Social Theory*, 7 (3): 355–69.
Baert, P. and Turner, B. (eds) (2004) American pragmatism and European social and political theory. Special issue of *European Journal of Social Theory*, 7(3).
Barnes, B. (1974) *Scientific Knowledge and Sociological Theory*. London: Routledge and Kegan Paul.
Barnes, B. (1982) *T. S. Kuhn and Social Science*. London: Macmillan.
Barnes, B. (1995) *The Elements of Social Theory*. London: UCL Press.
Barthes, R. (1973) *Mythologies*. London: Granada.
Bauman, Z. (1987) *Hermeneutics and Social Science*. London: Hutchinson.
Bauman, Z. (1988) *Legislators and Interpreters*. Ithaca: Cornell University Press.
Beck, U. (1992) *The Risk Society: Towards a New Modernity*. Cambridge: Polity.
Beck, U. (1995) *Ecological Enlightenment: Essays on the Politics of the Risk Society*. New Jersey: Humanities Press.
Beck, U. (1996) World risk society as cosmopolitan society? Ecological questions in a framework of manufactured uncertainties, *Theory, Culture and Society*, 13 (4): 1–32.
Beck, U. and Bonss, W. (eds) (1989) *Weder Socialtechnologie noch Aufklärung? Analysen zur Verwendung sozialwissenschaftlichen Wissens*. Frankfurt: Suhrkamp.
Beck, U., Giddens, A., and Lash, S. (eds) (1994) *Reflexive Modernization: Politics Tradition and Aesthetics in the Modern Social Order*. Cambridge: Polity Press.
Benton, T. (1977) *Philosophical Foundations of the Three Sociologies*. Routledge and Kegan Paul.
Benton, T. and Craib, I. (2001) *Philosophy of Social Science*. London: Routledge.
Berger, P. (1966) *Invitation to Sociology: A Humanistic Approach*. Harmondsworth: Penguin.

Berger, P. and Luckmann, T. (1966) *The Social Construction of Reality*. Harmondsworth: Penguin.

Bernstein, R. (1979) *The Restructuring of the Social and Political Sciences*. Oxford: Blackwell.

Bernstein, R. (1983) *Beyond Objectivism and Relativism: Science, Hermeneutics and Praxis*. Oxford: Blackwell.

Bernstein, R. (1991) *The New Constellation: The Ethical Horizons of Modernity/Postmodernity*. Cambridge: Polity.

Bhaskar, R. (1978) *A Realist Theory of Science*. Brighton: Harvester.

Bhaskar, R. (1979) *The Possibility of Naturalism*. Brighton: Harvester.

Bhaskar, R. (1986) *Scientific Realism and Human Emancipation*. London: Verso.

Bhaskar, R. (1991) *Philosophy and the Idea of Freedom*. Oxford: Blackwell.

Bhaskar, R. (1993) *Dialectic*. London: Verso.

Biervert, B. and Dierkes, M. (1992) Introduction: European social science, in M. Dierkes, and B. Biervert (eds) *Social Science in Transition: Assessment and Outlook*. Boulder: Westview.

Bijker, W. E. et al. (eds) (1987) *The Social Construction of Technological Systems*. Cambridge, MA: MIT Press.

Blaikie, N. (1993) *Approaches to Social Inquiry*. Cambridge: Polity.

Blau, P. (1964) *Exchange and Power in Social Life*. New York: Wiley.

Bleicher, J. (1980) *Contemporary Hermeneutics: Hermeneutics as Method, Philosophy, and Critique*. London: Routledge and Kegan Paul.

Bloor, D. (1991) *Knowledge and Social Imagery*, 2nd edn. Chicago: Chicago University Press.

Boden, M. (1979) *Piaget*. London: Fontana.

Bohman, J. (1991) *New Philosophy of Social Science: Problems of Indeterminacy*. Cambridge: Polity.

Böhme, G. (ed.) (1976) *Protophysik: Für und wider eine konstruktistische Wissenschaftstheorie der Physik*. Frankfurt: Suhrkamp.

Böhme, G. and Schäfer, W. (1983) Towards a social science of nature, in W. Schäfer, (ed.) *Finalization in Science*. Dordrecht: Reidel.

Böhme, G., van den Daele, W. and Hohenfeld, R. (1983) Finalization revisited, in W. Schäfer, (ed.) *Finalization in Science*. Dordrecht: Reidel.

Boltanski, L. and Thévenot, L. (1991) *De la justification: Les economies de la grandeur*. Paris: Gallimard.

Bottomore, T. (1975) *Sociology as Social Criticism*. London: Allen and Unwin.

Bourdieu, P. (1990) *The Logic of Practice*. Cambridge: Polity Press.

Bourdieu, P. (1995) *Sociology in Question*. London: Sage.

Bourdieu, P. (1996) Toward a reflexive sociology, in S. Turner, (ed.) *Social Theory and Sociology: The Classics and Beyond*. Oxford: Blackwell.

Bourdieu, P. (2004) *Signs of science and reflexivity*. Cambridge: Polity Press.

Bourdieu, P. and Wacquant, L. (1992) *An Invitation to Reflexive Sociology*. Chicago: University of Chicago Press.

Brante, T. et al. (eds) (1993) *Controversial Science: From Content to Communication*. Albany: SUNY Press.

Brown, R. (1989) *Social Science as Civic Discourse: Essays on the Invention, Legitimation, and Uses of Social Theory*. Chicago: University of Chicago Press.

Bryant, C. (1985) *Positivism in Social Theory and Research*. London: Macmillan.

Bryant, C. (1995) *Practical Sociology: Post-Empiricism and the Reconstruction of Theory and Application*. Cambridge: Polity Press.

Byrne, D. (1998) *Complexity Theory and the Social Sciences*. London: Routledge.

Calhoun, C. (1995) *Critical Theory of Society*. Oxford: Blackwell.

Castoriadis, C. (1984) *The Imaginary Institution of Society*. Cambridge: Polity Press.

Coleman, J. S. (1990) *Foundations of Social Theory*. Cambridge: Polity Press.

Collier, A. (1994) *Critical Realism: An Introduction to Roy Bhaskar's Philosophy*. London: Verso.

Daele, van den, W. (1977) The social construction of science: institutionalization and definition of positive science in the latter half of the seventeenth century', in E. Mendelsohn, et al. (eds) *The Social Production of Scientific Knowledge*. Dordrecht: Reidel.

Daele, van den, W. (1983) Science in a crisis of legitimation, in W. Schäfer, (ed.) *Finalization in Science*. Dordrecht: Reidel.

Daele, van den, W. (1992) Concepts of nature in modern societies and nature as a theme in sociology, in M., Dierkes, and B. Biervert. (eds) *Social Science in Transition: Assessment and Outlook*. Boulder: Westview.

David, M. (2005) *Science in Society*. London: Palgrave.

Davidson, D. (1984) On the very idea of a conceptual scheme, *Inquiries into Truth and Interpretation*. Oxford: Clarendon Press.

Delanty, G. (1999) *Social Theory in a Changing World: Conceptions of Modernity*. Cambridge: Polity Press.

Delanty, G. (2000) *Modernity and Postmodernity: Knowledge, Power, the Self*. London: Sage.

Delanty, G. (2001) *Challenging Knowledge: The University in the Knowledge Society*. Buckingham: Open University Press.

Delanty, G. and Strydom, P. (eds) (2003) *Philosophies of Social Science: The Classic and Contemporary Readings*. Buckingham: Open University Press.

Delmar, F. and McCarthy, T. (eds) (1977) *Understanding and Social Inquiry*. Notre Dame: University of Notre Dame Press.

Dettling, W. (1996) Fach ohne Boden: Brauchen wir überhaupt noch Soziologen?' *Die Zeit*, 5 January.

Dewey J. (1927) *The Public and its Problems*. New York: Holt.

Dierkes, M. and Biervert, B. (eds) (1992) *Social Science in Transition: Assessment and Outlook*. Boulder: Westview.

Dilthey, W. (1989) *Introduction to the Human Sciences (Selected Works vol. 1)*. Princeton: Princeton University Press.

Durkheim, E. (1978) *Institutional Analysis*. Chicago: University of Chicago Press.

Eder, K. (1996) *The Social Construction of Nature*. London: Sage.

Fay, B. (1975) *Social Theory and Political Practice*. London: Allen and Unwin.

Feyerabend, P. (1975) *Against Method: Outline of an Anarchistic Theory of Knowledge*. London: Verso.

Feyerabend, P. (1978) *Science in a Free Society*. London: New Left Books.

Flyvbjerg, B. (2000) *Making Social Science Matter: Why Social Inquiry Fails and How it Can Succeed Again*. Cambridge: Cambridge University Press.

von Foerster, H. (1981) *Observing Systems*. Seaside, CA: Intersystems Publications.

von Foerster, H. and Zopf, G. (eds) (1962) *Principles of Self-Organization*. New York: Pergamon.

Forester, J. (ed.) (1985) *Critical Theory and Public Life*. Cambridge, MA: MIT Press.

Foucault, M. (1970) *The Order of Things*. London: Tavistock.

Foucault, M. (1980) *The History of Sexuality*, vol. 1. London: Penguin.

Fuchs, S. (1992) *The Professional Quest for Truth*. Abany, NY: SUNY Press.

Fuller, S. (1992) Being there with Thomas Kuhn: a parable for postmodern times, *History and Theory*, 31: 241–75.

Fuller, S. (1993) *Philosophy, Rhetoric and the End of Knowledge*. Madison: University of Wisconsin Press.

Fuller, S. (1994) The reflexive politics of constructivism, *History of the Human Sciences*, 7 (1): 87–93.

Fuller, S. (2000a) *Thomas Kuhn: A Philosophical History for Our Times*. Chicago: University of Chicago Press.

Fuller, S. (2000b) *The Governance of Science*. Buckingham: Open University Press.

Furner, M. (1975) *Advocacy and Objectivity: Crises in the Professionalization of American Social Science, 1865-1905*. Lexington, Kentucky: University of Kentucky Press.

Gadamer, H.-G. (1979) *Truth and Method*. 2nd edn. London: Sheed and Ward.

Garfinkel, A. (1981) *Forms of Explanation: Rethinking the Questions in Social Theory*. New Haven: Yale University Press.

Gergen, K. (1994) *Realities and Relationships: Soundings in Social Construction*. Cambridge, MA: MIT Press.

Gergen, K. (2001) *Social Construction in Context*. London: Sage.

Gergen, M. and Gergen, K. (eds) (2003) *Social Construction: A Reader*. London: Sage.

Gibbons, M., Limoges, C., Nowotny, H., Schwartzman, S., Scott, P. and Trow, M. (1984) *The New Production of Knowledge*. London: Sage.

Giddens, A. (1974) *Positivism and Sociology*. London: Hutchinson.

Giddens, A. (1976) *New Rules of the Sociological Method*. London: Hutchinson.

Giddens, A. (1977) *Studies in Social and Political Theory*. London: Hutchinson.

Giddens, A. (1984) *The Constitution of Society*. Cambridge: Polity Press.

Giddens, A. (1987) Structuralism, post-structuralism and the production of culture, in A. Giddens, and J. Turner, (eds) *Social Theory Today*. Cambridge: Polity Press.

Giddens, A. (1990) *The Consequences of Modernity*. Cambridge: Polity Press.

Giddens, A. (1991) *Modernity and Self-Identity*. Cambridge: Polity Press.

Giddens, A. (1995) Comte, Popper and Positivism, in *Politics, Sociology and Social Theory*. Cambridge: Polity Press.

Giddens, A. (1996) *In Defence of Sociology*. Cambridge: Polity Press.

Gilbert, N. and Mulkay, M. (1984) *Opening Pandora's Box: A Sociological Analysis of Scientists' Discourse*. Cambridge: Cambridge University Press.

Giles, D. (1993) *Philosophy of Science in the Twentieth Century*. Oxford: Blackwell.

Goldmann, L. (1969) *The Human Sciences and Philosophy*. London: Cape.

Goudsblom, J. (1977) *Sociology in the Balance: A Critical Essay*. Oxford: Blackwell.

Gouldner, A. (1970) *The Coming Crisis of Western Sociology*. London: Heinemann.

Gouldner, A. (1979) *The Future of Intellectuals and the Rise of the New Class*. New York: Seabury.

Gulbenkian Commission (1996) *Open the Social Sciences: Report of the Gulbenkian Commission on the Restructuring of the Social Sciences*. Stanford: Stanford University Press.

Haan, N. et al. (eds) (1983) *Social Science as Moral Inquiry*. New York: Columbia University Press.

Habermas, J. (1971). Science and technology as ideology, in *Towards a Rational Society*. London: Heinemann.

Habermas, J. (1976a) The analytical theory of science and dialectics, in T. Adorno, et al. (1976) *The Positivist Dispute in German Sociology*. London: Heinemann.

Habermas, J. (1976b) *Legitimation Crisis*. London: Heinemann.

Habermas, J. (1977) *Theory and Practice*. London: Heinemann.

Habermas, J. (1978) *Knowledge and Human Interests*. 2nd edn. London: Heinemann.

Habermas, J. (1979) *Communication and the Evolution of Society*. London: Heinemann.

Habermas, J. (1981) Modernity versus Postmodernity, *New German Critique*, 22: 3–14.

Habermas, J. (1984) *The Theory of Communicative Action*, vol. 1, *Reason and the Rationalization of Society*. London: Heinemann.

Habermas, J. (1987) *The Theory of Communicative Action,* vol. 2, *Lifeworld and System: A Critique of Functionalist Reason*. Cambridge: Polity Press.

Habermas, J. (1988) *On the Logic of the Social Sciences*. Cambridge: Polity Press.

Habermas, J. (1989a) *The Structural Transformation of the Public Sphere*. Cambridge: Polity Press.

Habermas, J. (1989b) The new obscurity, in *The New Conservatism: Cultural Criticism and the Historians' Debate*. Cambridge, MA: MIT Press.

Habermas, J. (1990) *The Philosophical Discourse of Modernity*. Cambridge: Polity Press.

Habermas, J. (1993) *Justification and Application: Remarks on Discourse Ethics*. Cambridge, MA: MIT Press.

Habermas, J. (1996a) *Between Facts and Norms: Contributions to a Discourse Theory of Law and Democracy*. Cambridge: Polity Press.

Habermas, J. (1996b) Mikael Carleheden and René Gabriels, 'An interview with Jürgen Habermas' *Theory, Culture and Society*, 13, (3): 1–17.

Hacking, I. (1999) *The Social Construction of What?* Cambridge, MA: Harvard University Press.

Halberg, M. (1989) Feminist epistemology: an impossible project?, *Radical Philosophy*, 53: 3–6.

Hannigan, J. (1995) *Environmental Sociology: A Social Constructionist Perspective*. London: Routledge.

Haraway, D. (1988) Situated knowledges: the science question in feminism and the privilege of the partial perspective, *Feminist Studies*, 14 (2):12.

Harding, S. (1983) *Discovering Reality: Feminist Perspectives in Epistemology, Methodology and Philosophy*. Dordrecht: Reidel.

Harding, S. (1986) *The Science Question in Feminism*. Buckingham: Open University Press.
Harding, S. (1987) *Feminism and Methodology*. Bloomington: Indiana University Press.
Harding, S. (1991) *Whose Science? Whose Knowledge: Thinking Women's Lives*. Ithaca: Cornell University Press.
Harré, R. (1986) *Varieties of Realism: A Rationale for the Natural Sciences*. Oxford: Blackwell.
Hartsock, N. (1983) The feminist standpoint: developing the ground for a specifically feminist historical materialism, in S. Harding, and M. Hintikka, (eds) *Discovering Reality*, Dordrecht: Reidel.
Harvey, L. (1990) *Critical Social Research*. London: Unwin Hyman.
Haskell, T. (1977) *The Emergence of Professional Social Science*. Urbana: University of Illinois Press.
Hazelrigg, L. (1989) *Social Science and the Challenge of Relativism*. 2 vols. Gainesville: University Press of Florida.
Heilbron, J. (1995) *The Rise of Social Theory*. Cambridge: Polity Press.
Hill, C. (1988) *The World Turned Upside Down: Radical Ideas During the English Revolution*. Harmondsworth: Penguin.
Hill Collins, P. (1986) Learning from the outside within: the sociological significance of black feminist thought, *Social Problems*, 33 (6): 30–2.
Himmelstrand, U. (ed.) (1986) *Sociology: From Crisis to Science*. London: Sage.
Hindess, B. (1977) *Philosophy and Methodology in the Social Sciences*. Brighton: Harvester.
Hollis, M. (1995) *The Philosophy of the Social Sciences*. Cambridge: Cambridge University Press.
Holmwood, J. and Steward, A. (1991) *Explanation and Social Theory*. London: Macmillan.
Homans, G. (1958) Social behaviour as exchange, *American Journal of Sociology*, 63: 597–606.
Honneth, A. (1995) *The Fragmented World of the Social*. New York: State University of New York Press.
Horkheimer, M. (1972) Traditional and critical theory, in *Critical Theory: Selected Essays*. New York: Herder and Herder.
Horowitz, I. L. (1993) *The Decomposition of Sociology*. Oxford: Oxford University Press.
Jacob, M. C. (1994) *The Problem of Western Science, 1640–1990*. New Jersey: Humanities Press.
Jacoby, R. (1987) *The Last Intellectuals: American Culture in the Age of Academe*. New York: Basic Books.
Jameson, F. (1991) *Postmodernism or the Cultural Logic of Late Capitalism*. Durham: Duke University Press.

Joas, H. (1993) *Pragmatism and Social Theory*. Chicago: University of Chicago Press.

Joas, H. (1996) *The Creativity of Action*. Cambridge: Polity Press.

Keat, J. (1981) *The Politics of Social Theory: Habermas, Freud and the Critique of Positivism*. Oxford: Blackwell.

Keat, R. and Urry, J. (1975) *Social Theory as Science*. London: Routledge and Kegan Paul.

Köhnke, K. (1991) *The Rise of Neo-Kantianism*. Cambridge: Cambridge University Press.

Knorr Cetina, K. (1981) *The Manufacture of Knowledge*. Oxford: Pergamon.

Knorr Cetina, K. (1984) The fabrication of facts: toward a microsociology of scientific knowledge, in N. Stehr, and V. Meja, (eds) *Society and Knowledge: Contemporary Perspectives in the Sociology of Knowledge*. London: Transaction Books.

Knorr Cetina, K. and Mulkay, M. (eds) (1983) *Science Observed: Perspectives on the Social Studies of Science*. London: Sage.

Knorr Cetina, K. (1993) Strong constructivism – from a sociologist's point of view, *Social Studies of Science*, 23, 555–63.

Kuhn, T. (1970) *The Structure of Scientific Revolutions*. Chicago: University of Chicago Press.

Lakatos, I. (1970) Falsification and the methodology of scientific research programmes, in I. Lakatos, and A. Musgrave, (eds) *Criticism and the Growth of Knowledge*. Cambridge: Cambridge University Press.

Lakatos, I. (1978) *The Methodology of Scientific Research*. Cambridge: Cambridge University Press.

Lash, S. (1994) Reflexivity and its doubles: structure, aesthetics, community, in U. Beck, A. Giddens, and S. Lash, *Reflexive Modernization*. Cambridge: Polity Press.

Lash, S. et al. (eds) (1996) *Risk, Environment and Modernity: Towards a New Ecology*. London: Sage.

Latour, B. (1987) *Science in Action*. Milton Keynes: Open University Press.

Latour, B. and Woolgar, S. (1986) *Laboratory Life: The Construction of Scientific Facts*. Princeton: Princeton University Press.

Latour, B. (1993) *We Have Never Been Modern*. New York: Harvester Wheatsheaf.

Lenk, H. (1992) *Zwischen Wissenschaft und Ethik*. Frankfurt: Suhrkamp.

Lepenies, W. (1988) *Between Literature and Science: The Rise of Sociology*. Cambridge: Cambridge University Press.

Levine, D. (1996) Sociology and the nation-state in an era of shifting boundaries, *Sociological Inquiry*, 66, (3): 253–66.

Losee, J. (1993) *A Historical Introduction to the Philosophy of Science*, 3rd edn. Oxford: Oxford University Press.

Luhmann, N. (1984a) The differentiation of advances in knowledge, in N.

Stehr, and V. Meja (eds) *Society and Knowledge: Contemporary Perspectives in the Sociology of Knowledge*. London: Transaction Books.

Luhmann, N. (1984b) The self-description of society, *International Journal of Comparative Sociology*, 25: 59–72.

Luhmann, N. (1984c) The cognitive program of constructivism and a reality that remains unknown, in W. Krohn, G. Küppers and H. Nowotny (eds) *Self-Organization: Portrait of a Scientific Revolution*. Dordrecht: Kluwer.

Luhmann (1986) The autopoiesis of social systems, in F. Geyer and J. van der Zouwen (eds) *Sociocybernetic Paradoxes: Observations, Control and Evolution of Self-Steering Systems*. London: Sage.

Luhmann, N. (1988) *Erkenntnis as Konstruktion*. Bern: Benteli.

Luhmann, N. (1990a) *Die Wissenschaft der Gessellschaft*. Frankfurt: Suhrkamp.

Luhmann, N. (1990b) *Essays on Self-Reference*. New York: Columbia University Press.

Luhmann, N. (1995) *Social Systems*. Stanford: Stanford University Press.

Luhmann, N. (1996) On the scientific context of the concept of communication, *Social Science Information*, 35 (2): 257–67.

Lynd, R. S. (1937) *Knowledge for What? The Place of Social Science in American Culture*. Princeton: Princeton University Press.

Lyotard, J.-F. (1984) *The Postmodern Condition*. Manchester: Manchester University Press.

MacLean, M. and Winch, P. (1990) *The Political Responsibility of the Intellectual*. Cambridge: Cambridge University Press.

Maffesoli, M. (1996) *Time of the Tribes*. London: Sage.

Manicas, P. (1987) *A History and Philosophy of the Social Sciences*. Oxford: Basil Blackwell.

Mannheim, K. (1993) Competition as a cultural phenomenon, in K. Wolff (ed.) *From Karl Mannheim*. London: Transaction Books.

Manturana, H, and Varela, F. (1980) *Autopoiesis and Cognition: The Realization of the Living*. Dordrecht: Reidel.

Marcuse, H. (1977) *Reason and Revolution: Hegel and the Rise of Social Theory*. London: Routledge and Kegan Paul.

Martins, H. (1972) The Kuhnian 'Revolution' and its implications for sociology, in T. Nossiter et al. (eds) *Imagination and Precision in the Social Sciences*. London: Faber and Faber.

May, T. (2000) A future for critique: positioning, belonging and reflexivity, *European Journal of Social Theory*, 3 (2): 157–73.

May, T. and Williams, M. (eds) (1998) *Knowing the Social World*. Buckingham: Open University Press.

Mayntz, R. (1992) The influence of the natural science theories on contemporary social science, in M. Dierkes and B. Biervert (eds) *Social Science in Transition: Assessment and Outlook*. Boulder: Westview.

Medd, W. (2002) Complexity and the social world, *International Journal of Social Science Methodology*, 5 (1): 71–81.

Melucci, A. (1989) *Nomads of the Present: Social Movements and the Individual Needs in Contemporary Society*. Philadephia: Temple University Press.

Melucci, A. (1996) *Challenging Codes: Collective Action in the Information Age*. Cambridge: Cambridge University Press.

Mendelsohn, E. et al. (eds) (1977) *The Social Production of Scientific Knowledge*. Dordrecht: Reidel.

Merchant, C. (1989) *The Death of Nature: Women, Ecology and the Scientific Revolution*. London: Routledge, Kegan and Paul.

Merton, R. (1970) *Science, Technology and Society in Seventeenth Century England.* New York: Harper.

Miller, R. (1987) *Fact and Method: Explanation, Confirmation and Reality in the Natural and the Social Sciences*. Princeton: Princeton University Press.

Mills, C. W. (1970) *The Sociological Imagination.* Harmondsworth: Penguin.

Morrow, R. (1994) *Critical Theory and Methodology*. London: Sage.

Mulkay, M. (1979) *Science and the Sociology of Knowledge*. London: Allen and Unwin.

Nielsen, J. M. (ed.) (1990) *Feminist Research Methods: Exemplary Readings in the Social Sciences*. Boulder, Co: Westview.

Nowotny, H. (1992) Time in the social sciences, in M. Dierkes, and B. Biervert (eds) *Social Science in Transition: Assessment and Outlook*. Boulder, Co: Westview.

Nowotny, H., Scott, P. and Gibbons, P. (2001) *Knowledge and the Public in an Age of Uncertainty*. Cambridge: Polity Press.

Nüse, R., Groeben, N., Fritag, B. and Schreier, M. (1991) *Über die Erfindung/en des Radikalen Konstruktivismus: kritische Gegenargumente aus psychologischer Sicht*. Weinheim: Deutscher Studien Verlag.

O' Hear, A. (1989) *An Introduction to the Philosophy of Science*. Oxford: Clarendon Press.

O' Neill, J. (1995) *The Poverty of Postmodernism*. London: Routledge.

Oakes, G. (1988) *Weber and Rickert*. Cambridge, MA: MIT Press.

Olsen, M. (1965) *The Logical Collective Action*. Cambridge, MA: Harvard University Press.

Outhwaite, W. (1975) *Understanding Social Life: The Method Called Verstehen*. London: Allen and Unwin.

Outhwaite, W. (1983) *Concept Formation in Social Science*. London: Routledge and Kegan Paul.

Outhwaite, W. (1987) *New Philosophies of Social Sciences: Realism, Hermeneutics and Critical Theory*. London: Macmillan.

Outhwaite, W. (1996) Philosophy of the social sciences, in B. Turner, (ed.) *The Blackwell's Companion to Social Theory*. Oxford: Blackwell.

Palmer, R. E. (1969) *Hermeneutics: Interpretation Theory in Schleiermacher, Dilthey, Heidegger and Gadamer*. Evanston: Northwestern University Press.

Parsons, T. (1959) Some problems confronting sociology as a profession, *American Sociological Review*, 24: 547–59.

Poggi, G. (1996) *Lego Quia Innutile*: an alternative justification for the classics, in S. Turner, (ed.) *Social Theory and Sociology: The Classics and Beyond*. Oxford: Blackwell.

Popper, K. (1959) *The Logic of Scientific Discovery*, 2nd edn. London: Hutchinson.

Popper, K. (1972) *Conjectures and Refutations*. London: Routledge and Kegan Paul.

Popper, K. (1976) The logic of the social sciences, in T. Adorno, et al. *The Positivist Dispute in German Sociology*. London: Heinemann.

Purkhardt, C. (1993) *Transforming Social Representation: A Social Psychology of Common Sense and Science*. London: Routledge.

Putnam, H. (1975) *Mind, Language and Reality*. Cambridge: Cambridge University Press.

Radder, H. (1988) *The Material Realization of Science*. Assen/Maastricht: Van Gorcum.

Richard, S. (1983) *Philosophy and Sociology of Science*. Oxford: Blackwell.

Ricoeur, P. (1981) *Paul Ricoeur, Hermeneutics and the Human Sciences*, J. Thompson, (ed.). Cambridge: Cambridge University Press.

Romm, N. (1991) *The Methodologies of Positivism and Marxism: A Sociological Debate*. New York: Macmillan.

Rorty, R. (1979) *Philosophy and the Mirror of Nature*. Princeton: Princeton University Press.

Rose, H. (1983) Hand, brain and heart: a feminist epistemology for the natural sciences, *Signs*, 9 (1): 73–90.

Rosenau, P. (1992) *Postmodernism in the Social Sciences*. Princeton: Princeton University Press.

Rosenberg, A. (1988) *Philosophy of the Social Sciences*. Boulder, Co: Westview.

Rouse, J. (1987) *Knowledge and Power: Toward a Political Philosophy of Science*. Ithaca: Cornell University Press.

Ryan, A. (1970) *The Philosophy of the Social Sciences*. London: Macmillan.

Said, E. (1979) *Orientalism*. New York: Vintage.

Said, E. (1994) *Representations of the Intellectual: The 1993 Reith Lectures*. London: Vintage.

Sartre, J.-P. (1963) *Search for Method*. New York: Knopf.

Sayer, A. (1984) *Methodology in Social Science: A Realist Approach*. London: Hutchinson.

Sayer, A. (2000) *Realism and Social Science*. London: Sage.

Schäfer, W. (ed.) (1983a) *Finalization in Science*. Dordrecht: Reidel.

Schäfer, W. (1983b) Normative finalization, in W. Schäfer, (ed.) *Finalization in Science*. Dordrecht: Reidel.

Schelling, T. C. (1960) *The Strategy of Conflict*. Cambridge, MA: Harvard University Press.

Schelsky, H. (1975) *Die Arbeit tun die Anderen. Klassenkampf und Priesterherrschaft der Intellektuellen*. Oplanden: Westdeutscher Verlag.

Schmidt, S. J. (ed.) (1987) *Der Diskurs des Radikalen Konstruktivismus*. Frankfurt: Suhrkamp.

Schmidt, S. J. (ed.) (1992) *Kognition und Gesellschaft: Der Diskurs des Radikalen Konstruktivismus*. Frankfurt: Suhrkamp.

Scott, R. and Shore, A. (1979) *Why Sociology Does Not Apply: A Study of the Use of Sociology in Public Policy*. New York: Elsevier.

Simons, H. (ed.) (1990) *The Rhetorical Turn: Invention and Persuasion in the Conduct of Inquiry*. Chicago: University of Chicago Press.

Sismondo, S. (1993) Some social constructions, *Social Studies of Science*, 23: 515–53.

Skinner, Q. (ed.) (1985) *The Return of Grand Theory in the Human Sciences*. Cambridge: Cambridge University Press.

Smith, D. (1974) Women's perspective as a radical critique of sociology, *Sociological Inquiry*, 44: 7–13.

Smith, D. (1987) *The Everyday World as Problematic: A Feminist Sociology*. Boston: Northeastern University Press.

Snow, C. P. (1993) *The Two Cultures*. Cambridge: Cambridge University Press.

Stanley, L. and Wise, S. (1983) *Breaking Out: Feminist Consciousness and Feminist Research*. London: Routledge and Kegan Paul.

Stehr, N. (1994) *Knowledge Society*. London: Sage.

Stehr, N. (1996) The salt of social science, *Sociological Research Online*, 1, 1, <http://www.socresonline.org.uk/socresonline/1/1/1.html>

Stehr, N. and Meja, V. (eds) (1984) *Society and Knowledge: Contemporary Perspectives in the Sociology of Knowledge*. London: Transaction Books.

Stockman, N. (1983) *Antipositivist Theories of Science*. Dordrecht: Reidel.

Strydom, P. (2000) *Discourse and Knowledge: The Making of Enlightenment Sociology* Liverpool: Liverpool University Press.

Strydom, P. (2002) *Risk, Environment and Society*. Buckingham: Open University Press.

Strydom, P. (2005) Contemporary european cognitive social theory, in: G. Delanty, *Handbook of Contemporary European Social Theory*. London: Routledge.

Taylor, C. (1971) Interpretations and the sciences of man, *Review of Metaphysics*, 25(1): 3–10.

Thompson, J. B. (1981) *Critical Hermeneutics: A Study in the Thought of Paul Ricoeur and Jürgen Habermas*. Cambridge: Cambridge University Press.
Toulmin, S. (1953) *The Philosophy of Science*. London: Hutchinson.
Toulmin, S. (1992) *Cosmopolis: The Hidden Agenda of Modernity*. Chicago: Chicago University Press.
Touraine, A. (1977) *The Self-Production of Society*. Chicago: University of Chicago Press.
Touraine, A. (1981) *The Voice and the Eye: An Analysis of Social Movements*. Cambridge: Cambridge University Press.
Touraine, A. (1988) *Return of the Actor*. Minneapolis: University of Minnesota Press.
Touraine, A. (1995) *Critique of Modernity*. Cambridge: Polity Press.
Trigg, R. (1985) *Understanding Social Science: A Philosophical Introduction to the Social Sciences*. Oxford: Blackwell.
Trigg, R. (1993) *Rationality and Science: Can Science Explain Everything?* Oxford: Blackwell.
Tudor, A. (1982) *Beyond Empiricism: Philosophy of Science in Sociology*. London: Routledge and Kegan Paul.
Turner, B. and Baert, P. (eds) (2004) American pragmatism and european social and political theory, special issue of *European Journal of Social Theory*, 7 (3).
Turner, S. (ed.) (1996) *Social Theory and Sociology: The Classics and Beyond*. Oxford: Blackwell.
Turner, S. (2003) *Liberal Democracy 3.0*. London: Sage.
Turner, S. and Roth, P. (eds) (2003) *Philosophy of the Social Sciences*. Oxford: Blackwell.
Unger, R. (1987) *Social Theory: Its Situation and its Task*. Cambridge: Cambridge University Press.
Urry, J. (2003) *Global Complexity*. Cambridge: Polity Press.
Vattimo, G. (1992) *The Transparent Society*. Cambridge: Polity Press.
Wagner, P. (1994) *A Sociology of Modernity: Liberty and Discipline*. London: Routledge.
Wagner, P. (1996) Der Soziologe als Übersetzer, *Die Zeit*, 15 April.
Wagner, P. (2001) *Theorizing Modernity*. London: Sage.
Wagner, P., Weiss, C., Wittrock, B., and Wollmann, H. (eds) (1991) *Social Sciences and Modern States: Natural Experiences and Theoretical Crossroads*. Cambridge: Cambridge University Press.
Webb, K. (1995) *An Introduction to Problems in the Philosophy of Social Science*. London: Pinter.
Weber, M. (1949) *The Methodology of the Social Sciences*. Glencoe: The Free Press.
Weber, M. (1970) Science as a vocation, in H. Gerth, and C. W. Mills (eds) *From Max Weber*. London: Routledge and Kegan Paul.

Wellmer, A. (1967) *Critical Theory of Society*. New York: Herder and Herder.

Williams, M. (2000) *Science and Social Science*. London: Routledge.

Wilson, B. ed. (1970) *Rationality*. Oxford: Blackwell.

Winch, P. (1958) *The Idea of a Social Science and its Relation to Philosophy*. London: Routledge and Kegan Paul.

Woolgar, S. (1988a) *Science: The Very Idea*. London: Tavistock.

Woolgar, S. (1988b) *Knowledge and Reflexivity: New Frontiers in the Sociology of Knowledge*. London: Sage.

Wynne, B. (1996) May the sheep safely graze? A reflective view of the expert-lay knowledge divide, in S. Lash, et al. (eds) *Risk, Environment and Modernity: Towards a New Ecology*. London: Sage.

Index

Passim indicates numerous references within page range.

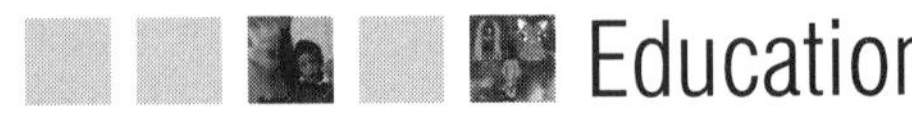
Education

Health & Social Welfare

Management

Media, Film & Culture

Psychology & Counselling

Sociology

Study Skills

OPEN UNIVERSITY PRESS
McGraw - Hill Education